Understanding World Christianity

Understanding World Christianity

China

China

KIM-KWONG CHAN

FORTRESS PRESS
MINNEAPOLIS

Contents

Introducing the Fortress Press Series:
Understanding World Christianity

The idea of a major project on world Christianity is timely. According to research from Pew, approximately two-thirds of the world's nations and territories are Christian majority.[1] Christianity continues to widen its global net, claiming the allegiance of well over two billion people. Of the ten largest national Christian populations—the United States, Brazil, Mexico, Russia, Philippines, Nigeria, China, Democratic Republic of the Congo, Germany, Ethiopia—only two are from the Western world. Around one-sixth of the human population holds membership in the Roman Catholic Church. The modern Pentecostal/Charismatic movement—only a century old—claims roughly 600 million people today. As Pew reports, "Christians are also geographically widespread—so far-flung, in fact, that no single continent or region can indisputably claim to be the center of global Christianity. A century ago this was not the case."

Of the eight cultural blocs of the world, Christianity is the largest religion in six of them: Latin America and the Caribbean, North America, Western Europe, Eastern Europe, Africa, and Oceania. Only in Asia and the Middle East is Christianity not the religion most people adhere to. However, some of the most important developments in world Christianity are happening

---

1. See "Global Christianity—A Report on the Size and Distribution of the World's Christian Population," Pew Research Center, December 19, 2011, https://tinyurl.com/ycsffdt7.

in Asia, and the Middle East will forever be the land of Jesus—where the gospel was unleashed. Furthermore, Islam—by far the most dominant Middle Eastern faith—can scarcely be understood apart from the history it shares with Judaism and Christianity. Christianity's influence in the world is profound, and there is little reason to think it is abating.

In the 1960s, esteemed church historian Stephen Neill began noticing that—for the first time in human history—there existed a truly *world* religion: Christianity. Neill was ahead of his time. Due to his globetrotting on behalf of the World Council of Churches, he was able to observe rather intimately how deeply Christianity was taking root in Africa and Asia, seemingly against all the odds. While the leviathan structure of European colonialism was collapsing, Christianity defied all predictions by indigenizing. Many thought that when the colonial administrators and missionaries left, Christianity would wither. But the opposite happened. When the Europeans and North Americans got out of the way, these people integrated the gospel into their cultures, into their own lands, on their own terms. And today, we are front-row observers to these events, many of which are still unfolding. Christianity is changing civilizations as civilizations change Christianity. These stories are fascinating, they are important, and they need to be told.

The Understanding World Christianity project addresses head-on the fact that many churches, colleges, and seminaries are struggling to come to terms with the reality that Christianity is now a worldwide faith, not just a Western one. There is a popular and hardened conception that Christianity is dependent upon the nations of Western Europe and North America. Some variants of the story prolong the worn-out narrative that Asia and Africa are being somehow held hostage by the white man's religion, and that Christianity has everything to do with colonialism and imperialism, and nothing to do with indigenization, freedom, and self-assertion. Thus, many students even take degrees in Christianity under a long-outdated curriculum: Christianity is born in the Middle East, Constantine makes it a Western faith, the Enlightenment ushers in a modern era, Christianity fades, and now we inhabit a *postmodern* world.

This Eurocentric paradigm is obsolete, for many reasons. First of all, Christianity has expanded terrifically. No longer is it centered in the West. It is now broadly spread out across the world, especially in Africa and Latin America. Second, the important modern European thinkers—Bonhoeffer, Tillich, Barth—who are typically required reading in Western seminaries do not adequately represent the world's Christians. Christianity is so much more diversified now. We are in great need of hearing the southern voices such as John Mbiti, Kwame Bediako, Oscar Romero, and M. M. Thomas. The Western academy needs to think more globally, given the striking changes the Christian faith has undergone in the last century. Third, in what some call an era of globalization, we are much more exposed to the non-Western world. Media, immigration, and increased international travel have made cultures intersect and cross-pollinate, creating a hybridity that was not so obvious a generation or two ago. This is especially the case for people who live in cities. Los Angeles, Dallas, Chicago, New York, and Miami are excellent examples of this diversification process, which has a trickle-down effect throughout America's smaller cities, towns, and villages. A woman in small-town New Mexico could very well have an Indian physician, a Vietnamese priest, and a Guatemalan housekeeper. These situations are increasingly common for the average American.

Thankfully, a corpus of research on Christianity's *global* history is proliferating, and there is a growing awareness that Christianity never was the exclusive possession of the Western world, and certainly is not today. In spite of the gains that have been made, there are fundamental questions that remain unaddressed or underaddressed. For example, what is the *meaning* of global Christianity? How will the drastic changes to Christianity's geography impact theology, mission, and ministry? Indeed, what does this new body of research have to say to the church? What can Christians do with this information? How must missionary work be reconceived? These are practical questions begging further investigation. It is critical that Christians respond to global Christianity in sensitive and thoughtful ways. The Understanding World Christianity series will equip specialists, leaders, and students with up-to-date, on-the-ground information that will help them get their heads around the stories and the data.

In the parable of the Sower, Jesus described a scene where seed was scattered on various types of soil. Some seed was unproductive, but some produced bountifully. Similarly, at the beginning of the twenty-first century, Christianity flourishes in surprising places. The continent of Africa is half Christian. China and the former Soviet Union are opening up to Christianity after decades of oppression. The 266th pope is from Buenos Aires. Korea is home to some of the largest Christian congregations in the world. Meanwhile, in Christianity's old heartland—Western Europe—it appears faith is receding. Who could have foreseen these astonishing developments a century ago?

In the early years of the faith, when Christian gentiles began to outnumber believing Jews, the faith began to take on a decidedly different identity. Led by the apostles' ambitious missionary work, the early church adapted capably, and grew exponentially. Peter and Paul profoundly shaped "the Way" by fashioning it into an institution open to all people, all nationalities and ethnicities alike. It was a blended family par excellence, albeit with considerable growth pains. Today we stand at a similar crossroads. The Global South has become the new heartland of a faith that was anchored in the West for centuries. The composition of Christianity—easily the world's largest religion—is changing, right before our eyes.

An important question remains, however. Is it a *fait accompli* that Christianity will continue to move south, with little for the Western churches to do but watch?

Scholars such as Robert Wuthnow contend there is much that the churches in the Western world can do, and in fact are doing. In *Boundless Faith: The Global Outreach of American Churches*, he shows that American churches now spend $4 billion annually on overseas ministry, more than ever, and the number of "full-time missionaries serving abroad has increased steadily." In contrast to paternalistic models of the past, where the sending church was the clear authority, mission work today follows a collaborative paradigm, "through direct partnerships with overseas congregations, engaging in faster and more efficient transcultural com-munication, interacting with a sizable population of refugees and immigrants, and contributing to large-scale international humanitarian and relief organizations."[2] Our mental maps of missionaries flowing from the West to the rest must be updated, as Brazil, Korea, and Nigeria are now sending nations with robust missionary programs. India, Vietnam, and the Philip-pines provide hundreds of Roman Catholic priests to serve in the United States. Indeed, Christians from the Global South are globally engaged, and North American churches are wise to partner with them.

The Understanding World Christianity series will contribute to this robust conversation in key ways. It will interpret these monumental changes for a larger audience. It will engage crit-ical questions arising from a global, interconnected Christian faith. And it will draw upon some of today's best special-ists—familiar with Christianity on the ground in their respective geographies—in order to create authoritative and readable com-posites of what is happening. Authors for the series come from a range of ecclesial backgrounds, including Orthodox, Roman Catholic, mainline Protestant, Evangelical, and Pentecostal.

The new era of world Christianity is impacting global politics, higher education, Christian ministry paradigms, and countless char-itable organizations. This project will help professors, pastors, stu-dents, and professionals understand that with the global spread of Christianity comes a new opportunity for sharing the ongoing story, informed by sensitivity to local and contextual differences. As our world flattens and as Christians globally become more inter-dependent, a rich complexity is developing. Worldviews are shifting, societies are transforming, and theologies are being rewritten. This project will help Christians to navigate through the differences more carefully and more thoughtfully.

Read more about the Understanding World Christianity series online at: fortresspress.com/uwc.

—Dyron Daughrity, General Editor
The Understanding World Christianity Series

---

2. Robert Wuthnow, *Boundless Faith: The Global Outreach of American Churches* (Los Angeles: University of California Press, 2010), 1–2.

Acknowledgments

In the spring of 1979, when I was in Beijing giving a seminar in clinical nutrition at the Beijing Capital Hospital (formerly Peking Union Medical College Hospital, founded by the Rockefeller Foundation in 1921), I encountered my first Christian in China, the matron of the hospital, Madam Lin Baoshang. After the lecture, I went to her dormitory for a simple dinner. She drew down all the curtains and listened carefully, making sure there was no one in the corridor, before she whispered a very moving grace over the meal. Later in the same year, I met some members of the Northwest Spiritual Band (see chap. 5), who took me under their wing to visit Christian remnants who had survived the Great Proletarian Cultural Revolution (1966–1976) in different parts of China. Through fellowship with them, I have had a rare glimpse of the Chinese Christians who, despite enduring many years of suffering for their faith, lived with an intense aura of faith, hope, and joy. I realized I had witnessed the mysterious power of the powerlessness of the cross, through which God lived with these Christians at the darkest hour of their life in a most profound way.

In 1981, after visiting dozens of Chinese Christian communities in more than a dozen provinces, I felt drawn to learn more of the spiritual reality of the Chinese Christians and to follow the reemergence this Christian community in socialist China. I also wanted to know more about China, especially about the sociopolitical context in which the Chinese Christians were situated, as China began to unleash its huge economic potential. I had since taken up studies in economics and theology in order to position myself as an observer of China and of the Chinese Christian community. During the past four decades, I have had the honor of witnessing the radical transformation of China from one of the poorest developing nations into one of the most vibrant economic entities in the world. More important, I have had the privilege of visiting hundreds of Christian communities (including Catholic and Orthodox) in every province in China, as well as meeting Christians from more than twenty different ethnic minority groups. The more I heard their stories, the more I felt humbled by them. When I visited them, I believed I was meant to strengthen them, yet I became the one who had been most blessed. If I were to list out all the names of these Christians whom I feel indebted to and wanted to acknowledge in this volume, the list would run into tens of thousands! In fact, every Chinese Christian whom I have encountered has in some way shaped this volume; to them this volume is dedicated.

I would like to particularly mention some colleagues in academia whom I have greatly benefited from: Dan Bays, Chen Cunfu, Alan Hunter, Graeme Lang, Paul Martinson, Gordon Melton, David Palmer, Tetsunao Yamamori, and Yang Fenggang; their ideas, passions, values, and knowledge have been alchemized into this volume. I would like to thank four people in particular who helped in the editing of this volume: Rose Chue of the Lutheran Theological Seminary in Hong Kong, who polished my English in the first draft; Louise Joachimowski of La Rouge Productions, who further worked on my final manuscript; Dyron Daughrity of Pepperdine University, who did the general editing to fit this volume into the Understanding World Christianity series of Fortress Press; and the editor at Fortress, Emily Brower, who transformed the manuscript into a presentable volume to the reader.

Kim-kwong Chan
March 6, 2019
Ash Wednesday

Introduction

A CAGED COMMUNITY

On October 1, 1949, Mao Zedong declared the founding of the People's Republic of China and ushered in a new socialist society in which Christians would be treated as undesirable elements of society. Since then, Christians have lived in a political cage. During this new nation's first three decades, Christianity experienced a series of devastating blows. Its population was reduced from four million in 1949 (three million Catholics, one million Protestants, and about 250,000 Orthodox) to almost zero in the mid-1970s, at which time Christianity publicly existed in only two chapels (one Catholic and one Protestant), mainly for the foreign diplomats in Beijing. Four factors contributed to such a reduction in the Christian population. First, the new Chinese government embraced an atheistic ideology with the objective of eradicating religion from the public domain. All Christian institutions, such as church-run schools or hospitals, were nationalized, and church activities were curtailed. Citizens were discouraged from embracing religion, thus greatly reducing the Christian population. Second, the new government launched a series of political campaigns attempting to actualize socialism in the shortest possible time span. These campaigns included a planned economy, collective production units such as the commune system, and the systematic dismantling of any force hampering such progress of socialism, such as religion, which was interpreted as a parasite living off of the blood of the peasants

1

and workers. Hence all Christian activities were further limited, clergy were sent to farms and factories, and many church venues were confiscated and converted into warehouses or buildings for other collective use, further reducing participation in Christian activities. Third, the People's Republic of China sided with the USSR during the Cold War period and regarded the West, and Western-affiliated groups such as Christianity, as the archenemy of China. Any affiliation with Christianity was suspect, as it might have been infiltrated by hostile forces looking to sabotage the Chinese regime. As a result, many missionaries from the West were expelled, and Chinese Christians associated with these missionaries were accused as enemy agents and charged as antirevolutionaries. Fourth, with the increasing political tension between China and the USSR from the late 1950s, the majority of Orthodox Christians still living in China, mostly Russian descendants, were forced to leave China, greatly reducing the Orthodox population. Together, these political forces shrunk the Christian community in China into a tiny remnant that lived under constant threat from civil authority. By the mid-1970s, the Chinese authority declared that religion in China had been confined into a museum, which officially marked the moratorium of Christianity in China.

In the late 1970s, China surprised the world by adopting a new "Reform and Open" policy, which replaced the planned economy with a market economy and called it socialism with Chinese characteristics. There was skepticism as to whether this was a trick that China was playing to disarm the West or whether China really did intend to reform its economic sector in order to catch up with the world. China began to open up to outside investment and learn various innovations and technologies from the West. With this liberal policy and the gradual lifting of the Bamboo Curtain, which allowed more people from abroad to visit China, church watchers began to hear news from Christians in China after a silence of more than two decades. The news was astonishing: this tiny community had not only survived under the harshest conditions but also grown into a sizable community within this political cage. In the early 1980s, the Chinese government estimated there were three million Catholics and three million Protestants in China. This government estimate suggested that Catholics had been able to maintain their population for three decades despite the almost total lack of clergy and sacraments and that Protestants had tripled in number in spite of the severe lack of virtually all Christian resources, especially the Bible.

For the past four decades, China has continued with this Reform and Open policy, transforming itself from one of the poorest nations into the world's second-largest economic entity. It has a burgeoning middle class, which has become the world's largest source of outbound tourists (130 million)[1] and the world's highest travel spending per capita (USD $5,425 in 2017).[2] Chinese goods are flooding into the world, and Chinese investments are seen globally. China now has the world's largest highway networks as well as its most extensive high-speed train system. Christianity in China, too, has surprised the Christian world to become the fastest-growing Christian group in recent history; there are about twelve million Catholics and perhaps as many as eighty million Protestants as reported by some mission agencies! China has also produced the largest number of Bibles in the world, with more than 150 million copies printed so far. The percentage of Christians in the general population is at its highest since the official introduction of Christianity into China in 635 CE. Furthermore, there are increasing numbers of Chinese Christians engaging in world mission to evangelize others beyond the borders of China. All of these phenomena are taking place within a politically caged environment imposed by civil authority, which limits Christian churches to operating within a confined time and space, constrains the type of Christian activities within a restrictive policy framework reinforced by various governmental regulations, and controls Christian leaders through various coercive measures.

China's rise has drawn much speculation as to its place in global affairs, from an ambitious dragon that will dominate the world to a friendly engine that will deliver global economic prosperity. In the same way, the Christian phenomenon in

---

1. Jason Tan, "China Outbound Tourism Hits Record High in 2017," Caixing Global, March 5, 2018, https://tinyurl.com/yalzrk5z.

2. "Average Budget of International Tourists on Vacation Travel in Selected Countries in 2017," Statista, April 2017, https://tinyurl.com/y7lc6jo8.

China also raises a plethora of ecclesial questions, such as the means of survival of Chinese Christians in a hostile environment, the spirituality that sustains this community, the role of the government's policy vis-à-vis church growth, the methods of evangelism developed by Chinese Christians, and so on. The rapid expansion of the Chinese Christian population also inspires much speculation as to the applicability of the Chinese ecclesial model in other parts of Christendom, the Chinese missionary as the next wave of global mission workers, the geopolitical implication of China becoming the largest Christian nation, and the significance to Catholicism after the signing of the Sino-Vatican Provisional Agreement on episcopal appointment in September 2018 between the world's largest religious institution and the world's largest atheist-agnostic country. However, before one can begin to answer these important questions, there are two major issues that must be explored and understood: the experiences of Chinese Christians and the factors that have contributed to their present ecclesial reality. Both issues are the intended foci of this volume. It also interprets the Christian community in the framework of Chinese society in order to gain a glimpse of the interactive dynamics between Christianity and contemporary China in the context of the present social reality. Based on these analyses, this writing will speculate on the future of Chinese Christianity both in the contexts of China and of global Christianity.

A PRIVILEGED OBSERVER

In early 1979, as the Bamboo Curtain had just lifted and religion was still not allowed to exist in the open, I had the privilege of giving lectures in Beijing as a nutritionist. I had a rare glimpse of a nation where almost everyone wore Mao suits and rode on bicycles. It was the China when food was rationed, travel was controlled, and churches and temples were all closed. Through some unintended connections, I encountered some Christians who had kept their faith in secret and connected me to other Christian groups that were still surviving. As I heard their stories, I was greatly encouraged and challenged by the faith of these

Christians. I also sensed an atmosphere of change, as Chinese people were eager to acquire any information of the outside world, including religion. Later, I witnessed the reopening of the second Protestant church in China, Moore Memorial Church in Shanghai, in September 1979, acquired a copy from the first batch of the reprinted Chinese Bible, and met with many Christians who had just been released from years in labor camps. By 1980, I had traveled to twenty provinces and listened to stories from hundreds of Christians of their experiences during the darkest period of their faith journeys. Their stories astonished me as they revealed a picture of many extraordinary religious experiences beyond human comprehension. I also found that China was a complex reality with ever-changing dynamics, within which the Christian community was situated: anything reported about China is probably true but not the whole truth. The more I traveled, the more I realized that I did not understand China, much less the Chinese Christian community. I then decided to be an observer of China, trying to find out how it could strive to catch up with the world and how Christianity could survive in this seemingly hostile environment.

I then embarked on an academic journey as a student both in Sinology and in theology. Because of family links, including a distant uncle who was the head of a provincial Christian council and many uncles- and aunts-in-law (from my wife's side, a Christian family for several generations) who were church leaders in both registered and nonregistered Christian groups, I was able to gain access to diverse Christian circles in China. From the mid-1980s until recent years, I have visited hundreds of Christian communities in every province of China to understand their situations. My service in an ecumenical agency, the Hong Kong Christian Council, further expanded my contacts with various Christian groups, including Orthodox Christians, in China. Owing to my training at Pontifical University specializing in Catholic theology, I was trusted by certain Catholic leaders in China, invited to teach in several seminaries, and allowed access to Catholic communities. These encounters with different Christian communities helped me to understand the theological self-understandings, challenges, and aspirations of Chinese Christians in their sociopolitical realities in different parts of China under various local authorities. Besides visiting Christian communities, I have also taught sociology and religious studies at universities in China; such teachings and dialogue with Chinese academia helped me to develop a sociological interpretation of Christianity in China, especially in the context of China's sociopolitical dynamics. All of these privileged positions have gradually formed my understanding of Christianity in China from both ecclesial and social dimensions, as illustrated by this volume.

THE UNFOLDING JOURNEY

The first chapter ("Chronological") begins with a general historical account of the introduction of Christianity into China in the seventh century CE and various later attempts at evangelization by different Christian groups, along with their impact on China. It is followed by the general experiences of the three main Christian traditions, Protestant, Catholic, and Orthodox, in contemporary China from the beginning of the People's Republic of China to the current time, including their interaction with the Chinese authorities, interecclesial tensions, adaptations, development since the 1980s, current status, impact on Chinese society, and ecumenical relations. All chapters in this volume, except chapter 3, include Catholicism, although Protestantism remains the main focus because the Protestant population constitutes the majority of the total Christian population in China. Orthodox Christianity is included when it is relevant to the discussion.

The second chapter ("Sociopolitical") looks at the Chinese government's ideology on religion and its policy on religious affairs, namely the political framework within which Christians in China live. It outlines the developments and changes of this policy, studies different implementations of the very same policy, and describes the diverse ecclesial responses toward such a policy, which has resulted in different factions (such as the division between the underground and official groups). It also looks into the intraecclesial dynamics among these factions and the multiple ecclesial self-understandings among Chinese Christian communities.

The third chapter ("Denominations") describes the various denominations and traditions of Protestantism that existed in China before 1949 and their gradual merging into the post-denominational framework of the current China Christian Council, the independent Chinese indigenous denominations and their development, the unregistered house church movement, the quasi-ecclesial communities, and the newly developed independent urban churches, as well as various extensions of international denominations in China. All of these different traditions have been woven into a complex mosaic of ecclesial patterns that makes up the Protestant community in China.

The fourth chapter ("Geographical") looks into the various manifestations of faith by different Christian communities living in diverse economic and cultural zones due to geographic differences. It examines how Christian expressions differ between rural and urban populations and takes an in-depth look into the region where the Christian population is highest proportionally in China: the municipality of Wenzhou, also known as the Jerusalem of China. It also examines the Christian faith among ethnic minorities, who live mostly around the peripheral areas of China.

The fifth chapter focuses on the spirituality of Chinese Christians through the witnesses of four individuals (three Protestant and one Catholic): an almost illiterate peasant who embraced the Christian faith in its most simple and practical form; a young lady with no formal training in music yet who has written hymns that have touched the hearts of millions of Chinese Christians; a pastor who left no writing behind and was commemorated along with Rev. Dr. Martin Luther King Jr. and Rev. Dr. Dietrich Bonhoeffer at Westminster Abbey as one of the ten Christian martyrs of the twentieth century; and a Jesuit from Shanghai who spent more than twenty years in jail and ended up as a bishop recognized by both the Chinese authority and the Holy See. Their spiritual journeys echo with the pilgrim journeys that millions of Christians in China have traveled.

The final chapter reflects on various theological issues such as the different ecclesial motifs of the Chinese church, the contribution of Chinese Christian experiences to church-growth theories, the ecclesiological challenges to the universal church vis-à-vis the Petrine office of the Catholics, the emergence of missionaries from China and their impact on world mission, the societal and religious significance of the Christian population in China, and emerging issues facing Chinese Christianity in local and global contexts.

As an observer of Christian communities in China for four decades, I confess that when it comes to China and Christianity, there is still more that I do not know than I do know. This volume is my somewhat ambitious attempt to portray the rise of this Christian community as yeast in a dough, in the Chinese society under strong governmental constraints. My attempt is meant to be a small step toward an understanding of the continuous interactive dynamics between the Christian community and Chinese society in the sociopolitical framework of the People's Republic of China, or in religious terms, the unfolding mystery of God's work in China. The credit of this volume belongs to the millions of Chinese Christians, regardless of their traditions, who have struggled to be genuinely faithful to their belief, relevant to their sociopolitical environment, and loyal toward their country and cultural heritage.

Regarding transliterations, there are different Romanization systems to transliterate Chinese names and places into English, such as the Wade-Giles, the Pinyin system developed by the Chinese government since the 1950s, and the Cantonese system used by the British authority in Hong Kong. I have used the Pinyin system as much as possible, such as "Mao Zedong" or "Zhejiang." I have included the commonly used English transliterated terms for certain persons or places in brackets, especially when a certain term appeared before the Pinyin system was developed, such as "Deng Yiming (Tang Yee-Ming)." When an English transliterated name is conventionally not known in its Pinyin form, the English name is used instead of its Pinyin form, such as "Hong Kong" instead of "Xianggang."

1.

Chronological

Despite centuries of laborious efforts by many missionaries, supported at times by vast resources, the combined population of Christians in China until the second half of the last century was still less than 1 percent of the Chinese population. Since 1949 China has been ruled by a government that not only promotes atheism as state orthodoxy but also exerts tight control over all religions, and especially over Christianity, which is regarded as a Western intrusion undermining Chinese nationalism. Consequently, Christianity gradually diminished under this new Chinese socialist society and even seemingly totally disappeared in the 1970s. It was not until 1979 that Christianity began its humble reappearance from a remnant that had survived brutal suppression. This small community grew at an astonishing rate, with high estimates placing the number of Christians today at one hundred million (7 percent of the 1.4 billion Chinese population). Some experts predict that China is likely to become the largest Christian population in the world by 2030, and this in a country where Christianity is tightly controlled by the authorities, and Christians are banned from public proselytizing.[1] Furthermore, this powerless community seems to be achieving phe-

1. In an interview, Professor Yang Fenggang of Purdue University predicted there will be 240 million Christians in China by the year 2030. "China Will Have the World's Largest Christian Population in 2030," *The Kukmin Daily*, June 22, 2016, https://tinyurl.com/y8ufmdkl.

nomenal growth without any aid from evangelistic resources or campaigns familiar to Christians in the West.

This chapter will first look at the historical presence of different Christian traditions in China to provide a general background of Christianity before the formation of the People's Republic of China. It will then describe the experiences of three branches of Christian tradition, Protestant, Catholic, and Orthodox, in two distinct phases within the realm of the People's Republic of China. The first phase will be the gradual diminishing of Christianity from 1949 to 1978, and the second phase will be the rapid development of Christianity from 1979 until the present day. The subsequent five chapters will focus on different aspects of the ecclesial dynamics during the period of the phenomenal growth of Christianity in China.

THE EARLY PRESENCE

Although there are legends and speculations about the presence of Christianity in China as early as the first century CE, following the discovery of some cross symbols in tombs, there is as yet no credible proof to support these theories. Records of Armenian Christians in China as early as the fifth century CE do exist; however, their presence did not seem to have any Christian influence beyond their own community, as there is no Chinese record of their faith, and no Chinese joined this faith. The first documented Christian community was set up by missionaries from the Assyrian Church (commonly known as the Nestorians), who officially came to China in 635 CE. The Chinese emperor granted favors, such as a piece of land in the capital on which to build their church. These missionaries were emissaries from the Sassanid Empire of Persia. When Islamic Arab forces conquered the Sassanid Dynasty and established the Islamic Caliphate in 651 CE, the Sassanid Empire disintegrated. Some Sassanid princes and their followers (a number of whom were Assyrian Church members) sought asylum in China and built Persian communities in exile based on the Assyrian Church community established earlier by these missionaries. These Persian exilic communities were funded and supported by the Chinese emperors for about two hundred years and eventually integrated into Chinese society. These Assyrian missionaries, with exiled Persians and some local converts, maintained a small community that lasted for a few hundred years.

Although there were some hymns and liturgical texts translated into Chinese, the Assyrian Church kept the old Syrian language as their ecclesiastical language. The Assyrian Christians in China were mostly not Chinese (Han) people;[2] many were Sogdians, Uyghurs, and Mongolians living at the periphery of Chinese culture and life. The community gradually died out due to two major factors: first, the Assyrian Church was declining rapidly in Eurasia due to the downfall of its patron—the Persian Sassanid Empire—and thus the Assyrian Church rendered little support to its counterpart in China. Second, at the same time, there was a rapid emergence of Islam in central Asia, which converted many people who were hitherto Christian or Buddhist. Islam became the dominating religion in Central Asia and remains so today. The last known occurrence of Assyrian Christians in China was in the mid-nineteenth century as recorded by a Russian Tsarist Army officer in the far northwestern part of China (Xinjiang) bordering Kazakhstan. These Christians were reported as nomads with no fixed abode. Since the 1980s, other than a few visits made by clergy of the Assyrian Church to China, there has been no other record of an Assyrian Christian presence in China.

Catholic missionaries first came to China in the thirteenth century. They established a small Catholic church headed by the Italian Franciscan Archbishop Giovanni di Monte Corvino in Beijing, converted some Chinese to the Catholic faith, trained a choir to sing the Latin mass, and translated part of the Bible into Chinese. Catholicism ceased to exist after around a hundred years, when Han Chinese overthrew the Mongolian Empire. However, Marco Polo's travelogue, published after he returned to Europe, generated continual European interest in China. In the late sixteenth century, Catholic missionaries such as Mateo Ricci reappeared alongside maritime expansion by the Spanish and Portuguese into the far east, which brought the latest Euro-

2. Han is the majority ethnic group, and it comprises over 90 percent of the general population. Chapter 4 will elaborate more on the ethnicity of the Chinese.

pean scientific and technical innovations as well as the Christian faith to the Chinese court. After establishing some small Catholic communities and gaining favor from the emperors of the Manchu Dynasty (Qing), the Catholic missionaries had a disagreement among themselves on their doctrinal stance regarding the Chinese traditional practice of ancestral veneration. It was known as the Chinese Rite Controversy. Eventually there was a papal ruling that banned the practice, deeming it idol worship. The Chinese emperor felt that this papal ruling was disrespectful to the Chinese culture and that anyone who did not respect Chinese traditions was not welcome in China. The emperor then issued a ban for all Catholic missionary activity in China.

It was not until the mid-nineteenth century that Catholic missionaries from the West, taking advantage of a politically weak Qing Empire and the presence of strong Western forces, were able to come en masse to China. It was also in this period that Western colonial powers were able to substantially project their political powers into Asia, Africa, and Latin America. Many mission orders, such as the Jesuits, Dominicans, Franciscans, and Maryknolls, eventually established a strong presence in China. With the aim of converting the Chinese to Catholicism, they set up schools, orphanages, hospitals, convents, monasteries, and seminaries.

During the Chinese Republican era, which began in 1911, Catholicism continued to grow with an increasing Western presence in China. Due to the political effects of the Bolshevik Revolution in Europe and the subsequent formation of the communist USSR, the Catholic missionaries usually took a very strong anticommunist stance, regarding communism as the anti-Christ. The Chinese Catholics thus naturally supported the pro-Western Chinese Nationalist Party and the nationalist government that it operated. Chinese Catholicism gradually grew in local leadership. Chinese bishops were consecrated starting in the 1920s, and in 1946 the Chinese Catholic Church hierarchy was formally established. This signified the indigenization of the Chinese Catholic community even though at that time, the majority of the bishops in China, 114 out of 140, were still foreigners. In 1950 there were more than three million Chinese Catholics, which was at that time the largest branch of the Christian tradition in China.

The Orthodox Church (Slavonic) was formally established in China in 1685 when the Qing imperial army took Russian Tsarist prisoners of war in Siberia. The Qing government transferred these captives to Beijing and allowed them to settle there. Among them was an Orthodox priest, Maksim Leontbev, who brought with him an icon of Saint Nicholas and a few religious texts. An ecclesiastical mission was established in 1715 under the Orthodox Church in Russia. This Orthodox community in China grew in size as it attracted Chinese converts, and many Russian men married local Chinese women. The membership of the Russian Orthodox Church in China greatly increased in the 1920s as many Russians fleeing the Bolshevik Revolution ended up in exile in China. In fact whole cities, such as Harbin, the provincial capital of Heilongjiang Province in northeastern China, were built by these Russian émigrés. In the early 1930s there were more than twenty parishes in Harbin alone that celebrated the Slavonic liturgy. Attempts were made to translate some of the church prayers, liturgies, and Bible into Chinese by the Orthodox Mission in Beijing. However, the church liturgy had always been in Slavonic as the church catered mainly to the Russian community and their descendants (many of whom were Eurasian) in China. By 1949, there were at least 250,000 Russian Orthodox adherents and a total of 109 parishes all over China. These were under different spiritual authorities; some adhered to Orthodox bishops in Shanghai, Beijing, and Harbin, while others opted to be under the authority of the Moscow Patriarch, which had been pro-USSR, and still others submitted to the Russian Orthodox Church abroad that opposed the pro-Soviet Moscow Patriarchate.

The first Protestant mission to the Chinese was led by Dutch missionaries from the Dutch Reformed Church, who converted some Chinese populations in the Dutch colony of Batavia (now Jakarta of Indonesia) in the early seventeenth century. They later tagged along with the Dutch East Indian Company (VOC) to the colony of Dutch Formosa (Taiwan) during the mid-seventeenth century to gain Protestant converts.[3] Some of these Dutch missionaries were killed by the local population while trying to convert them into Protestant faith. The catechist Daniel Hendrickx was perhaps one of the first Protestant missionary martyrs to China. Within thirty years, the Protestant community in Dutch Formosa had more than one thousand converts, mainly from among the aboriginal people. The missionaries built churches and schools and even managed to translate the Gospels into the local languages, which they helped create using Latin phonetic forms.[4] These Dutch missionaries were expelled by Chinese military forces in 1662, but the Protestant community that they had established remained active until in the mid-nineteenth century.

The first Protestant missionary to China, as stated by most historical books, was Robert Morrison of the London Missionary Society, who came to Macao, then a Portuguese colony, in September 1807. A few days after he arrived in Macao, he was expelled by the Macao authorities, who were Catholic and hostile toward Britain. He managed to arrive at the fenced-off foreign merchant enclave known as the Foreign Factories (Shamian), a sandbank island just outside of Canton (now called Guangzhou) of China, and sought refuge with American merchants, hiding out for several months before he returned back to Macao the following year. Due to this exploit, he was regarded as the first Protestant missionary to set foot in China. However, such a claim would imply that Taiwan was not part of China, and it also implies that the foreign merchants' compound near Canton, where no contact with Chinese was actually allowed except for some servants, was a mission field in China. Robert Morrison did later convert a few Chinese, master the Chinese language, and translate the whole Bible into Chinese.

It was not until 1842, when China signed the Treaty of Nanking after losing the Opium War to the British, that mis-

3. Vereenigde Oostindische Compagnie (VOC) was more than just a commercial company. It had been the colonial extension of the Dutch government both in a political and commercial sense.

4. For details of Dutch missionary work in Taiwan, see William Campbell, *An Account of Missionary Success in the Island of Formosa*, vol. 1 (London: Trübner, 1889).

sionaries were allowed to stay in the treaty ports to evangelize the Chinese and eventually freed to travel to the hinterland of China. Soon scores of Protestant missionaries from a wide range of denominations and different nationalities, as well as their Catholic counterparts of different mission orders, flooded into China. These missionaries participated in the height of the foreign mission movement immediately following the Great Awakenings in the United States and the United Kingdom. The missionaries came to expand the kingdom of God as well as to discharge the white man's burden by propagating a superior Christian culture in this ancient land. Due to these motivations, the missionaries generally regarded China as a land full of heathens needing to be liberated from backwardness, superstition, and pagan worship. The missionaries met with strong resistance from intellectuals and the Chinese elite who perceived this foreign religion, Christianity, as incompatible with Chinese culture. Many local conflicts erupted between some of the missionaries, their new Chinese converts, and the local population. However, the missionaries were protected under extraterritoriality laws (not under local court and law). The Qing government bent over backward to cater to the demands of the foreigners, fueling further resentment and hatred against foreign missionaries as well as Christianity, a religion perceived by the Chinese as a colonialist intrusion into China undermining Chinese sovereignty and dignity. These conflicts sowed seeds of resentment against foreigners, particularly missionaries, leading to anti-Christian sentiments becoming popular among many Chinese nationalistic intellectuals.

By 1900, China had become the largest Protestant mission field with more than ten thousand Protestant missionaries in the country, yet less than a quarter of a million Chinese Protestant converts. Despite their small number, these Chinese Protestant converts played an important role in shaping the history of China. The founding father of the Republic of China, Dr. Sun Yat-sen, was a baptized Protestant who had a profound spiritual experience when he was abducted by Qing Embassy officials in London and eventually rescued. This spiritual experience seemed to him an affirmation of God's will in his life that he should be a revolutionary and build a modern China.[5] A disproportionately high percentage of the early martyrs of the Republican Revolution to overthrow the Qing Empire were Protestants. Some of the Protestant churches, such as the Anglican Church in Changsha in Hunan Province, even gave sanctuary to these anti-Qing Chinese revolutionaries.

By 1930, there were more than twenty thousand Protestant missionaries laboring to promote the gospel. The number would have been much higher had it not been for the crisis looming over Europe that eventually led to the Second World War. Attempts to indigenize the Chinese Protestant churches were met with a mixed response from the missionary communities. Some independent Chinese churches had emerged since the 1920s as a Protestant response to the rise of Chinese nationalism. Many prominent leaders of the Chinese Nationalist Party (Kuomintang, or KMT, the ruling party) were Protestants, such as Generalissimo Chiang Kai-shek. He married the daughter of a Chinese Methodist preacher and also embraced the Protestant faith himself. Despite the strong Protestant influence among the political leaders and perhaps the intellectuals, the number of Chinese Protestants was still rather insignificant, numbering less than half a million in the midst of the large Chinese population, which had grown to almost four hundred million.

From the Japanese invasion of China in 1931 until the Japanese attack on Pearl Harbor in 1941, most missionaries (both Catholic and Protestant) in China had been told by their mission boards or orders to take a politically neutral stance and not condemn the Japanese military invasions in China, since their respective countries were still on good terms with Japan.[6] Some

5. In 1896, in a letter written to Revd. Au Feng-Chi, Sun wrote that he felt it was the grace of God that led to his being rescued from the Qing government's embassy in London, and so he would continue to follow the will of God to accomplish this revolution. This handwritten letter was reproduced in the book edited by Dr. Lilly Sun Sui-Fong (granddaughter of Dr. Sun Yat-sen), *An Album in Memory of Dr. Sun Yat-sen* (Macao: Chinese International News Press, 2003), 24.

6. One exception was Ms. Gladys Aylward, who was then under the China Inland Mission and who openly condemned the Japanese atrocities in an interview with *Time* magazine by Henry Luce. She acted against the strict orders from the mission board of keeping political neutrality. She even renounced her British nationality and took up Chinese citizenship, an act that infuriated many of her Western colleagues in China. Her story was published by the BBC writer Alan Burgess in a book titled *The*

countries, such as the United States, traded with Japan in war materials right up to the end of 1941. At the same time, however, Chinese national sentiment was high, and there was national resistance to the Japanese. Therefore the missionary-operated church enterprises kept a politically neutral stance, and many church-run schools even prohibited students from being involved in any anti-Japanese (regarded as patriotic) movements. It was not until the Western nations declared war on the Japanese that foreign missionaries from the Allied nations in China began to share the aspiration to fight against the Japanese invasion. By then, missionaries were either fleeing from the Japanese Army invasion along with Chinese refugees into the hinterland of China, where the KMT government was still in control, or detained in internment camps in Japanese-occupied areas.[7] Meanwhile, amid the large numbers of Chinese who had fled from coastal and central areas to the frontier regions of China were Protestants who took their faith with them. With the presence of these Chinese Protestants, Protestantism began to take root among ethnic minorities who lived in those frontier areas and in remote regions hitherto unreached by missionaries.

Following the end of World War II, China suffered a bloody civil war between the Communist Party of China (CPC) and the Nationalist Party (KMT), which led to the defeat of the latter in 1949. The KMT typically portrayed communism as an antireligious and anti-Chinese culture. Most Chinese Protestants and missionaries sided with the KMT, and many Protestant leaders left China in 1949 as they feared that the new communist regime would suppress religion in China. Some of them followed the

Little Woman. In 1958 it was made into a movie, *The Inn of the Sixth Happiness* starring Ingrid Bergman. On the Catholic side, there was Father Vincent Lebbe, who took up Chinese citizenship and organized a Catholic stretcher-bearer team helping the Nationalist Army fight against the Japanese in the battlefield. Incidentally, both had briefly met with each other in 1938 in Shanxi Province, where both were facing Japanese invasion.

7. One of the missionaries during this period was the Scottish missionary Eric Liddell, winner of two medals at the 1924 Paris Olympics, who had been a missionary in China serving under the London Missionary Society since 1925. He died in a Japanese internment camp in 1945, just a few months prior to the liberation of that camp. He could have been released earlier through secret prisoner exchange deals between the British and the Japanese, but he gave up his place to a pregnant woman. The movie *Chariots of Fire* (1981) is about his story as an athlete.

KMT members exiled to Taiwan, while many others went to other dispersed Chinese groups to establish new Protestant communities. By 1949, when the CPC had won the civil war—or liberated China, depending on one's political adherence—there were just less than one million Protestants left in the country. After more than a century of mission labor and investment, less than a quarter of 1 percent of the Chinese population had converted to Protestantism. If one combined all of the Christian populations in China (Protestants, Catholics, and Orthodox), it was about four million, less than 1 percent of the population among 450 million Chinese. All three branches had relied heavily on foreign support in terms of personnel and finance through close ties with their foreign supporting mission bodies.

CHRISTIANITY IN THE PEOPLE'S REPUBLIC OF CHINA (PRC), 1949–1978

On the eve of the founding of the People's Republic of China (PRC) in 1949, there was an exodus of KMT government officials and military forces, rich tycoons, foreign expatriates, and Christian leaders and missionaries all trying to flee the communists. Typical Cold War propaganda by the KMT portrayed the communists as monsters. When the Korean War began in 1950, the PRC was at war with the US-led military forces that were fighting under the flag of the United Nations and regarded the countries behind these forces as enemy states. The Chinese government called this conflict the "Anti-America Aid-Korea" War, and it soon organized a nationwide Anti-America Aid-Korea political campaign to rally support for the war effort.[8] The name carried a strong political implication of a Sino-US confrontation via Korea. The real enemy seemed to be America, which was also backing the renegade regime of the nationalist government (Republic of China–ROC) exiled in Taiwan. The newly established PRC government soon confiscated all US assets in China and expelled most of the remaining Westerners from China,

8. Unless stated otherwise, the terms *China, government, Chinese authority,* or *Chinese regime* are hereafter referred to as the Government of the People's Republic of China (PRC).

among them a significant portion of missionaries who were suspected of serving enemy states.[9] As the PRC allied itself with the USSR in the context of the Cold War, most Western countries sided with the USA in recognizing the ROC government in Taiwan as the legitimate representative of China. They regarded the PRC as a group of communist outlaws and bandits—the archenemy of the democratic world. The US also imposed economic sanctions on China and blocked it in the international arena. The battleground between China and the Western world soon extended from the Korean Peninsula into the international community, as most Western nations backed the US-led economic-political sanctions against China.

The majority of Christians in China had long been led, influenced, and supported by missionaries and showed hostility toward the new Chinese regime, and the government naturally suspected the loyalty of the Chinese Christians. With the escalation of Sino-US hostility, Christians in China were forced to demonstrate their loyalty to the state by renouncing their relations with their Western counterpart, denouncing the West—especially the US-led forces in Korea—and pledging allegiance to the new communist government. In fact, not only Christians, but all civil organizations in China had to terminate their relationship with their Western counterparts in what were deemed enemy states, otherwise they would be charged with treason and regarded politically as unpatriotic to the motherland. Very soon this de-Westernization campaign, as part of the nationwide nationalization program, took effect as major funding and support of various church-run social institutions was terminated, and these institutions were forcibly taken over by the government. All the formerly church-run hospitals and schools were soon nationalized under the control of the civil authorities.

The three branches of Christian traditions had different experiences under the new Chinese communist government. The

9. In 1950, some Catholic missionary priests were arrested and put on trial as spies trying to assassinate communist leaders in Beijing. Later many US missionaries in China, mainly the Maryknoll Fathers, were arrested and also tried as US spies. See Beatrice Leung and William Lau, *The Chinese Catholic Church in Conflict: 1949–2001* (Boca Raton, FL: Universal, 2004), 64–65.

Orthodox Church in China experienced intense internal rivalries, and in 1949 the Orthodox communities in China were split into three different authorities based separately in Harbin, Shanghai, and Beijing. With the departure of Bishop Ioann Maksimovich of Shanghai and his flock to the Philippines and the arrest of Metropolitan Nestor of Harbin (later deported to the USSR by the Chinese government and tried for anti-USSR activities), Archbishop Victor of Beijing remained as the sole ecclesiastical authority over the rapidly diminishing Orthodox community in China as Russian émigrés were also leaving China in growing numbers. Archbishop Victor was pro-Moscow and thought the USSR would support the Orthodox Mission in China. With a declining number of Orthodox priests, in 1950 Patriarch Aleksij of Moscow consecrated the first Chinese Orthodox Bishop, Simeon Du. Bishop Simeon went to Shanghai and immediately ran into conflict with the Russian priests there. Bishop Simeon wanted to develop a united Chinese autonomous Orthodox diocese, whereas the Russian priests of the Orthodox Mission wanted to retain services mainly for the Russians still in China. Bishop Simeon established a new seminary and a new Chinese publication, and actively converted several hundred Chinese to the Orthodox faith within two years (1951–1953). However, such encouraging growth could not compensate for the loss of thousands of Russian Orthodox members all over China.

By 1954, the Moscow Patriarchate closed the Orthodox Mission in Beijing, leading to disputes over the church's property. Without informing the Chinese bishop and clergy, Moscow decided to hand over most of the church property to the Chinese government, which was then enjoying a honeymoon period in its relationship with the USSR. Bishop Simeon resisted the order from Archbishop Victor, who was acting on behalf of the Moscow Patriarchate. Moscow decided to consecrate another Chinese bishop, and Bishop Vasilij Shuang eventually became the Bishop of Beijing alongside the rebellious Bishop Simeon in Shanghai, as Archbishop Victor had left China in 1956. In 1957, after almost three hundred years of Orthodox presence in China, the Moscow Patriarchate finally granted the Chinese Orthodox Church autonomous status, and it became the youngest autonomous Orthodox Church in the Ecumenical Orthodox communion.

By then the Chinese Orthodox Church had been reduced to a small community with perhaps fewer than fifty thousand parishioners, with the largest concentration in Harbin. In 1962, while China was politically at odds with the USSR, the few remaining Russians in China were forced to leave. Some chose to go to the USSR, but most left for Australia via Hong Kong. With their departure, most of the Orthodox churches in China were left vacant. When Bishop Vasilij died in 1962, followed by Bishop Simeon in 1965, the Chinese Orthodox Church effectively ceased to exist except for a few priests who still managed to perform some liturgical functions. During the Cultural Revolution from 1966 to 1976, all external signs of religion were destroyed, and the zealous Red Guards demolished many of the remaining Orthodox churches. The few surviving clergy were rounded up and sent to farms and factories for reeducation. All Orthodox liturgies ceased to be performed. The Orthodox Church in China seemed to have disappeared from the face of China.

Most of the Orthodox Church property in Beijing, including the former Orthodox Mission, had been given to the Soviet government. It was, ironically, the Russian, not the Chinese authorities, who decided to destroy these historical Orthodox buildings within the mission compound. In the early 1950s, the new ambassador of USSR to China, Pavel F. Yudin, ordered the buildings of the Orthodox Mission, including the famous Church of the Holy Martyrs with relics from the Chinese Orthodox Martyrs and the Tsar's family members, to be demolished. Yudin also ordered the Mission library to be burned down, along with its books, which had been collected for almost three hundred years. It was a deliberate destruction following the religious suppression campaign of the USSR in the late 1950s. Today the Russian embassy stands on the ground where these Orthodox historical buildings once stood, and the embassy garage is where the Church of the Holy Martyrs once existed.

As for the Catholics, they went through an intense struggle with the Chinese authority on the issue of ecclesial versus civil authority, resulting in an almost-schismatic Chinese Catholic

Church.[10] This struggle took place in the context of post–World War II Europe when the Soviet Union was competing against the USA and its Western allies over the control of Europe. The communist parties in Greece and Italy were gaining ground, and many Eastern European countries had already joined the communist bloc. Fearing increasing communist influence over Italy, the Holy See issued a series of orders to Italian Catholics, threatening the Catholics with discipline and urging them to resist the Italian Communist Party that was increasing in popularity. The Vatican regarded such a confrontation as a religious, not political, issue.

The Chinese Holy Hierarchy was established in 1946, signifying the independence of the Catholic Church in China from the control of the Mission Orders. However, in the following year, the Internuncio in China, Archbishop Riberi, replaced the Synod Commission with the Catholic Central Bureau (CCB). Riberi issued orders through the CCB to various ordinaries in China, thus assuming the role of the Primate of the Chinese Catholic Church. Riberi feared the increase of Chinese communist influence over China and wanted to prepare the Chinese Catholic Church for a holy war against communism. Under his leadership, the Catholic Church in China was moving on a collision course with the Chinese communist authorities.

In 1950, following directives from Rome, Riberi issued orders that were originally intended for Italian Catholics to Chinese Catholics prohibiting them from any association with the new Chinese communist government. These prohibitions included joining the army to fight in the Korean War, participating in social programs, attending government-run schools, joining a union, serving as a civil servant in the government, or even reading the government newspaper or government literature. Riberi, and perhaps many others in the West, believed that the new People's Republic of China would not last long and that the US-backed ROC exiled in Taiwan would soon reclaim China back into the democratic fold of the free world. The Chinese Catholics would have to endure hardship for a while, but

10. For details, see Chan Kim-kwong, *Struggling for Survival: The Catholic Church in China from 1949–1970* (Hong Kong: Christian Study Center on Chinese Religion and Culture, 1992).

they expected that life would be back to normal soon without this communist nuisance. The Chinese government interpreted these ecclesiastical orders of the Catholic Church as an imperialistic intrusion by hostile political forces from the West against the sovereignty of China, which intended to undermine the newly established Chinese regime. The Chinese Catholics were caught in a dilemma: to obey Rome against the Chinese government, actions regarded by the civil authority as treason, or to support the new Chinese regime and face the possible penalty of excommunication by the Church.

In November 1950, some Chinese Catholics openly issued a declaration for the self-support and reform of the Church, which implied that they would no longer depend on foreign support and would reject foreign control. Riberi immediately denounced this declaration. In early 1951, a Chinese vicar general, Li Weiguang, called for the autonomy of the Chinese Catholic Church and the termination of the Vatican's intervention in Chinese internal affairs. Rome excommunicated Li, and he became the first Chinese clergy to face such discipline. By 1954, nearly all foreign missionaries had been expelled from China, and many Chinese Catholic prelates, such as the only Chinese Cardinal at that time, Paul Yu Pin, had left for Taiwan with the KMT government. The ecclesiastical burden of the Catholic Church had fallen on the few Chinese bishops who still remained in China. By then, Pope Pius XII had issued two encyclicals urging Chinese Catholics to resist any autonomous movement, which effectively heightened the tension of the dilemma facing Catholics in China. In 1955 the government launched a nationwide anti-counterrevolutionary campaign to eradicate any forces still resisting the Chinese government. Some prominent Catholic leaders, such as Bishop Ignatius Kung Pin-Mei (Gong Pingmei) of Shanghai (cardinal *in pectore* since 1979 and made public in 1991), were arrested, followed by many other Catholics who were also resisting the government. In 1957, as an increasing number of the Chinese Catholic leaders who had replaced those who were arrested began to embrace a pro-government stance, the government called for a national Catholic representative meeting and formed the Chinese

Catholic Patriotic Association with branches in all dioceses. This Catholic Patriotic Association effectively replaced the ecclesiastical authority of the Chinese Holy Hierarchy that still followed orders from Rome. Chinese Catholics were divided between those who joined the Patriotic Association, also known as the Patriotic Church, and those who remained loyal to Rome, or the Loyal Church.

The departure of foreign bishops left behind a large number of vacant sees. More sees were then left vacant by the incarceration of the Chinese replacements appointed by Rome. In 1957 some dioceses held episcopal elections to try to fill those vacancies. They asked Rome for ratification of their candidates, but they not only failed to get approval from Rome but also were threatened with excommunication of those very same episcopal candidates. Nevertheless, in 1958 a couple of dioceses held independent episcopal consecrations producing valid, yet illicit, Chinese Catholic bishops. Later in the same year, Pope Pius XII issued another encyclical to the Chinese Catholics condemning the Patriotic Association as schismatic and rejecting the "illicit" consecrations with *ipso facto* excommunication. Some Chinese bishops tried to explain their extenuating circumstances to Rome, but they did not receive any official reply. From then, the physical link between the Chinese Catholic Church and Rome was terminated. After that, little was known about the Chinese Catholic Church other than some news on the consecration of more illicit bishops, at least fifty by 1965, and the ordination of priests. In the 1960s, the government launched a series of attacks on the Vatican during its national anti–Religious Superstition Campaign. These attacks revealed that there were some priests and bishops, or their appointees, who had refused to join the Patriotic Church, were still not incarcerated, and had clandestinely ministered to Catholics refusing to receive sacraments from the clergy of the Patriotic Church. Just prior to the Cultural Revolution in 1966, there were still Catholic churches operating in major cities celebrating the Tridentine Mass in Latin and at least one seminary training priests. At the beginning of the Cultural Revolution, all Catholic activities in public were banned. As the Chinese Catholic Church was living behind the

Bamboo Curtain, it had also missed the *aggiornamento* of the Second Vatican Council.

The Protestants have a different ecclesiastical structure from the Catholics or Orthodox, as there is no central ecclesiastical authority in Protestantism. Protestants are clustered under various religious authorities of different denominations and independent congregations. Prior to 1949, the National Christian Council of China represented most mainline denominations. This council participated in the founding council of the World Council of Churches in 1948. There were also numerous independent congregations and a few Chinese indigenous groups, such as the Local Church and the Jesus Family. Theologically, the majority of Chinese Protestants could be classified as fundamentalists, and few embraced the social gospel, popular in the first half of the last century. Politically, most Chinese Protestants held an anticommunist view, demonstrated by the fact that many Protestant church leaders fled China as communist forces took over the country.

From the late 1940s, a few Chinese Protestants openly suggested that Protestants could cooperate with the communists to build a new China. One of these was Wu Yaozong, who was regarded as a politically progressive Protestant. This phenomenon had been a minority yet audible voice in the Chinese Protestant circle. A few months after the formation of the PRC and with increasing confrontation between China and the West, Wu and others issued a manifesto calling for the condemnation of Western missionary enterprises, the purging of imperialist elements in the Chinese church, and a declaration of loyalty to the new Chinese government. This manifesto, commonly referred to as the "Three-Self Movement" (self-support, self-propagation, self-governance), was adopted by the National Christian Council of China. In 1951 the government issued stringent regulations limiting contact with foreign churches and nationalized formerly church-operated social institutions, such as schools and hospitals. The government also encouraged church leaders and laities to denounce their former missionary mentors and support the Chinese war effort on the Korean peninsula—a nationwide sociopolitical program involving almost all civil groups. In 1951, the Three-Self Movement incorporated the political elements of Cold War anti-Americanism and renamed itself as the "National Preparatory Committee of the Anti-America and Aid-Korea Three-Self Reform Patriotic Movement for the Protestant Church of China." This title implied that a Chinese Protestant in the new regime would not be regarded as patriotic unless there was total dissociation from the West and absolute alliance with the regime.

After the cessation of hostilities on the Korean peninsula,[11] this committee dropped the "Anti-America Aid-Korea" from its title and later became commonly known simply as the Three-Self Patriotic Movement (TSPM), or Three-Self Movement. In 1954, this organization replaced the National Christian Council of China as the only government-recognized national Protestant representation. Soon all Protestant churches were forced to join this Three-Self Movement to make sure the Chinese Protestant community would follow the government's political direction under the banner of patriotism.

Parallel with the Catholic experience in China, Protestants who opposed the TSPM organization were considered antigovernment or antirevolutionary, a serious political crime in China subject to harsh punishment and long sentences in labor camps. Congregations that failed to join TSPM were to be disbanded. By 1958 all denominations in China were outlawed and forced to merge into the TSPM. Churches with different methods of traditional worship had to hold united services, since many churches were closed due to the rapid decline in church attendance. Seminaries and Bible schools were closed and amalgamated into a few schools. Those who refused to join the government-sponsored Protestant body—often referred to simply as the Three-Self Church—chose to have their own worship or meetings, often clandestinely, at homes as a spontaneous expression of their devotion to their faith. These Protestant groups were later known as "family gatherings" and eventually referred to as the house church or family church—a unique ecclesial phenom-

11. As of March 2019, even after the second Trump-Kim summit in Hanoi, the Korean War still has not officially ended. There was just the ceasefire agreement signed in 1953, as well as the ceasing of hostility agreement between North and South Korean governments made in September 2018.

enon that had a profound influence on shaping Chinese Protestantism in later years.

From 1958 until 1961 almost all churches were closed or ordered to stop worship services as China launched the catastrophic Great Leap Forward Campaign (1958–1961), which tried to boost production to compete with the West. Pastors were sent off to farms or factories to enhance production. Although there was a brief liberal period from 1962 to 1965 for the country to recuperate from the disastrous campaign that had led to the loss of tens of millions of lives, few found interest or consolation in the Three-Self churches, which were advocating a form of Christianity that justified the sociopolitical stance of the Chinese government. By 1966, the Protestant community in China, as seen in public, seemed to have diminished to just a few churches in major cities, attended mostly by the older generation.

During the Great Cultural Proletarian Revolution (1966––1976), the Chinese regime, often by force, took a radical political position. Among the main targets for destruction were old traditions and cultures, including religion. Virtually all religious venues were confiscated for other purposes, and religious symbols were demolished or destroyed by zealous Red Guards, save for a few hidden or protected by the local population or items deemed to have important historical significance. Religious personnel were sent for reeducation or to labor camps. Priests, nuns, and monks were forced to renounce their vows of celibacy and marry. And many religious believers were forced to recant their faith or face adverse consequences, even death. Similar to the Chinese Catholic Church, Protestantism ceased to exist in China, at least in public, except for a handful of people who attended the only Protestant church still remaining open in Beijing for members of the foreign diplomatic corps. In the mid-1970s, the Chinese government even declared that religion in China now belonged in museums. Despite government oppression, there were rumors that some Protestants still kept up their faith in secret gatherings at home or in the field. Though there was hope, there was at that time no concrete news of Protestant existence in China during this harsh period when all religions were suppressed by the government. Ironically some liberal theologians in the USA theologized that the Chinese communists had successfully established a new heaven and earth in China and created the new man envisioned by St. Paul in Ephesians 4:22–24. They suggested that God had achieved this task through Mao Zedong of communist China in just a few decades, while the church had failed to accomplish this after centuries.

REAPPEARANCE AND PHENOMENAL GROWTH OF CHRISTIANITY SINCE 1979

In 1978, Deng Xiaoping announced that China would adopt a new Reform and Open policy, signifying a new era of China heading toward socioeconomic reform. One of the elements of this policy was allowing religion to resurface in order to rally religious believers to contribute to this reform. In 1979, the government returned some church buildings to both the Protestant and Catholic communities and at the same time reestablished the long-dormant TSPM and the Catholic Patriotic Association. Some Christians were astonished at such a policy change. While some flocked back to the newly opened churches, others were skeptical. They believed it could be a trick to draw them out into the open in order to persecute them, so many opted to remain clandestine. Still, to the surprise of all, many Christians resurfaced. As information on Christian experiences under that harsh suppression emerged due to increasingly open access to China, an astonishing picture began to appear of Christianity in China during that seemingly dark period.

On the Catholic side, all churches had been closed to the public since 1966, all priests were prohibited from performing their pastoral functions, and most priests, along with many laypeople, were sent to labor camp or prisons. Most of the memoirs from this time—such as the one by Archbishop Dominic Tang Yee-Ming (Deng Yiming) of Guangzhou—reflected that Catholics were actually strengthened in faith from these hardships. He and others regarded this time as a trial through which to purify their faith—an important spiritual experience that provided strong spiritual capital to the Loyal Church against the Patriotic

Church. Although priestly formation had been suspended, those who felt called to the priesthood vocation had remained celibate while hoping that one day they could go to a seminary and eventually join the priesthood. Catholic parents would secretly have their babies baptized, and on occasion, Catholics would gather in secret to recite prayers, such as the rosary, and sing hymns. Despite the lack of sacraments, the Catholic faith remained steady among most of the Catholic communities and grew in secret among their immediate family members. However, there were some priests and nuns, mostly from the ranks of the Patriotic Association, who had openly denounced their faith. Some, such as the late Bishop of Beijing Michael Fu Tieshan, had entered into marriage, as they believed that Catholicism would no longer exist in China. In fact, Catholicism remained in the shadows, hidden from the public eye, and was forged into an enduring faith. There is no accurate number, but the government's own estimation of three million Catholics in 1982 strongly suggests that the Catholic community in China at least remained at the same numerical strength as in 1949, despite more than thirty years of systematic suppression with a severe shortage of clergy. However, this community was split into two factions—those who followed the government-sponsored Patriotic Association along with its affiliates, such as the Catholic Affairs Committee (later disbanded and formed as a division under the Bishops' Conference) and its own Bishops' Conference not recognized by Rome, and those who followed the directives from Rome issued by Propaganda Fide as early as 1978 to continue the Rome-recognized Chinese Holy Hierarchy along with its appointed ordinaries.

Differing from the Catholic Church, the Protestant community could continue to operate without any ordained clergy, as the Reformation claimed priesthood for all. This theological distinction allowed the Protestant community much more flexibility in organization and development. Beginning in the mid-1950s, many Protestants met in their households away from the public eye. With the Cultural Revolution, even the government-sponsored TSPM churches closed; however, Chinese Protestants continued to gather together in secret, often in family households, and retained the most basic forms of Christian activities such as praying, Bible study, and hymn singing. The situation varied from one place to another depending on the local political climate. Many reports suggested that there had been massive conversions to Protestantism during the early 1970s at the height of the Cultural Revolution, especially in the rural areas where many city youths had been sent. The actual number is not known, as most of the converted were not baptized, no records were kept, and no census was ever taken. Also during this period, many Protestants were forced to leave their homes to work in remote regions and soon witnessed to their faith in their new location. New Protestant groups even began to appear in places where hitherto no Protestant faith had even been present. These new groups later became the foundation of many new Protestant churches. Often Protestants would share their testimonies and draw many to seek spiritual comfort in Christian teachings. Some would listen to gospel radio in secret, a severe crime if caught. Many claimed that they had experienced miracles, especially physical healings, after praying to God. Others would copy Bible verses and chapters by hand to circulate, as most Bibles had been confiscated and burned. Hymns and devotional writings were also produced to reflect the Christian sentiment during this period. Many who lived through this period experienced spiritual revival and witnessed that their faith was deepened and strengthened through suffering. Thus a spirituality of suffering and endurance slowly took shape among these Protestants.

By 1976, the Communist Party of China was searching for new directions for the country, and social controls were relaxed. Many Protestants began to emerge into the semi-open during this major political transition period in China. As early as 1978, some gatherings took place in public, such as the many Protestants that met every Sunday in the East Is Red Public Square of Hangzhou (later named the People's Square) to sing hymns and pray in the open. In 1979, the government officially allowed the Protestant community to resume operations and returned some church buildings. In 1980, the government helped to reconstitute TSPM and formed a parallel organization with TSPM called the China Christian Council (CCC). Together with TSPM, this group was called the Two Organizations (Lianghui) or TSPM/

CCC. The TSPM/CCC began to gain momentum in reopening churches, reestablishing seminaries and Bible schools, reprinting Bibles and hymn notes, and building a nationwide organizational structure with branches in almost all of the provinces and municipalities. Along with the growth of the TSPM/CCC, many house churches continued to operate independently from TSPM/CCC and from each other.

In 1982, a Communist Party internal policy paper (Document No. 19) estimated there were three million Protestants and three million Catholics in China. Given that the Chinese population was eight hundred million at the time, this estimate put Christians at 0.38 percent of the entire population. This was a surprising number, as most people thought that Christianity had almost been eradicated in China under severe political suppression. This authoritative estimate of the Party suggested a higher figure in percentage of population than the 1949 estimate of one million among 450 million (0.22 percent). It was the first time the government admitted that Protestantism had actually grown in China during the thirty years of harsh suppression and strong antireligious education. This conclusion coincides with my own impression in the early 1980s that in almost all the places I visited, in more than twenty provinces, the Protestant population was much higher than the recorded Protestant number of thirty years before. Many Protestant communities had moreover developed in locations where there had been no Christian presence in 1949.

A similar process also took place with Chinese Catholicism, and the Patriotic Church reestablished seminaries, ordained priests, consecrated bishops, and opened convents through its government-recognized institutions. Those who were loyal to Rome formed their own ecclesiastical structure under the authority of Rome. The same aforementioned Party document estimated that there were three million Catholics, the same number as in 1949. As for the Orthodox, there were but a handful of surviving priests, with no bishop or national organization. Several Orthodox churches were reopened under the auspices of the local authorities. Estimates suggest there were a few thousand Orthodox followers in China, most of whom were ethnically Russian or Chinese-Russian Eurasians.

From the 1980s until the 1990s, there were many reports of widespread conversions to Christianity, especially in rural areas. These conversions became known as the Christian Fever phenomena, often attributed mostly by Protestants to signs and miracles. The churches began to give figures of their members through the local branches to the national TSPM/CCC, and the total reported official figures were several million in the 1980s and around ten to twelve million in the 1990s. These numbers did not include those who were not part of the TSPM/CCC network, which may have had as many as, if not more than, the number of Protestants claimed by TSPM/CCC. Furthermore, local congregations tended to report a lower number, which was then further deflated by local government officials when the figures were transmitted to the senior administrative level. Therefore the actual number of practicing Protestants at the end of the last century could perhaps have been at least twenty-five million. During the first decade of this century, there was a rapid increase in Protestants in urban areas, as new urban churches sprouted up. Catholic numbers are more accurate because of the baptismal records kept by the parishes; by the end of the last century, there were estimated to be around five to six million Catholics, including both the Patriotic and the pro-Rome faction.

The Chinese Protestant community experienced a meteoric rise, with the official count at three million in 1982 (0.38 percent of population), ten million in the 1990s (1 percent), twenty-three million in 2010 (2 percent), and thirty-eight million in 2018 (2.7 percent). With an unofficial estimate of fifty million in 2015 (4 percent) or even ninety million (8 percent) by the Pew Research Center,[12] the Protestant church has demonstrated an almost twenty-fold increase (using the general estimate) or thirty-three-fold increase (taking the high estimate) in thirty-five years. This may well be the fastest-growing Protestant community in recent history, and its numbers are still increasing. Such a dramatic rise, as well as the huge difference between the official and unofficial count in the number of Protestants in

12. Pew Foundation's estimate of one hundred million includes ten million Catholics. Therefore it gives ninety million Protestants. See C. Hackett et al., *Global Christianity: A Report on the Size and Distribution of the World's Christian Population* (Pew Research Center, 2011).

China, certainly raises attention as to the difficulty of determining how many Protestants there are in China.

In the early 1990s, many quoted sixty million as the accurate number of Protestants in China, since this figure was allegedly sourced from the Chinese authorities.[13] Instead, however, this number came from a person who defected to Hong Kong from China and claimed that one of his relatives working at the State Statistics Bureau saw such a figure by accident in a nationwide, classified census report that happened to be lying on the desk of his colleague. No one could verify if such a report had existed, and no one else since then has claimed to see or know of this report. I later asked more than one hundred Protestant leaders in more than twenty provinces if such a census had ever taken place, and no respondent said that they had ever heard of it. Determining the number of Protestants who participate in non-registered groups is also difficult. Many of these groups report a high number of followers, but these numbers are almost all unverifiable due to the lack of exact head counts by these groups.

Even so, it is possible to estimate the size of these groups. Many of the house church leaders, not necessarily trained in statistics but instead rather pious in their hearts, share the number of their followers with those outside China, often in round figures. For example, they provide numbers such as fifty thousand, half a million, one million, three million, or even as many as five million. Those who collected these numbers from Christian mission agencies would take these numbers at face value as statistically sound figures and add them together on top of the official figure from TSPM/CCC to arrive at a figure as high as the ninety million Christians cited by Pew Research Center, as mentioned above. This large estimate also coincides with the hundred million copies of the Bible that have been published and distributed in China since the 1980s; it is suggested that a majority who got a copy of the Bible would be Christian.

In 2012, the TSPM/CCC gave the official figure of Protestants as at least twenty-three million; however, their figures are often regarded with a high degree of skepticism. This figure

13. This figure was reported by Jonathan Chao (1939–2004) of the Chinese Church Research Center, who had pioneered studies of Christianity in communist China since the 1980s, and had been widely quoted as an authoritative figure.

came from a two-year research project done by the Chinese Academy of Social Science. The Academy commissioned several small teams of researchers to (1) gather figures from several provincial government offices, (2) interview unregistered church groups, (3) interview selected registered churches in rural and urban areas, and (4) use the gathered data to project a nationwide figure. However, interviewees may not have reported true figures to the government, and the vast difference in Protestant density between provinces and cities was not taken into account. For these reasons, even though this figure of twenty-three million has been vigorously justified by both TSPM/CCC and the Chinese government, it is most likely a rather deflated figure. The Amity Foundation, once the official spokesperson for the TSPM/CCC, tabulated all available published figures from provincial TSPM/CCC figures and came up with several million more than the number the national TSPM/CCC had claimed.

Several qualifying factors have to be taken into consideration as one tries to make sense of the gulf between the twenty-three million reported by the TSPM/CCC and the ninety million calculated by researchers at Pew Research Center. The first to consider is interecclesial crossover. There are many points of intersection between the TSPM/CCC and nonregistered groups. Often a person may be baptized in a TSPM/CCC church, later attend a nonregistered group, but still make occasional appearances at TSPM/CCC churches and is thus counted by both as their member. Alternatively, an individual may attend several nonregistered groups but be counted by each group as a member. This situation has become rather common in recent years as the lines between different camps became blurred.

Second, internal migrants affect the numbers. Currently, there are about 250 million internal migrants in China who live less than half of the time in their own homes. The majority of these migrants are peasants from rural areas seeking menial jobs in the city or working at factories in coastal cities in the production process of all kinds of Chinese-made goods now flooding the global markets. Significantly, the majority of Chinese Protestants are rural peasants, and thus a large portion of the country's Protestant population does not consistently live at home but instead works from different locations. For example, in a heavily Protestant populated municipality in a rural part of China, Zhoukou City of Henan Province, the local leader estimated Protestant figures of eight hundred thousand (out of a total population of ten million in the area), or 8 percent of the population. However, in this particular municipality, 45 percent of the population are internal migrants living elsewhere during most of the year. In other words, there are only 450,000 Protestants living there most of the time, and the other 350,000 are actually living elsewhere. Nevertheless, the latter were counted as far as the church is concerned as part of the local congregations' lists. These very same Protestant internal migrant workers were also counted as part of the local Protestant population in the urban centers at Protestant gathering points near the factories in which they work. Such double counting is typical. Given the aforementioned factors, the actual number of Protestants would most likely be less than ninety million.

One of the most reliable figures on Protestant population in China was established by a team of sociologists from Peking University in 2016 using sophisticated methodologies by tapping into two huge national survey databases: the Chinese Family Panel Studies (CFPS), a total of four surveys with a sample population of more than fifty thousand people in twenty-five provinces, and the Chinese General Social Survey (CGSS), a total of seven surveys from 2001 to 2015. Both surveys asked about religious affiliation and religious practices in different forms. Drawing from these data, the team established that the Protestant population ranges from twenty-eight million who had openly confessed their Christian faith to thirty-eight million, which includes the hidden Christians, those who hide their identity in public yet exhibit some forms of Christian manifestation.[14] In April 2018 the government gave the figure of thirty-eight million Protestants in China in a white paper issued by

14. Yunfeng Lu and Zhang Chunni, "Observation in Present Situation of Contemporary Chinese Christian: Based on the Survey Data from CGSS and CFPS," in *The World Religious Cultures* 1 (2016): 34–46. After visiting Christian communities in almost all the provinces in China during the past forty years, I estimate there are at least fifty million practicing Protestants in China, and if I err, it would be on the conservative side. My estimate is higher than the figure of thirty-eight million, close to the high estimate of the research estimated by Lu and Zhang, as quite a large num-

the State Council on freedom of religious belief in China, a figure most likely based on the research by this team from Peking University.[15] Immediately the TSPM/CCC changed their figure from twenty-three million to thirty-eight million and gave no explanation for the sudden increase of the Protestant population. Meanwhile, the current estimate of Chinese Catholics, combining two factions, is about twelve million; the Orthodox, around twenty thousand.

In 1980, Christians, hitherto thought to be extinct, emerged from the ruins of the Cultural Revolution and soon developed into an amazing community that captured the attention of the entire Christian world. Protestants grew from a humble three million to tens of millions within three decades and Catholics from three million to twelve million. All this growth took place in a sociopolitical environment hostile to religion in general; the state orthodoxy is atheism, and the state is hostile to Christianity in particular as a religion often associated with the Western imperialism that devastated and humiliated China. The phenomenal growth in the number of Christians in China may also have a significant impact on the global Christian community.

IMPACT ON GLOBAL CHRISTIANITY

As the Chinese Catholic Church reemerges into Chinese society, one of the most important concerns is whether the Chinese Catholic Church can be in full communion with the Roman Catholic Church, or if it will become a schismatic ecclesial entity like the Old Catholics or the Anglican Church. If it is the former, which most of the stakeholders—Rome, Beijing, and Chinese Catholics—desire, then whether Rome or Beijing will have the ultimate authority over the Catholic Church in China—especially episcopal appointments, as the bishop is the ultimate authority over a diocese—is a challenging issue over religious authority versus secular sovereignty. In order to tackle

ber of house church members would simply refuse to acknowledge their religious situation to any public survey.

15. The Chinese government published a document in April 2018 titled *China's Policies and Practices on Protecting Freedom of Religious Belief* (Beijing: State Council, 2018), https://tinyurl.com/y96shhpr.

this issue, Rome and Beijing have held official bilateral talks since the 1990s. Sino-Vatican relations are an important issue for the Vatican, from the late Pope John Paul II, to Pope Benedict XVI, to the current Pope Francis. Although the two parties have faced their equal share of rumors and political complications, both sides have taken a realistic approach to working out agreements over a number of issues on ecclesiastical authority, especially the appointment of a bishop, as a new ground for the normalization of the Chinese Catholic Church. The laborious negotiations finally resulted in the signing of the *Provisional Agreement* between China and the Vatican over the episcopal appointment on September 22, 2018, which signifies the first major step toward the normalization of the Chinese Catholic Church. It is the first time since 1958 that all Catholic bishops in China are in full communion with the Pope. He has accepted all the illicit bishops into his fold and exercised his authority as the head of the Chinese Catholic Church by immediately establishing the Diocese of Chengde, an act that in the past may have been challenged by the Chinese authority as foreign interference into China's internal affairs. The Chinese immediately sent two bishops to attend the Ordinary General Assembly of Synod of Bishops in October 2018 in Rome, the first Chinese episcopal delegates from mainland China to attend the Synod of Bishops. Although there are still many important issues over the ecclesial normalization of the Catholic Church in China to be resolved, such as the fate of underground bishops, diocesan boundaries, the role of the Patriotic Association, the canonical status of the bishop's conference, or the cooperation between the official and underground factions, just to name a few—the rejoining of the Chinese Catholic Church back into the Catholic communion bears significant ecclesial influences that cannot be underestimated in the Roman Catholic Church. In the Roman Catholic communion, where the centrality is gradually shifting from Europe and North America toward Africa, Latin America, and Asia, the important role that the Chinese Catholic community plays should not be discounted. It numbers more than the Catholics in Ireland, and its faith has been tested through trials and sufferings for decades.

The Orthodox Church in China had once been ignored, as few would have thought the survival of this seemingly dying community possible. However, this small denomination within Chinese Christianity struggled in about two dozen parishes in inner Mongolia, Heilongjiang, and Xinjiang, as well as through a few clusters of Orthodox followers in Beijing and Shanghai. These communities were sustained by a few aging Chinese Orthodox priests in the 1980s and 1990s. Occasionally Orthodox priests and bishops from Russia, and some via Hong Kong, would come and offer help. In 1997, the Moscow Patriarchate passed a Synod resolution to place the Chinese Orthodox community under its spiritual jurisdiction. Furthermore, various Russian presidents raised their concern for the Chinese Orthodox Church to Chinese leadership. At this time, there were also more than a dozen young people who had finished theological training in Moscow and St. Petersburg and were ready to enter into church ministry. The lack of a Chinese Orthodox bishop prevented these young candidates from entering into priesthood because Chinese government regulations decreed that Chinese religious bodies couldn't function under foreign domination, such as receiving priesthood from a foreign bishop. This stalemate finally broke in 2013 when President Xi officially invited Patriarch Kirill to visit China. He became the first world religious leader invited by the Chinese government and the first religious leader ever granted an interview with the president of China. Through this gesture, China hoped to foster positive Sino-Russian relations. With Kirill's visit, the Chinese government formed a working group with the Russian Orthodox Church to help the Chinese Orthodox Church and granted permission to Russian bishops to ordain Chinese Orthodox priests to continue the ecclesial function of this community in China. The first priest was ordained in 2015, and many Chinese seminarians are training in Russia to prepare for the priesthood. Furthermore, there has been an increased interest, especially among intellectuals in China, in Orthodox belief. Currently, there are at least twenty Orthodox parishes in China with about twenty thousand Orthodox followers, and there is an increasing number of clusters of newly converted Orthodox believers. They mostly found this new faith through the internet, books, or travel abroad and eventually managed to get baptized either abroad or by foreign Orthodox priests who happened to be available in China. This small representation of the Christian Orthodox tradition seems to have embarked on a new and exciting journey. It may perhaps lead to the reconstitution of the Autonomous Chinese Orthodox Church, suspended in 1965 when the last Chinese bishop, Simeon of Shanghai, passed away. If a new Chinese Orthodox bishop is consecrated, this youngest and smallest Orthodox family member may rejoin the Orthodox Ecumenical Communion.

As for the Chinese Protestant community, the TSPM/CCC is part of the World Council of Churches family and is represented in the WCC's Central Committee, which influences global Christian orientation. Beyond the representation and influence of Chinese Protestantism in the WCC, the sheer number of Chinese converts within such a short period in the context of an unfavorable socioreligious environment with virtually no resources challenges many current modes of evangelism. The unique ecclesial mode of the house church—simplistic, devoid of liturgy, laity centered—provides a new ecclesial paradigm challenging many present ecclesial practices. Furthermore, the potential of Chinese missionaries participating in global mission is being noted in mission circles, as there are already hundreds of Chinese missionaries now laboring in especially hard-to-access countries (such as the Muslim world). These Chinese missionaries often base their strategies on their past ecclesial experience of operating in unfavorable environments. It seems that Chinese Protestants are now integrated into the fabric of the global Christian family and will contribute to the shaping of Christendom in the years to come.

2.

Sociopolitical

In China, the rights of the citizen traditionally belong to the state, and it is up to the civil authority to dispense even basic human rights within political conditions supportive of the ruling regime. For example, in the constitution of the PRC, a citizen can enjoy all the rights stated in the constitution, such as freedom of belief in religion. However, in order to be qualified as a "citizen," one has to affirm absolute support for the rule of the Communist Party over China and the socialist political system. Therefore human rights in China are conditional rights that individuals can only enjoy in exchange for political loyalty to the ruling authority. Within this framework of conditional rights and a regime that is not favorable to religion, Christianity has faced various sociopolitical challenges during different periods of political dynamics in China. This chapter will first look at the development of religious policy by the Chinese Communist Party, the administrative apparatus governing religious affairs, and the diverse implementation of the religious policy.[1] It will then examine Christianity's response to the government's religious policy in two distinct phases: before 1980, and from 1980 to 2018.

1. Many of the themes and ideas in this chapter are accredited to Chan Kimkwong and Graeme Lang, "Religious Diversity and the State of China," in *The Politics and Practices of Religious Diversity: National Contexts, Global Issues*, ed. Andrew Dawson (London: Routledge, 2016), 82–98.

CHINESE GOVERNMENT POLICIES AND
ADMINISTRATION ON RELIGION

China has a long tradition of state control over religion. Historically, Chinese society did not have a dominant religion, and many religions coexisted for centuries under the rule of civil authorities that usually embraced a nonreligious ideology based on ideas and texts associated with Confucianism as the basis for governance.[2] The perpetual aim of the imperial regimes was to control religious groups and to keep them loyal, or at least subservient, to the governing authorities and to minimize interreligious conflicts, which could compromise social stability. As such, China has a governance tradition of state supremacy over and supervision of religions that can be dated back more than 1,500 years. This supremacy was accomplished in many different ways; various governments provided support to religious groups in exchange for their loyalty and often even subtly encouraged the groups to compete for government favor. The current Chinese government is no exception to this long governance tradition, except that it is the first regime in China's history that made atheism the state's official ideology, whereas most Chinese dynasties had not endorsed a particular belief as the state orthodoxy.

The formation of the People's Republic of China (PRC) in 1949 ushered in a new sociopolitical era as the new government attempted to follow the socialist Soviet blueprint to transform China from a feudalistic society into a modern one. There are two main components of the Chinese governing authority: the Party, which decides on policy, and the Government, which executes policy. The Communist Party of China (CPC) contains a major division called the United Front Work Department (UFWD), which was originally tasked with rallying all the noncommunist factions to support the Party to form a united front against the Japanese aggression during the Sino-Japanese War but continued operations after the war. The UFWD has

2. C. K. Yang, *Religion in Chinese Society: A Study of Contemporary Social Functions of Religion and Some of Their Historical Factors* (Prospect Heights, IL: Waveland, 1961).

branches in all administrative divisions down to the county level. Its current main task is to guide all noncommunist groups—such as religious denominations, other minor political parties, influential public figures such as established artists, athletes, or prominent scholars, Chinese citizens who live abroad, and Chinese civil institutions overseas such as the Confucius Institutes—to support the Party and to promote its current political policy. This department also formulates different policies, including the policies for religious affairs. On the government side, the Chinese government modeled itself after the USSR and established various administrative divisions, including the Religious Affairs Bureau (RAB). The RAB has branches at different administrative levels of the government and implements the religious policies formulated by the UFWD.

The national ideological policy on religion from the 1950s until 1966 was a gradual promotion of atheism and continual denunciation of religion as a form of unscientific superstition, but at the same time it allowed religious believers who were politically submissive to hold limited religious activities. Such a policy is designed to drive people away from religion by categorizing faith as a politically unfashionable and scientifically unsound worldview. During this period, religious groups soon shrank rapidly in size and influence; members were seemingly mainly elderly and uneducated. This policy and practice was in place until 1966 when the Great Proletarian Cultural Revolution (1966–1976) radicalized all social policies; the Religious Affairs Bureau was disbanded, and all religions were suppressed by force as the Revolutionary Committee (the governing body during the Cultural Revolution) felt that religion hindered the progress of socialism and thus needed to be eradicated—by force if necessary.

CHRISTIAN RESPONSES TO RELIGIOUS POLICY
FROM 1949 UNTIL 1980

Within the general framework of the religious policy of the Chinese government, the Protestant community gave various responses at different periods. Such responses gradually shaped the present ecclesial self-understanding of the Chinese Protestant community. In the 1950s, the newly established People's Republic of China underwent a socialist transformation, including the nationalization of all private sectors and de-Westernization of all institutions. The Chinese churches had to cut off links with the West and join the only government-sanctioned Protestant organization: the Chinese Protestant Three-Self Patriotic Movement (TSPM). Churches that joined this movement were considered politically patriotic and were allowed to operate openly, albeit subjected to strong political control by the government. Those who joined the TSPM tended to denounce those who did not join and vice versa. Those joining the TSPM justified their decision by claiming that because Western missionaries brought the gospel along with Western imperialism to China, the Chinese church had to remove the latter influence in order to build a true Chinese church. Further, patriotism is an integral element of Christian belief; therefore, just as the churches in US, as commonly believed by the Chinese, support the American government, so the churches in China should support the Chinese government. The denouncing of fellow Protestants who refused to join TSPM was seen as a political purification process helping to cleanse the imperialistic toxins left behind by Western missionaries; however, it had severe consequences as denounced Protestants frequently received long jail sentences for being antirevolutionaries.[3]

These TSPM church leaders considered themselves politically progressive and tried to construct a new brand of Christianity that would not only survive in socialist China but also live out a form of Christian ecclesial aspiration in harmony with the general Chinese national aspiration, especially in the 1950s and 1960s when the newly established Chinese government was embarking on an idealistic social experiment. These Protestants even attempted to reinterpret biblical stories to support current political movements, such as stressing Jesus as a member of the working class (son of carpenter) who recruited the pro-

3. Ms. Lim Wei-zi reported on a seminar given by Professor Ying Fuk-tsang of Chinese University of Hong Kong on Christians who betrayed fellow Christians in China in her article "The Understanding of Being a Stooge during the Revolutionary Era," http://www.csccrc.org/newsletter/26/113.pdf.

letarians (fishermen), denounced the greedy capitalists (money changers in the temple), and sided with the oppressed class (healing the leper). Their theological attempts, generally brushed off by Western theologians as mere communist propaganda, incidentally read like a proto-form of the liberation theology that appeared much later in Latin America. Despite their enthusiastic support of the new Chinese regime, their submission to the authority, and their voluntary restraining of their activities, there was no sign that the Chinese authority would give more allowance to TSPM in spite of their loyalty. Instead, the government's general social policy gradually constrained the TSPM's arena of operation until 1966, when all forms of public religious activity were banned. Even most TSPM leaders were gradually arrested as potential antirevolutionaries and sent to various labor reform camps for years of reeducation. Some, in their private conversations, showed regret for their naive wish that their patriotic stance would gain enough government favor to allow the Protestant community to operate freely in the open.

Churches that refused to join the TSPM were forcibly closed, while their leaders were jailed, their congregations disbanded, and their activities deemed illegal. They considered those who joined the TSPM, the same group that betrayed them to the civil authority, the Judas of the church. Many organized their religious activities at home or in clandestine settings by retaining only the most essential form of religious devotions such as prayers, testimonies, Bible readings, and some hymn singing. Their gatherings continued to flourish even after the TSPM churches were closed. In fact, many Protestants who had formerly attended TSPM churches later joined, or even established, these house gatherings. The fact that house gatherings flourished and even attracted new converts who hitherto had had no contact with the Protestant faith affirms their claim of representing the true body of Christ in China. Such experiences and claims laid important theological groundwork for the huge schism between TSPM and the house churches in the 1980s, a schism that remains the most important characteristic of Protestantism in China.

Those who gathered in homes often identified themselves with the early Christians, who lived through persecution from the Roman Empire. They generally believed in the separation of church and state and were rather apolitical in their theological self-understanding, avoiding any political involvement by holding a dualistic worldview. However, under China's authoritarian regime, one cannot hold a neutral political stance, for even an apolitical position was usually interpreted as unpatriotic. Nevertheless, these Protestants held on to their uncompromising position and believed that suffering would purify their faith. Many even suffered death—one of the ten Christian martyrs in the twentieth century commemorated by Westminster Abbey was Pastor Wang Zhiming, who was executed by the Chinese authority in Yunnan Province after a public trial in 1967 for the crime of believing in the Christian faith.[4] Although well known among Christians abroad due to his commemoration at Westminster Abbey, his story has been banned by the TSPM/ CCC, and few Protestants in China have heard of him. Similarly, the stories of Chinese Protestants suffering persecution were, until recently, generally banned by the government and the TSPM/CCC. These stories, like many stories from Protestants in clandestine and persecution situations, are mostly unverifiable; however, they are often circulated in private, with some being mythologized for didactic purposes to encourage others.

Catholic responses during this period ran parallel to Protestant reactions, with the splitting of their community into two factions: the Patriotic Church under the government's leadership in defiance of Rome's authority, and the clandestine pro-Rome faction. However, unlike Protestantism, where every believer can be a self-proclaimed ecclesial leader with no fixed structure or centralized authority to be accountable with, Catholic doctrine is based on the sacraments and relies on the clergy as the center of ecclesial operations and full communion with the Pope as the apex of ecclesiastical authority. Therefore, the canonical status of those who joined the Patriotic Church has been a hotly debated canonical, theological, and emotional issue within the Chinese Catholic community. Some Catholics considered clergy who joined the Patriotic Association apostates, their sacraments invalid, and any association as carrying the risk of excommu-

4. See "Wang Zhiming," Westminster Abbey, https://tinyurl.com/yysrblfq; also "Martyrs of the Modern Era," BBC, July 9, 1998, https://tinyurl.com/jmw5fl5.

nication. Ironically, the Patriotic faction argues that they have been always part of the Roman Catholic Church under the spiritual authority of St. Peter's successor, but they had to take extreme yet justifiable measures, such as the independent consecration of bishops, to ensure their survival in a hostile environment. They tried their best to retain their Roman Catholic identity by following the prescribed liturgies and Catholic practices to demonstrate that they were not schismatic like the Anglicans in reference to Rome. Despite their efforts to consecrate new independent bishops and ordain priests, they were not popular among the Chinese Catholics, and church attendance continued to drop. In 1966, all Catholic churches were closed. Similarly to their counterparts in the Protestant church, Catholic religious leaders, even those who had joined the patriotic faction, were arrested and sent to labor reform camp. Some publicly renounced their faith, and many Catholic religious turned their back on their vow of celibacy and married.

In the pro-Rome faction, because of the constant arrest and detention of noncooperative clergy and their successors, ecclesiastical functions soon came to a halt because there were very few priests still available to exercise the sacramental duties. Without sacraments or priests, Catholic religious life came to a standstill. Many pro-Rome Catholics resorted to saying prayers, such as the rosary, at home with family or relatives. Theologically speaking, these gatherings were not an ecclesial function as no sacrament was performed. Due to the lack of priests, there was little growth or development of the Catholic community during the Cultural Revolution. Unlike their Protestant counterparts, very few Catholics claimed to experience miracles. Most of the spiritual experiences recorded were those of clergy who endured long jail sentences. A few brave priests even managed to establish secret parish ministries among the Catholics in their labor camps.

It is interesting to note that many of these jailed pro-Rome clergy, such as Bishop Aloysius Jin Luxian of Shanghai and Archbishop Dominic Deng Yiming of Canton, both recalled that one of their very comforting moments in jail was the encounter with imprisoned Protestants who, through their testimonies, hymn singings, and open witness of their faith, greatly encouraged their fellow prisoners.[5] Before these encounters in prison, Protestants and Catholics in China considered each other archenemies; however, the shared experience of persecution and suffering accentuated the core value of Christian faith—hope and comfort from God—that transcended differences in traditions and doctrines and bonded these jailed Christians. It was a serendipitous situation that instilled an ecumenical union in the midst of suffering.

ADMINISTRATIVE APPARATUS ON RELIGIOUS AFFAIRS: 1980S UNTIL THE PRESENT

In the late 1970s, the government rehabilitated the RAB and the UFWD. The RAB was then a branch within the UFWD and later, in the early 1980s, was transferred from the Party apparatus to the Government as a subministry under the State Council. In the 1990s, the RAB at a national level changed its name to State Administration of Religious Affairs (SARA), and all its branches at the lower administrative level (Provincial or below) were known as the RAB. There have been attempts to merge SARA/RAB into other ministries as part of the government's downsizing program, such as the Ministries of Civil Affairs and the National Affairs Commission, yet SARA/RAB has been able to maintain its importance within the complex of Chinese bureaucracy and maneuver away from merging or redundancy. In March 2018, the Chinese government transferred SARA back under the Party's UFWD in order to streamline government administration as well as strengthen its political control over religion.

The revised constitution of the PRC in 1982 states that all citizens have the right to believe or not to believe in religion, and all religions in China have to be autonomous and not under foreign dominion. The same constitution affirms that the Communist Party of China (CPC) is the only ruling Party that governs China with communist ideology and that Marxism-Leninism is

---

5. For example, see Aloysius Jin Lu-xian, *The Memoir of Jin Luxian*, vol. 1, *Learning and Relearning 1916–1982*, trans. William Hanbury-Tension (Hong Kong: Hong Kong University Press, 2012).

the only state orthodoxy of the PRC, which makes atheism the official ideology adhered to in all public institutions, including schools and mass media. Based on this constitutional framework, the UFWD formulated a "Freedom of Religious Belief" policy to define the role, function, and space that religion could occupy within Chinese society.[6] In general, this new religious policy allowed citizens to have freedom in religious belief as a personal matter but emphasized the importance of the national sovereignty of Chinese religious organizations, which means that there would not be any foreign dominion or influence over religious groups in China. Religious organizations are expected to give unquestioning support to the political leadership of the CPC. Religious activities are also confined to specified locations—officially registered "religious activity sites." Despite these regulations, in practice, religious activities have proliferated both within and outside these officially registered sites.

The general division of labor between UFWD and RAB remains similar to how it had been in the past: the UFWD still formulates and refines policy on religious affairs. The policy is executed by the State Administration of Religious Affairs (SARA) at the national level and various Religious Affairs Bureaus (RAB) at different administrative levels (provincial, municipal, and usually down to the county and even township level). These bureaus translate the policies from UFWD into administrative measures and implement them by imposing these measures on respective religious bodies through administrative regulations and decrees. The RAB has different divisions to deal with the five major religions recognized by the government: Buddhism, Daoism, Islam, Catholicism, and Protestantism. In 2011, it also added a new division to deal with religious schools and all minor religions found in China other than those five major groups, such as the Orthodox Church, the Baha'i, the Latter-day Saints Church (Mormon), local folk religions such as shamanism or followers of the goddess Mazu, as well as other world religions, such as Judaism, found mostly among expatriates in China. The five primary religious bodies also have their

6. Chan Kim-kwong and Eric R. Carlson, *Religious Freedom in China: Policy, Administration, and Regulation—A Research Handbook* (Santa Barbara, CA: Institute for the Study of American Religion, 2011).

respective national associations, as well as branches at all admin-istrative levels corresponding to the relevant level of RAB and the UFWD, mirroring the multilevel governing structure of China, and acting as a bridge between the government and the religious bodies. All religious groups that belong to one of the five major religions are supposed to be officially affiliated with a branch of these religious bodies, which in turn are supervised by the respective RAB and guided by the Party's UFWD. This is a comprehensive administrative system to ensure the full monitor-ing and regulation of all religious activities in China.

Unregistered religious groups, such as the house churches of the Protestants or pro-Rome/Underground Catholic factions, are technically not under the RAB, for these groups have already violated the law by functioning without an affiliation with the government-sanctioned religious bodies and are thus legally under the purview of the Ministry of Public Security; however, this typically functions as more of a gray area. Foreigners in China who conduct illegal religious activities, such as spreading religious messages without permission, and whose acts violate the principle of the autonomy of Chinese religion come under the Ministry of National Security, which deals with espionage and foreign infiltration. At times, the Public Security Bureau may take action to arrest leaders of an unregistered religious group without consulting the local RAB, a common situation in Chinese bureaucracy where there may be as many as a hundred ministries and agencies with overlapping jurisdictions.

Other than SARA/RAB, the Ministry of Public Security, and the Ministry of National Security, there are other branches of the Government or the Party that are also involved with reli-gious affairs. Since 1999, there has been a specific Anti-Cult unit under the Party apparatus, commonly known as the 610 Office,[7] to deal with groups identified by the government as evil cults. Currently there are more than a dozen religious groups in China

7. June 10, 1999 (or 610 in short) was the date when more than twenty thousand Falun Gong members gathered in a silent protest around Zhongnanhai, the residen-tial district of the Politburo in Beijing. This act infuriated the top leadership, and subsequently China declared Falun Gong an "evil cult" targeted for suppression and formed this office to deal with the matter. Later this office expanded its scope of operation to include many other sects that the government had defined as evil cults, among which most are Christian-related sects.

classified as evil cults, which are prohibited by the government and prosecuted by the authority under a law designated to eliminate these groups. These groups include some extreme Christian sects like The Church of the Almighty God.[8] In March 2018, the government merged this 610 Office into the Ministry of Public Security and placed the office under the political leadership of the Party's Political and Judiciary Commission. The Ministry of Foreign Affairs has been actively involved in Catholic affairs in China as it regards the Vatican as a sovereign state, and any relations between Chinese Catholics and Rome would have political implications for China's foreign affairs. The Taiwan Affairs Offices of the State Council also claims some interests in Catholic affairs, as the Vatican is the only remaining European nation that retains full diplomatic relations with the Republic of China (ROC, Taiwan). The Nationality Affairs Commission often intervenes in the policy and administration of religious affairs when such religion is closely associated with a particular national minority group, as in the case of Buddhism among Tibetans and Mongolians, or Islam among the Uyghur. In fact, the administration of religious affairs in China can be a rather confusing issue, as many Government and Party divisions claim a stake over it, and each division operates with its own institutional interest in mind. Therefore SARA/RAB is not the sole authority on religious affairs in China, and often it has difficulty exercising its authority, since all the divisions mentioned above outrank the SARA/RAB in both political and administrative authority.

CHANGES IN ATTITUDES AND POLICIES TOWARD RELIGION FROM 1980 UNTIL THE PRESENT

Between 1980 and 2010, each decade included some kind of fundamental shift in basic attitudes toward religion that affected the interaction between religion and society. Until 1990, religion was regarded as an inferior and distorted worldview. The Party believed that religion would naturally die off as Chinese

---

8. The official list of Evil Cults by the Public Security Bureau is available online at https://tinyurl.com/ybrkfblu.

society advanced. Therefore, there was no active measure to either suppress or promote religion. However, religion was not allowed to have influence in the public domain and could only operate within government-sanctioned venues. Despite these constraints, all religions in China experienced growth during those ten years. From 1990 to 2000, the government regarded religion as a sociocultural force in human civilization. The government also allowed the academic study of religion as a cultural phenomenon and permitted religious groups to provide limited charity services, such as running clinics or elderly homes, to the public. More people in China had access to religion, and all religious groups reported a steady growth. From the beginning of the twenty-first century to around 2010, as China achieved tremendous economic progress, new social issues emerged, such as urban poverty and income polarity. Pragmatically, the government allowed nongovernmental organizations, including religious groups, to address social needs. In the religious realm, the government made specific appeals, and even demands in some regions, for religious groups to operate charitable social projects such as building schools, providing scholarships, running free clinics, or doing voluntary work to help the needy population, as a means to support the government's sociopolitical and economic objectives. Since then, religion has reached Chinese society on an unprecedented scale and gained increasing visibility in the public domain. Intellectuals, businesspeople, entertainers, media celebrities, and even family members of prominent party leaders have been drawn to religion. Indeed, religion has become a rather fashionable trend at the expense of the Party's popular influence. It seems that religion, and Christianity in particular, has enjoyed astonishing growth in these three decades despite various shifts of governmental position on religion, a growth somewhat parallel with the phenomenal economic boom of China during the same period.

Since 2010, there has been a significant ideological shift in China, resulting in more active government intervention in religion in general and a tightened grasp on Christianity in particular. Three factors contribute to this shift: national security, the political theory of "Peaceful Evolution," and the model of religious ecology. First, in 2013, under the leadership of Presi-

dent Xi Jinping, the Chinese government established a National
Security Committee, which, among other fields such as education, media, and national minorities, included religion within
its jurisdiction on the grounds that religion could have political implications that might threaten national security. Since
then, religion is no longer treated as a cultural phenomenon
or a social group but as a social element with implications for
national security. This new view of religion falls in line with
the ideological shift of the Chinese government, which empha-
sizes strengthening the Party's ideological control and rejecting
foreign ideological influences, particularly Christian influences.
Therefore, Christianity has since been considered a potential
base for hostile foreign forces bent on undermining China,
which has to be dealt with as a matter of national security.

Second, the theory of "Peaceful Evolution" has resurfaced in
China. After the fall of the Berlin Wall and the collapse of
the USSR, in the early 1990s the Chinese government commissioned a team of social scientists to investigate the causes.
The purpose was to ensure that China would not fall into the
same fate as the USSR, especially given the infamous events
at Tiananmen Square on June 4, 1989, which echoed similar
cases of unrest in Eastern Europe. The analysts concluded that
the collapse of communist rule in Europe was primarily due
to the long-term coordinated efforts of the US and NATO in
undermining the basic structure of socialist countries in Europe
through cultural, political, religious, and economic means on
various levels.[9] The Chinese named this Western strategy
"Peaceful Evolution" (heping yanbian). Christianity allegedly
played an important part in this strategy through the role of the
Polish Catholic Church in support of the Solidarity Movement,
and the Lutheran Church in East Germany harboring political
dissidents.[10] Wang Zuoan, director general of SARA, in his book
on religious policy in China suggested that in order to protect

9. From the personal communication of the author with scholars who conducted
these studies in 1992 and 1993. Subsequently dozens of books were published in
China using this term heping yanbian—"peaceful evolution"—as the main theme or
even the title of the books.

10. See Jiang Zemin's "Party Secretary Jiang Zemin's Talk on Resist Peaceful Evolution and Strengthen the Building of the Party," in Beijing Youth Daily, August 23,
2001.

the security of China, the country must be wary of such "peaceful evolution" in the area of religion (particularly Christianity).[11] Since the beginning of the twenty-first century, the government has limited the contact of Chinese Christians with their Western counterparts who might promote ideas such as human rights, freedom, and democracy, as well as with those who support Christian communities not under the administrative authority of the government. Even so, the "Peaceful Evolution" theory was not popular in the Party's ideological circles until 2013, when it was adopted as part of the new national policy. Since then Christianity has been openly suspected as a potential base for antigovernmental political activities.[12]

Third, the government has embraced a model of religious ecology in which all religions are seen as different plants in a garden. The civil authority, functioning as the gardener, needs to manage this garden so that all the different types of plants have a fair chance to grow. The government interpreted the fast growth of Christianity, compared to the growth of other religion, as unhealthy. If unchecked, such progress would inhibit the growth of other religions, leading to an unhealthy ecological environment. The government further attributed the rapid growth of Christianity to seemingly heavy support from abroad. Therefore, the government, regarding itself as the gardener, took measures to curb the growth of Christianity by controlling mission activities in China and limiting Christian groups from receiving support from abroad. At the same time, the government encouraged the growth of other religions by funding and

11. Wang Zuoan, *The Religious Issues and Religious Policy of China* (Beijing: Religious Cultural Press, 2002), 398.

12. In October 2013 the National Defense University of the People's Liberation Army released a movie titled *Silent Contest*, which represented the thinking of the current leftist faction in China. At the beginning of this movie, the Chinese Communist Party's view on the Cold War is reiterated: the collapse of the USSR was the result, not the end, of the Cold War. It then carries on to suggest that China is the United States' next target of the Cold War. This movie went viral in China and was briefly suspended during the Party's Central Committee meeting in November 2013, but it has now become the rallying point for the leftist faction in China. It is generating numerous serious discussions among Chinese citizens but at the same time dismissed as rubbish by the West. The movie is readily available on the internet: National Defense University Information Management Center, *Silent Contest*, October 2013, https://tinyurl.com/y2lcvbwk.

promoting international events for Buddhism and Daoism, so that all religions in China would have equal resources for competitive development and China could develop a balanced religious ecology within which all religions live in harmony with each other.

In March 2016, the government called for a National Religious Work Conference chaired by none other than President Xi himself and presided over by six of the seven politburo members (the seventh member was out of the country on a state visit on that date). Other than using this occasion to consolidate Xi's leadership position and to accredit himself as the architect of China's latest religious policy, this conference affirmed the following new directives in religious policy: (1) the government would direct, instead of guide, all religions in China and thereby take a more active role in controlling religious groups; (2) all religious groups in China should be Sinicized, meaning religions cannot embrace or promote values of the Western world and must incorporate social values as advocated by the Chinese government; (3) the administration of religious affairs would expand from departmental (SARA/RAB) control to a higher administrative level, where the coordination of many ministries, such as education, public security, and others, would also have a role in overseeing religious affairs. A few months after this conference, the government circulated a draft of the new administrative regulations on religious affairs, articulating much tighter control over religion than the current regulations, that have been in effect since February 1, 2018. Since the implementation of this new regulation, Christianity has experienced much tighter control, as many local authorities have removed Christian signs from public, banned church summer camps, prohibited all minors from entering churches, and closed Christian-operated kindergartens and schools. It seems that Christianity, which has traditionally borne a foreign image, will face much tighter control in the days to come.

DIVERSITY IN THE IMPLEMENTATION OF STATE POLICIES ON RELIGION

Religious dynamics are rather diverse in China due to the wide sociopolitical variations in different regions within the vast country. Therefore, the various RABs and Public Security apparatus act differently in different locations, even though they are supposed to follow the same policies issued by the Central Government in Beijing. For example, in areas where there are large concentrations of Muslims, such as Qinghai or Ningxia, preferential treatment has been given to Muslims in some instances at the expense of other religions such as Protestantism, and some Protestants in those areas have faced difficulties in gaining registration or permission to hold religious activities in comparison with Protestants in other provinces. The local authorities in these two provinces often refuse permission for Protestants to run training programs because these programs might promote evangelistic work targeting Muslims, which in turn would antagonize the local Muslims who constitute the predominant population. At the same time, however, Muslims are allowed to run madrasas and religious courses for their believers. The local officials rationalize their discriminatory actions as a means to attaining a higher goal of social stability, as they would be held responsible for any social disturbances or mass protests raised by the Muslims as a result of Christian proselytizing in these areas.

In areas where there may be ethnic tensions or the possibility of religiously motivated terrorist or separatist activities, such as in the case of the Uyghur-dominated areas of Xinjiang, there are strict measures to curb religious activities that do not generally appear in other parts of China or in areas inhabited mainly by Hui (Sinicized Arabs) Muslims.[13] For example, in January 2015 Xinjiang implemented a new Religious Regulation, which forbids the listening to, storage of, and dissemination of any religious message that might contain elements with the potential to destabilize society. Further, there are measures in place that curb traditional religious observations, such as coercing Uyghur

13. Dru C. Gladney, *Dislocating China: Reflections on Muslims, Minorities, and Other Subaltern Subjects* (Chicago: University of Chicago Press, 2004).

students to eat in the daytime during Ramadan.[14] Authorities in Xinjiang justify this act as a way of discouraging religious extremism, but such measures could easily encourage a separatist mentality as the Uyghurs could feel that they are discriminated against by the ruling Hans. However, no such measure is observed in other Muslim-concentrated areas in China, such as Ningxia. The fear of Uyghur separatism fueled by religious enthusiasm is not baseless, as the Islamic State leader Abu Bakr Al-Baghdadhi in July 2014 announced that the Islamic State intended to expand their operation in China.[15] Chinese Islamic State soldiers have been captured on battlefields, and in 2014, Malaysian officials reported that several hundred Chinese nationals passed through Malaysia while in transit to the Middle East to fight for the Islamic State in Syria and Iraq.[16] The current number of Islamic State soldiers from China may well reach several thousand.[17] At the same time, in order to pacify the Muslims, the Xinjiang government does not allow the formation of any provincial-wide network of Protestant bodies. Some regional governments, such as the Kashgar government in southern Xinjiang, officially declare the nonexistence of Christianity so that local Christian groups cannot even register and instead have to report to the authority regularly. From the example of Xinjiang, one can easily see that the implementation of a religious policy is a highly complex affair depending on the local socioethnic and political situation. Often, the religious policy implemented in one location may be radically different from the implementation of the same policy in another region, though they are all within the political realm of China and supposedly under the very same policy on religion.

The government's attitude on "native" religions such as Buddhism, Daoism (i.e., the officially registered and accepted Chinese versions of Buddhism and Daoism), and "folk religion" is

14. "Islamic Fasting Month, China Pushes 'Eat and Drink' to Test Uighur Loyalty," *Liberty Times Net*, June 16, 2016, https://tinyurl.com/zc32lcv.

15. Alex Olesen, "China Sees Islamic State Inching Closer to Home," *Foreign Policy*, August 11, 2014, https://tinyurl.com/yyonr62e.

16. Kristine Kwok, "Malaysia Transit Hub for China Jihadists," *South China Morning Post*, January 23, 2015, A-1.

17. Ben Blanchard, "Syria Says up to 2,000 Chinese Uyghur Fighting in Militant Groups," Reuters, May 11, 2017, https://tinyurl.com/y4kkpohj.

not as burdened with suspicions about foreign infiltration or influence as Christianity and Islam. Indeed, it appears that some government officials, up to and apparently including President Xi Jinping, pay respect to these "native" religions as cultural and religious alternatives to Christianity for Chinese citizens. They have expressed such support in various speeches and in government sponsorship for conferences devoted to the promotion and study of those religions.[18] Such endorsement for "native" religions seems to be in line with a religious ecology model that encourages certain religions in competition with others that might receive support from outside the country.

Examining the state-religion interaction at the local level makes it clear that there are a variety of local government accommodations regarding local religious organizations that do not always follow official policies and regulations. For example, local advocates for the construction or reconstruction of Daoist, Buddhist, and folk-religion temples and related religious activities can use the rhetorical tools of "cultural heritage" and "promoting tourism" to support the building of new edifices. They are also able to bring intellectuals and officials to public religion-related events as an excuse to support Chinese cultural heritage. However, there are times that a local variance may become a pilot project; if it is proven feasible, it may become a benchmark for others to model. For example, in Protestant-dominated areas such as in Zhejiang, local officials would have, in the past, turned a blind eye to church buildings clearly constructed in violation of building permits or regulations. However, there has been a government campaign since 2014, with hastily passed building ordinances, to forcefully demolish building structures with obvious Christian symbols, such as the cross, in order to curb the increasing influence of Christianity. This campaign began as a local policy by Zhejiang Party Secretary General Xia Baolong, a protégé of Xi Jinping, and drew international attention, though it was confined basically to Zhejiang. However, with the implementation of the new and more restrictive national religious regulations in 2018, and the promotion of Xia Bao-

---

18. Fenggang Yang, *Religion in China: Survival and Revival under Communist Rule* (New York: Oxford University Press, 2012).

long from provincial government to the central government in Beijing, some provinces such as Henan also have begun to remove crosses from church buildings. These provincial authorities may have read such seemingly extreme actions as politically correct measures in line with Xi's current governance as demonstrated from the case of Zhejiang. As to whether the government's forceful removal of crosses from church buildings is now a national policy by the central authority or a regional measure as initiated by local administrators may well be an academic question; however, it is indeed a political reality in China. Such diversity in government practices often conveys, especially to outsiders, a rather confusing and contradictory picture of religion in China. The contradictions reflect the differences in implementation of religious policies depending on which groups and local officials are involved and when they take place.

RESPONSES TO RELIGIOUS POLICY FROM 1980 TO THE PRESENT

In 1980, the government allowed the reemergence of religions and organized the Protestants to form a joint organization with TSPM called the China Christian Council (CCC). The two organizations were together named *Lianghui* or TSPM/CCC. The TSPM/CCC began to gain momentum in reopening churches and reestablishing seminaries and Bible schools, reprinting Bibles and hymnals, and establishing nationwide organizational structures with branches in almost all provinces, municipalities, prefectures, and counties—all with the support of the government. It also established links with the global Christian community by joining the World Council of Churches in 1993, becoming part of the Global Christian Forum in 2014, and actively participating in ecumenical affairs. Since the 1980s when there were just a handful of reopened churches with perhaps three million believers, the current official membership in TSPM/CCC is more than thirty million.[19] The TSPM/CCC issues church policy and regulation, effectively connecting tens of thousands of TSPM/CCC churches into one large block of

19. See the official website of TSPM/CCC at https://tinyurl.com/y376fwx2.

Protestant community—perhaps the largest single block of Protestants in China. These TSPM/CCC churches register with the government, receive guidance from the civil authority, and operate within the framework established by the authority. Their personnel appointments are often decided by the government, though perhaps based more on political loyalty than religious competency. Government-recognized religious institutions, such as TSPM/CCC, have a monopoly over their respective religion. Officials of these recognized religious organizations are treated as government officials on par with ranking civil servants who have special subsidies, privileges, and benefits. In some provinces, such as Yunnan, the government often sends its own staff to take up positions at the provincial TSPM/CCC office and assist these organizations. These offices are government-organized nongovernment organizations and a de facto government's governing apparatus extended in the Protestant community.

Members of the TSPM/CCC take a pragmatic stance to justify their full cooperation with the government. They stress the theological conviction of obeying the government as God's ordained authority on earth. They follow the priority of love of the nation above the love of the church as they generally argue that without China, there would not be the Chinese church. They also attribute the rapid growth of the Chinese church to the government's religious policy of freedom of religious belief. Further, they argue that the present state of the TSPM/CCC as being free from foreign domination or interference, as opposed to the past when foreign missionaries dominated the church in China, is an authentic expression of a mature and independent Chinese church. Such an expression of indigenization is also accredited to the Communist Party of China's striving for Chinese political sovereignty, especially within the Chinese church. Some of the TSPM/CCC leaders theologize their political stance. Chen Zeming, a former faculty member of the Nanjing Jinling Union Theological Seminary, advocated a theology of reconciliation, suggesting that Christianity had sinned against China through its imperialistic aggression and needed to repent and be reconciled with China in order to be accepted by Chinese society. Bishop Ding Guangxun (K. H. Ting) advanced the notion of justification by love (not faith), urging Chinese Protestants not to discriminate against the atheistic communists. His theological stance implied that communists with good deeds would not necessarily end up in hell but instead may be found in heaven. However, whether an atheist would appreciate being accepted into the Christian heaven is another theological matter upon which Ding did not elaborate. Despite the promotion of such theological ideas by official TSPM/CCC machineries and resources, they seem to have had little impact on daily Protestant living in China. Protestants within the TSPM/CCC, other than those who are at the top of the hierarchy, are more concerned with a stable and open environment in which to conduct their religious activities than these official theological stances.

There is also a wide range of church-state relations exercised by the network of churches that are registered within the umbrella of the TSPM/CCC. Some TSPM/CCC leaders may be hostile to communism, but they still have to maintain a pragmatic working relationship with the local authorities. Their activities are regulated by the local governments, and restrictions vary depending on the local authorities' attitudes toward Christianity. Many of these TSPM/CCC groups also run house gatherings for practical reasons: insufficient space in the church building, greater convenience in meeting at the homes of believers who live far away from the officially sanctioned church venue, and in some cases, a long tradition among local Protestant groups of meeting in people's homes rather than in church buildings. Many of these house gatherings operated by TSPM/CCC groups are not registered and are technically illegal; however, local authorities usually exhibit a high tolerance toward these ecclesial operations as long as the TSPM/CCC notifies the authorities. I once spoke to a pastor at a TSPM/CCC church in a provincial capital who said that they had reported to the government that he ran seven house gatherings under his church, but added that in fact he runs twenty-one such gatherings. This TSPM/CCC situation is very typical; officially all of its activities are under the civil authority, but in fact it keeps some activities outside of the official jurisdiction.

There are also many churches that are in the process of registration for provisional approval but are not yet fully registered, or they are acknowledged by the authorities and are closely liaising with them. Such situations are common, especially with newly established Protestant communities in areas where no Protestant church has existed or newly established urban house churches with few connections to local Protestant groups, TSPM/CCC or otherwise. Many do not want to join TSPM/CCC but instead link directly with the government, as in the cases of some house church groups in Jiangsu and Jilin provinces.[20] Many more nonregistered groups began to follow this new trend—legally registered but autonomous from TSPM/CCC—but can no longer do so as the new religious regulation from 2018 leaves little room for such an option.

There are also many Protestant communities formally registered with the government who remain outside the TSPM/CCC network, such as the churches in Xinjiang Uyghur Autonomous Region. These registered churches exist outside of the TSPM/CCC network and deal with the local civil and even military authority directly, as some Protestant communities live within the Construction Corp of Xinjiang under the jurisdiction of the Military Commission. Additionally, there are Protestant groups that are formally under government supervision and yet are not allowed to register. However, despite their supervision, the local authorities deny their formal existence because of the lack of registration. One such case is the church in Kashgar of Xinjiang. The local authority demands that this church make a weekly report to the government on its activities, even though the church supposedly does not officially exist on paper.[21] Therefore, even within the legal registration framework of China, there

20. As early as 1995, there were many churches in Yanbian Korean Autonomous Prefecture of Jilin Province who had already registered with the government independently from TSPM/CCC, calling themselves Yanji Christian Church; they even ran their own theological training center. One of their faculties in training had been a ThM student of mine while I taught at Trinity Theological College in Singapore as a guest faculty member. Since 2013, Jiangsu Province has also registered many house churches that have also refused to join the TSPM/CCC.

21. I visited this church in 2003 and 2004. The local authority assured me that there was no Protestant presence in the whole region of Southern Xinjiang in which Kashgar is situated, for there was no record of any Protestant group that had been noted. At the same time, there was a notice posted at the church by the local authority ordering them to make weekly reports to the authority on their activities. This is government administration with typical Chinese characteristics.

exist vast gray areas among registered churches, and many officially acknowledged groups are still on the fringes of the law.
As for the nonregistered sector, since the 1980s often referred
to as "house churches," the situation is equally complex as that
of registered groups, if not more so. In the early 1980s, many
Protestant groups survived as remnants following harsh governmental suppression after 1949 and opted not to join the
reestablished TSPM/CCC. They believed that they should not
compromise their stance by falling under the supervision of the
TSPM/CCC, a group that once allied with the government to
suppress these very churches. In the 1980s, Protestantism experienced rapid expansion in rural areas in provinces such as Henan
and Anhui, reportedly stimulated in part by stories of "faith-
healing" miracles by Protestant preachers.[22] In spite of these
humble beginnings, these Protestant groups soon swelled, and
their house gatherings could no longer accommodate such large
numbers of worshipers. While some split into smaller groups,
some began to meet at buildings specially constructed or dedicated for larger groups, such as barns or warehouses. However,
such groups are still referred to as "house churches" or "family
churches," even though many of the meetings no longer take
place in someone's home. Some of these "house church" meetings gather in buildings that can hold several hundred people
and supposedly operate training facilities that can accommodate
a hundred or more students. Most of these are known and mon-
itored by the authorities, as it is almost impossible to hide a regular gathering in a highly populated country like China, and
there is really no secret in China! The term "autonomous Christian communities,"[23] or ACCs, versus those who registered with
the TSPM/CCC, may reflect more accurately the ecclesiological reality of these nonregistered Protestant groups than the term
"house church" conveys.

In the past three decades, there has been huge growth among
the ACCs, both in rural and urban areas, as China likewise has
experienced rapid urbanization. There are, however, many divisions among these ACCs due to theological differences—from

22. Alan Hunter and Chan Kim-kwong, *Protestantism in Contemporary China*
(Cambridge: Cambridge University Press, 1993), 145–54.

23. Hunter and Chan, *Protestantism in Contemporary China*, 178.

strict fundamentalism to extreme charismatic beliefs, as well as leadership styles and personality clashes. All this adds to the diverse development of this ecclesial movement both in strength and in variety. Since these ACCs do not fall under the supervision of the civil authorities like TSPM/CCC, they have a high degree of flexibility and mobility in their expansion, training, development, and recruitment. Very often, a zealous believer who has evangelized a few dozen friends, relatives, and neighbors begins to organize such gatherings, which eventually evolve into a "house church." If this new Protestant leader is affiliated with a larger group, then this new group is likely to become part of a larger network. Although there are no accurate statistics on the number of adherents in ACCs, estimates vary from just a few million suggested by TSPM/CCC up to sixty million or more by others as discussed in the previous chapter. Although strong in number, ACCs, by the very nature of their autonomy, do not have a unifying structure; instead, there are tens of thousands of groups ranging from small household gatherings to sophisticated structures with a national network of millions of members.

Despite the vast differences, these ACCs do share many things in common. Theologically, they usually oppose the TSPM/ CCC on church and state relations, considering the TSPM/ CCC to have compromised the integrity of the church by not only betraying the church to secular authority but also submitting the church under a civil authority instead of God's. Legally, they are not under the direct supervision of the Religious Affairs Bureau; however, many ACCs retain certain liaisons with their local civil authorities, such as the local public security office or neighbor committee. Socially, although ACCs have no legal social status and are not under the direct control of the government, most ACCs, just like other spheres of livelihood in China, are under the monitoring system of the Public Security apparatus. This disadvantageous social position does not prevent people from joining their ranks. In fact, many ACCs have recently launched missions or church planting programs, even abroad, thus giving birth to new Protestant communities both in China and in other countries. Ecclesiastically, they are not bound by any denominational polity; they are mostly led by leaders with charisma. They are flexible, hidden from the public domain, and stress the separation between church and state. They also teach that the church should not be submissive to civil authorities. The major disagreement between these two factions is the issue of church-state relations. In recent years, there have been encouraging signs that the two sides are beginning to cooperate with and accommodate each other, which will be elaborated upon in the following chapter.

International Protestant groups, mission agencies, and denominations often contribute to this interecclesial tension by taking sides with either camp. Since the TSPM/CCC is a member of the World Council of Churches (WCC), many national councils of churches and the traditional mainline denominations, such as the Lutheran World Federation or the Anglican Communion, often endorse TSPM/CCC as the sole Protestant representative in China, a move resented by ACCs. Evangelical circles tend to support ACCs, especially the many Protestant ministry organizations and mission groups that have established clandestine ministerial cooperation with ACCs. The involvement of these overseas Protestant groups often strengthens the entrenched positions of either TSPM/CCC or ACCs and brings the battle between these two groups into ecumenical circles.[24]

It is sad to observe that often the institutional interest of some

24. The Lausanne 2010 Conference is an example of such conflicts. The Conference organizer had first invited ACCs to attend, and this upset the TSPM/CCC. It later invited TSPM/CCC, and ACCs did not like it. Just prior to the conference, the executive chairman of Lausanne Movement, Doug Birdsall, went to China and clandestinely visited some of the invited ACC delegates but without paying a visit to the TSPM/CCC invitees. The TSPM/CCC invitees felt disrespected and suspected a possible conspiracy trying to humiliate them at the conference. In the end, the Chinese government received help from the South African Embassy in China as the embassy marked the South African visa on the ACC Chinese delegates' passports with special stamps that could alert the Chinese border guard as these delegates tried to exit China, and this managed to stop all the invitees of the ACCs in China who participated as full delegates from leaving China. The TSPM/CCC invitees—invited as observers—refused to attend to avoid possible confrontation with pro-ACC participants at the conference. This incident escalated the already existing hostility between TSPM/CCC and ACC and extended the schism into international Protestant agencies. The Lausanne movement later totally sided with ACCs and burned its bridge with TSPM/CCC. I was personally involved in the communications between the Lausanne Conference organizers and some of the Chinese delegates.

overseas Protestant groups seems to supersede the important goal of unity in the Chinese Protestant church.

Catholic responses to governmental control are similar to the Protestant ones: the Patriotic faction is predictably identical to their TSPM/CCC counterpart, whereas the underground group aligns more with the ACCs. However, due to the different ecclesiastical structures of the Catholic and Protestant churches, the tension between the Patriotic and the pro-Rome factions has been gradually deescalating as Rome and Beijing are negotiating for normalization of their relations. When the Catholic Church was allowed to reappear in 1979, the Vatican had already issued a special order—in 1978—to grant Chinese ordinaries special privileges, such as shortening the training period of priests and giving the authority to appoint an episcopal successor without prior approval from Rome in emergency circumstances in order to continue the episcopal succession. Other than the ecclesiastical and pastoral issues of the Chinese Catholics, the Vatican also wanted to normalize diplomatic relations with China so that it could formally intervene in the division among the Chinese Catholics, whom the Holy See considered as all under one Catholic Church. The challenges to the Holy See are manifold, including the escalation of diplomatic tension with Taiwan, since the Vatican has recognized the government of the Republic of China (ROC, Taiwan) as the sole representation of China, the only European nation to maintain such a diplomatic link with Taiwan. Any closer ties with China would add stress to the Vatican-Taiwan relation. Also, if the Vatican is negotiating a closer relation with China, it has to recognize many independently consecrated bishops who have clearly violated the canonical order of Rome. This would lead to the need to pacify underground Catholics who paid a high price to stay loyal to Rome, but were eventually required to share glory and power with patriotic factions, whom they considered traitors. The Vatican would also have to share authority with Beijing on matters of ecclesial sovereignty, especially on episcopal appointments, which the Holy See has regarded as its prerogative. All of these challenges bear profound political, canonical, pastoral, and theological implications not only for the Catholic Church in China but also for the global Roman Catholic communion.

As for the Chinese authority, a unified Chinese Catholic Church may bring harmony to Chinese society. However, it also raises concern, as a unified church would have a strong bargaining position with civil authorities and may leave little room for the government to leverage one faction against the other. Also, if normalization takes place, the government has to allow the Vatican, via the Nuncio or its representative, to exercise ecclesiastical authority over the Chinese Catholic Church. This is an issue of sovereignty that was seemingly nonnegotiable in the past as stated in the Constitution of China. However, if the largest atheistic nation is officially connected with the largest single and organized block of religious believers in the world, China may be regarded not only as an economic giant but also as a respectful nation that accepts the great civilizations and religions of the world.

Against all odds and after more than thirty years of engagement, both covert and public, and during the reign of three pontiffs and three Chinese presidencies, intentions from both sides have led to the historical Provisional Agreement signed in September 2018. First, since 2014, both sides have called for a halt to hostility: China stopped the independent consecration of bishops, and Rome ceased the excommunication of those disobedient bishops who received independent consecration, as well as having no new appointment of underground bishops. Second, the majority of bishops currently operating in the open, which numbers about seventy, have also received approval and recognition from Rome before being consecrated in public under the government's order, Thirdly, some underground bishops have been recognized by the Chinese authorities. Fourth, the Catholic Church in Taiwan is well prepared for the Vatican to switch its diplomatic presence from Taipei to Beijing. Fifth, and most important, both sides reestablished formal contact, which gave rise to a joint working group paving the way for Sino-Vatican normalization and tackling the technical issues. The two sides reached a general framework of agreement on episcopal appointment in November 2016, a major step toward establishing a unified China Bishop Conference as the sole ecclesiastical authority from which the two factions will gradually merge into one single, ecclesiastical entity. Both sides have been working hard to resolve many outstanding issues prior to the signing of Provisional Agreement, such as the ecclesial status of the several illicit bishops in the Patriotic faction, of whom some are openly excommunicated. Some allegedly have spouses and children, yet all are backed by the Chinese authority. There are also several dozen legitimate bishops of the underground faction, some still in government detention, who are regarded as illegal under the law of China. On September 22, 2018, both sides resolved most of the thorny issues and signed the Provisional Agreement on episcopal appointment. This is the first major step toward the normalization of the Chinese Catholic Church since the break between Rome and the Chinese Catholic community sixty years ago, when the Chinese Catholic Church consecrated its first independent bishop against specific orders from Pope Pius XII on April 13, 1958, in Hankou of Hubei Province. Immediately the pope pardoned the illicit bishops and established a new diocese in China to exert his papal authority as the head of the Chinese Catholic Church. There will be a whole range of difficult issues, such as the legitimization of underground bishops by the Chinese authority, that will test the good faith of both governments in the spirit of the agreement.

For the twelve million Chinese Catholics, despite decades of internal ecclesial tensions caused by sociopolitical forces, there is hope for a united Chinese Catholic Church through the efforts of both the Vatican and the Chinese government. It seems that Catholics in China have been taken hostage by various political forces in the past as pawns in the international political arena, be it anticommunist forces in China during the Cold War or as a way for the Chinese authority to enhance its international image. The experience of the Catholics in China reflects the strong political control of the Chinese authority over religion and the powerlessness of religious groups in China at the mercy of civil authority.

The tiny Chinese Orthodox community has benefited from the new geopolitical dynamic at work in China. When religion was permitted again in the early 1980s, this small community was scattered throughout various provinces, each with merely a handful of believers. The lack of active priests also severely limited Orthodox religious activities. Some Orthodox followers in China sought religious services across the border in Russia, and often Russian Orthodox priests would perform religious services with tacit agreement from the civil authority. Because of the insignificance or lack of impact of this community in Chinese society, the government did not pay much attention to it. In fact, some in the government decided to ignore it, expecting that it would die off eventually when the last priest passed away.[25]

However, this seemingly dying community gained support from the Moscow Patriarchate, which took the Chinese Orthodox community under its wing. Furthermore, Russian political leaders consistently appealed to their Chinese counterparts on behalf of this on every possible occasion, though often with no response until 2012, when China decided to enhance Sino-Russian relations as a major diplomatic policy. The first state visit made by the newly ascended Chinese President Xi was a high-profile visit to Moscow in March 2013. Prior to his visit, the Russians made it clear that they would raise their concern for the Orthodox community in China, hoping to have at least some positive gesture from the new president. Xi not only met with Patriarch Kirill but also invited Kirill to China in May 2013, an unprecedented invitation from a Chinese communist leader to a world-recognized religious leader. Since Kirill's visit, the Chinese Orthodox Church has been revived, and new Chinese Orthodox clergy are now being prepared with approval from China and support from the Russian Orthodox Church. Similar to their Catholic and Protestant counterparts, the Chinese Orthodox Church has been affected by the political dynamics of the Chinese government. In this case, it served as a token of a positive gesture in foreign relations with Russia. It seems that the importance of foreign relations supersedes the so-called sovereignty issue stressed in China's religious policy, as China has accepted the involvement of the Russian Orthodox Church into Orthodox affairs in China. As for the continued development of the Chinese Orthodox Church, it is dependent on several factors: support from the Russian Orthodox Church, which rides on the current positive Sino-Russian political relations; the

25. Conversation with the director of Provincial RAB in Heilongjiang, December 1999.

incorporation of new Chinese Orthodox converts into the Chinese Orthodox Church, especially those from intellectual circles; and the transformation of the current Chinese Orthodox self-identity from a cultural rediscovery toward a religious identity of the Orthodox spiritual tradition.

Different Christian traditions in China have experienced similar fates under the communism of the People's Republic of China during the first three decades of social experimentation by the Communist Party of China since 1980. While most thought Christianity had been eradicated from China, during the past three decades, a resilient Chinese Christianity has risen from the ruins and rapidly grown into a significant community, which is much larger than before. Despite the government policy of religious control, containment, and constraint, which is compounded by frequent interecclesial tensions regarding church-state relations, this seemingly powerless community, which includes all three main Christian traditions, is silently growing with unprecedented depths of penetration across Chinese society, reaching tens of millions. It is indeed a new chapter of Christianity in China, a chapter filled with the struggles of Chinese Christians torn between loyalty to the church or to the state, and between immanence in or transcendence from this world.

3.

Denominational

VARIOUS PROTESTANT TRADITIONS BEFORE 1949

When China opened the door to Protestant missions in the mid-nineteenth century, almost all major Protestant denominations sent missionaries and tried to establish their presence. It was common for a denomination to send different missionaries from their churches located in different nations. For example, there were at least a dozen different Lutheran mission groups from countries such as Finland, Norway, and the US, among others, with respective and unrelated mission establishments in China. There were also at least a dozen Presbyterian missions from various English-speaking countries. These denominational mission boards generally established churches as replicates of their home congregations. Usually these denominational missions were well vested with resources and would build schools, orphanages, hospitals, and chapels using architectural blueprints from their home countries. It was not uncommon to find a Gothic-style church building with clergy wearing full European vestments in a small town in rural China, juxtaposed with Chinese temples, mud huts, serene rice paddy fields, and curious Chinese peasants peeking through the stained-glass windows at the pews and altar table of the church.

Beside denominational mission boards, there were many

independent and interdenominational mission organizations, such as Basel Mission, London Mission Society, or China Inland Mission, in China from the mid-nineteenth century. These groups were later joined by literally thousands of smaller mission groups often composed of a handful of people who were supported by a few sending patrons or congregations. Most of these independent mission groups would establish mission stations, which later evolved into churches that had little resemblance to the major denominational churches in terms of ecclesiastical architecture and policy. The mandate of these mission groups was primarily to make converts rather than to develop church institutions such as church polity, order, authority, and sacraments. However, these mission stations or preaching points would often operate some simple form of a church service, and some eventually developed into new ecclesial communities, thus giving rise to new denominations. For example, in the 1920s the US-based Christian Missionary Alliance (CMA) was a mission-sending agency with a presence in China. The congregations that the CMA missionaries established in China later became a denomination called the Chinese Christian Missionary Alliance Church. Other than these independent denominations set up by mission groups, whenever there was an ecclesiastical split within a mainline Western denomination—such as the tension over fundamentalism and liberalism among the Presbyterians in the US during the 1920s—these divisions caused splits within the newly established Chinese churches and generated more Protestant groups and new denominations in China.

By 1949, not only could one find almost all the major Protestant denominations and their various splinter groups within the Chinese Protestant community—Anglicans, Baptists, Congregationalists, the Salvation Army, and Seventh-Day Adventists (SDA)—but there were also nationally distinct groups of the same denomination appearing as separate Chinese Protestant denomination entities. For example, the Swedish Free Church, the American-Swedish Free Church, and the Norwegian Free Church all bore distinctive Chinese names and operated their Chinese missions separately from each other, yet they all belonged to the same theological and ecclesiastical genre. There were also missionaries establishing new denominations, such as the Rhenish Church or the Christian Missionary Alliance Church, that were not found in their mission-sending home countries. In fact, the Chinese Protestant church became one of the best places to find a good collection of not only the Protestant denominational representations that one can find in the West but also new denominations found only in China's mission field.

Other than denominations transplanted or established by the missionaries, Chinese Protestants also developed some unique ecclesial forms, especially following the 1920s when strong nationalistic aspirations emerged in China, and denominational alignment was seen as almost equivalent to religious Western imperialism. Many Chinese Protestants attempted to build indigenous Chinese Protestantism both to be free from Western cultural influence or control as well as to be authentic to Chinese cultural heritage and social aspirations. These indigenous ecclesial attempts varied from an independent congregation splitting from a missionary-controlled establishment, to a congregation wholly established by Chinese pastors, to a group of congregations established by local Chinese Protestants with ecclesial characteristics differing from those established by the missionaries. Among many indigenous Chinese churches, the Church of Christ in China, the Local Church, the True Jesus Church, the Jesus Family, and the Spiritual Band Movement were of theological significance because they were all genuine attempts to find an authentic expression of Protestantism within the Chinese sociopolitical milieu and to avoid denominationalism. Each of these developed into some form of a sustainable ecclesial community bearing unique characteristics. The impact of these denominations can still be felt today not only within but also beyond the Chinese Protestant community. The following is a general description of these groups, with their current status both in China and abroad.

The Church of Christ in China

In the 1920s, many Chinese Presbyterian and Reformed churches joined together to form a coalition called the Chinese

Presbyterian Church. The name was later changed to the Church of Christ in China (CCC) at the General Assembly in 1927, which invited churches from other non-Presbyterian organizations such the Baptists, Methodists, and the United Brethren to join. It modeled itself after contemporary ecumenical church establishments such as the United Church of Canada in 1925 or the United Evangelical Church of the Philippines in 1929. The church polity was based on Presbyterianism, divided into conferences and councils, and ecclesial control was in the hands of Chinese. There was no major theological or ecclesiastical breakthrough other than the transfer of church property and authority from the foreign missionaries into Chinese ownership. This ecclesial establishment emphasized ownership by nationals and Christian unity, and it had little theological and ecclesiological innovation. It was a hybrid of Presbyterianism and Congregationalism with some latitude for a Reformed theological orientation. By 1949, it had become one of the largest Chinese Protestant groups and rivaled the missionary-controlled denominations. During the 1950s, many of the CCC leaders supported TSPM, and the Church of Christ in China was soon absorbed into TSPM. Currently the only Church of Christ in China is the CCC Council in Hong Kong, which developed independently from its counterpart in China since 1950.

The Local Church

During the 1920s, a young Chinese church leader, Watchman Nee Tuosheng, and others called upon Chinese Christians to leave the denominational churches, which they considered unbiblical. Nee's biblical vision of the church was of small groups assembled at home or common hall and led by the laity, with only one church allowed in each location or city—a simplistic form of ecclesial gathering modeled after some of the New Testament ecclesial models. Nee's ecclesial movement was known as the Local Church, Little Flocks, or Assembly Hall. A prolific writer, Nee wrote many volumes on spirituality influenced by Plymouth Brethren teachings, such as J. N. Darby's dispensationalism, the French mystic Madam Guyon's writings, and many others. These volumes drew many readers from among Chinese Protestants and convinced many to join the Local Church as an ecclesial community spiritually superior to the denominational ecclesial establishments. By 1949, this church constituted as much as 10 percent of all Chinese Protestants. One can easily see the unique ecclesial characteristics of the Local Church, small group gatherings at a member's home, as the ecclesial precursor of the house church movement that later evolved in China.

In the early 1950s, the Local Church held a strong anticommunist and anti-TSPM stance, and its ecclesial model—meetings in households for a simple form of worship that emphasized personal devotion—became the ecclesial norm for those who refused to join the TSPM. Some of their leaders followed the nationalist government to Taiwan. Nee was arrested by Chinese authorities in 1952, charged with being an antirevolutionary along with many other crimes, and died in a labor camp in 1972. Many of his colleagues were arrested, but some joined the TSPM as the "Reformed Local Church," denouncing Nee and others who refused to join this new group. Many attribute the survival of Chinese Protestantism under severe communist suppression to the Local Church and its ecclesiology, which enabled Chinese Protestants to survive without the traditional denominational institutions such as church buildings, polity, liturgy, and clergy.

Some Local Church leaders left China in 1950 and continued the movement, first in Taiwan and Hong Kong, then in the US. One of these, Witness Li, developed his own theological and ecclesial characteristics, including the controversial "shouting" of the name Jesus, which led to his followers becoming known as the Shouters.[1] Some evangelicals in the US published books

1. In the early 1980s, this "shouting" practice was introduced to the Local Church in China, and the Chinese government described those who practiced such shouting as "Shouters." The government banned this and categorized the practitioners as members of an evil cult. In the early 1980s, some members of the Shouters were even executed by the authority. This Shouter category has been used by many local government authorities to suppress many dissenting Protestant groups, especially the followers of the Local Church. The Local Church has stopped this practice, and the relevant government authorities have clearly been informed of this fact, but they still keep Shouters on the list of the Evil Cults at China's Anti Evil Cult Association

accusing Witness Li and the Local Church he led of heresy; Li and his followers accused those evangelical writers of libel in court and eventually won the case. Currently many evangelical groups, including Fuller Theological Seminary, accept the Local Church as an authentic Protestant denomination adhering to orthodox Christian beliefs compatible with the evangelical faith. Today the Local Church, with its Living Stream Ministry headquarters located in Anaheim, California, numbers more than ten million followers in more than fifty countries, with the majority of the members being non-Chinese. It even has its own version of the Bible: *The Holy Bible Recovery Version*. The Local Church, which started as an indigenous movement of Protestants in China, has now become an international Protestant group. It began in order to replace denominationalism with its own ecclesial vision; through its success, the Local Church ironically turned itself into a de facto denomination with ecclesiastical authority, structure, polity, and practice, and a set of established doctrinal understandings distinguishing it from other Protestant traditions. In China, it functions as an autonomous group in which some of the individual churches operate within the TSPM/CCC structure and some outside the TSPM/CCC framework.

The True Jesus Church

In 1917, influenced by Pentecostal missionaries, three Chinese pastors formed a Sabbatarian Pentecostal Church called the True Jesus Church (TJC) with practices and beliefs such as speaking in tongues, foot washing, oneness Pentecostalism (baptism only in the name of Jesus, not the Trinity), Sabbath observance, faith healing, baptism with the Holy Spirit, and water baptism with frontal immersion in natural living water. The TJC quickly gained popularity and has been entirely operated by Chinese nationals since its beginning. In the mid-1920s, the TJC began to send missionaries overseas to spread this brand of Chinese

website. For more, see China Anti-Cult Association, "Be Alert to All Kinds of Cults That Endanger the Public," ChinaFXJ, September 18, 2017, https://tinyurl.com/y4doqrbo.

Pentecostalism, mainly among the Chinese in diaspora. By 1949, the TJC claimed to have 120,000 members in China, which meant that as many as one out of eight Protestants in China at that time belonged to this denomination. Since the 1950s, TJC has been absorbed into the TSPM, but its churches usually operate independently and use different venues as they meet on Saturdays rather than on Sundays. TJC churches not in mainland China have formed the TJC International Assembly, based in Taiwan, to govern all the TJC churches in different countries. The majority of TJC members are in Taiwan, and they constitute perhaps the third-largest Protestant group in Taiwan after the Presbyterian Church and the Local Church. Currently, the TJC is the largest Chinese Pentecostal denomination and numbers 1.5 million followers in more than fifty countries on five continents. It is a global Pentecostal denomination established by Chinese Protestants with an increasing number of non-Chinese followers.

The TJC in mainland China operates as a separate ecclesial entity from other groups. It is clustered mostly in Fujian Province with some churches scattered in neighboring provinces. It has joined the TJC International Assembly. TJC seminarians are trained at local seminaries with special provisions, such as a special prayer time and venue. TJC's ecclesial practices, like speaking in tongues and faith healings, are often frowned upon by other Chinese Protestants as well as thegovernment, as the TSPM/CCC generally has taken an anticharismatic stance, and the government interprets faith healing as unscientific superstition. However, the TJC is increasingly accepted by the Protestant community in China as the charismatic movement now affects the entire spectrum of Protestant communities in China.

The Jesus Family

In 1908, there was a Christian revival in Shangdong Province, and many accepted the gospel. Influenced by this revival, a young Protestant named Jing Dianying began to organize the Saints Cooperative Society, a Protestant mutual help fellowship, in his home village of Mazhuang in Taian City. At the same time, some Assemblies of God missionaries nearby experienced the baptism of the Holy Spirit and became members of this society. Later Jing himself had a similar experience of the Holy Spirit. In 1927 he formally established the Jesus Family, whose initial membership came from members of his cooperative who also had the experience of being filled by the Holy Spirit. This new group was meant to be a community that embraced the apostolic lifestyle of the Jerusalem Christians recorded in the book of Acts. All those who joined had to break away from their old family network, surrender all personal possessions to this community in order to live a frugal lifestyle, obey the head of the Family, and be ready to die for Jesus. Furthermore, they prayed in tongues, expected signs and miracles, conducted group and personal devotions and prayer meetings several times a day, and discharged assigned daily work. There was no private ownership as material goods were shared in common and allocated by the head of the Family on the basis of need. If one left the Family, he or she could take nothing away, and the Family would cut off all relations with that person. It resembled a religious order of the Catholic tradition, like the Franciscans, except that many joined as a whole family unit and retained their family structure within the larger Family. The head of the Family, like a Superior or an Abbot in the Catholic order, assumed the ultimate authority in both spiritual and temporal matters, and he would often act as a matchmaker to pair up single members for marriage.

The ecclesial model of this Jesus Family may sound like a cult in a contemporary socioreligious framework. However, it gained huge popularity in China when it first started and not only attracted many poor and uneducated peasants but also drew some intellectuals and professionals to join its ranks. During the 1930s and 1940s, there were wars and famines in China, and the majority of the population lived in extreme poverty as their homes had been destroyed by war or natural disasters. This type of communal life enabled survival, even in extremely harsh conditions. Some of these families, numbering several hundred people, would migrate to other places due to famine, natural disaster, or war; they became refugees and often ended up in the remote hinterland of China. I have met some of the remaining Jesus Family members in Hami, Xinjiang, who recounted their migration experience from the Yellow River Flood of 1938 where hundreds of thousands lost their lives, and millions became refugees.[2] This Jesus Family community from Henan Province traveled on foot for hundreds of miles, carrying all their possessions on their back until they reached Hami in the middle of the dry Turpan basin, one of the hottest places in China, where there were still some lands available for cultivation and settlement. Many refugees from Henan perished on this gruesome journey. This Jesus Family survived the journey and managed to reestablish their community by growing melons and vegetables. Their success was probably due to the strict communal rules regarding sharing everything in common, a frugal lifestyle, and being sustained by a strong conviction in God's sovereignty. This Jesus Family became the second Christian presence in Hami after the disappearance of the Assyrian (Nestorian) Church about a thousand years ago; in the 1990s, an archaeological team excavated in Hami and discovered an Assyrian Christian chapel dating from more than a thousand years ago. By 1949, there were several hundred such communities observing the same ecclesial practices, using the same hymnolgy, following the spiritual authority of Jing and his senior colleagues through their writings, and spreading all over China to even remote frontiers where no Christian had ever ventured. These groups—charismatic in theology, communal in living, frugal in lifestyle, and pietistic in spirituality—became some of the most influential indigenous Protestant communities in China.

In 1950, many leaders of the Jesus Family endorsed the TSPM's declaration, supported the new regime, and soon joined the TSPM movement. Most were able to maintain their ecclesial lifestyle until the introduction of the commune system in the late 1950s. The Jesus Family even dispatched a special medical team

2. The nationalist government attempted to slow down the rapid advance of the Japanese Army in Central China by demolishing the dikes of the Yellow River and flooding huge areas of farmland in Henan Province. It caused not only hundreds of thousands of deaths and millions of displaced persons but also a huge famine across central China that lasted for several years. Steven I. Dutch, "The Largest Act of Environmental Warfare in History," *Environmental and Engineering Geoscience* 15, no. 4 (November 2009): 287–97.

to join the Chinese Volunteer Army to support the war effort of the Chinese government fighting against the UN troops in the Korean War theatre. In the late 1950s, when China converted all farms into collective communes, the Jesus Family was supposed to be disbanded and administratively merged into the commune system. However, some Jesus Families conveniently just converted into being production brigades—production subunits of a commune—and managed to maintain some of their unique communal features and structures throughout the whole period of the Cultural Revolution.[3] In fact, the Jesus Family had been successfully operating as a sustainable farming-production unit long before the introduction of the commune experiment by the communist Chinese authorities, which operated very similarly to the Jesus Family's model, albeit with a different ideological driving force.

Today, there are still some Protestants in China who have kept the ecclesial vision of the Jesus Family, such as the display of charismatic gifts, the simple and frugal lifestyle, the apostolic ecclesial mode of sharing all possessions, and living as a production community with no personal ownership. For example, there are some highly educated Chinese Protestants in Liaoning Province inspired by the Jesus Family who live as a community through the creation of business farming co-ops to produce organic rice and other high-end farming products. They live together, dress in simple uniforms, own and share everything in common, and conduct devotions in the morning before work and Bible studies and worship at night. They utilize the latest farming technology, invest in research and development, employ innovative marketing skills, and produce high-end organic farm produce, which is eagerly sought after by the market. Their company is one of the best organic farming corporations in Liaoning. It seems that the spirit of the Jesus Family still carries on in China and has reappeared in modern forms.

3. In 1979, I came across some commune production brigade members in Shandong in which the brigade members were all Protestants (all from Jesus Family background). Officially, these brigades were called Production Brigade Number One, Production Brigade Number Two, and so on. However, they referred to themselves as Number One Prayer Brigade, Number Two Prayer Brigade, and so on. They reported that they had held onto the Jesus Family structure while merged into the commune system.

Spiritual Ministry Band

In the early 1940s, more than half of the Chinese population was directly affected by war, and tens of millions lost their homes, if not their lives. The eschatological theme of the second coming gained popularity, fueling a new mission movement by Chinese Protestants based on a proactive, pretribulationist, premillennial eschatology, which was the most popular school of eschatology among Chinese Protestants.[4] One of the earliest founders of spiritual workers' bands was Reverend Zhang Guquan of the North China Theological Seminary, who, in the early 1940s, formed the Northwest Spiritual Ministry Band with a few colleagues and some theological students. Inspired by the Jesus Family, the Band was a faith mission group where members shared everything in common and had no personal possessions. Their mission objective was to spread the gospel in the northwestern part of China, which was considered the frontier area at that time. They would fast and pray for days for direction and deliberately avoid administrative structures and planning. Therefore they could claim that wherever they went, whomever they met and evangelized, and whatever support they received were all part of the divine plan, not human desire. Most of their members were from Shandong, with some from Henan, Shaanxi, and Shanghai.

This band had no clear geographic objective in mind, no map, and no funding, but they kept wandering toward the northwest region, and most ended up in Xinjiang, the most northwest province, taking shelter with the local Protestant congregations. Along the way they targeted Han Chinese for evangelism instead of the local Uyghur, who were the majority population and all Muslims, as none of the members attempted to learn the local Uyghur language. The band wrote many hymns with moving words expressing their romanticized experiences of suf-

4. It is a literal interpretation of Matt 24:14 that the end time will arrive, that is, the second coming of Jesus, when the gospel is preached around the world beginning from Jerusalem in the first century CE and finally back to Jerusalem. Based on this interpretation, Jesus has not come back because the gospel has not been preached around the world. Therefore one can speed up the second coming by actively spreading the gospel toward the direction of Jerusalem.

ferings and hardship while serving the Lord in remote places. Those hymns and the testimonies of the members were widely circulated. Very soon, the Northwest Spiritual Ministry Band had become a legend among mission-minded Chinese Protestants, and many formed mission groups modeled after them. At its height, this band had about forty members; many joined but eventually left for various reasons, such as going back home for family needs, illnesses, or staying in a locale as the pastor for new converts. In 1950, this band was disbanded by the new Xinjiang government, because Xinjiang was liberated by the Chinese Communist Red Army and became part of the newly established People's Republic of China. Reverend Zhang was arrested, and he later died and was buried in Xinjiang. Most of the remaining members stayed and eventually also died in Xinjiang.

Influenced by the story of the Northwest Spiritual Ministry Band, Reverend Mark Ma Ke of the China Inland Mission Bible School in Fengxiang, Shaanxi, and some of his students embarked on fasting and prayer. During their prayers, some students felt moved to preach the gospel starting in northwest China, moving through central Asia and on to Mount Zion in Jerusalem as the penultimate event of the second coming of Christ. They organized the Preaching the Gospel to All Places Band (later translated in English by Helen Bailey in England as the Back to Jerusalem Band) modeled after the Northwest Spiritual Ministry Band. They had a clear objective to preach the gospel along the way from China to Jerusalem and then to wait there for the second return of Jesus at Mount Zion. It began with only a few members and eventually numbered about two dozen. They went to Xinjiang and attached themselves mostly to the local Han Chinese congregations already established by the Christian Native Evangelistic Crusade (CNEC).[5]

5. This denomination later renamed itself as Christian Nationals' Evangelism Commission, as the term *Crusade* would be too provocative, especially to the Muslims in Xinjiang. It established the first Protestant church in the capital of Xinjiang in 1946 (then called Dihua and now Urumqi) at Mingde Road, conducting services in Chinese, Uyghur, and Russian. The church still stands today with a new building, and it is the largest congregation in Xinjiang. By 1950, this denomination had established several more churches in Xinjiang, with the furthest one in Yiling just next to the Soviet Kazakhstan.

Similar to the Northwest Spiritual Ministry Band, they did not attempt to evangelize the local Uyghur, and none learned or spoke the local language. Their mission concept was to travel through these regions passing out gospel tracts (in Chinese) and holding open-air evangelistic rallies along the way. In 1949, a couple of their members eventually arrived in Kashgar, in the far western part of China next to Afghanistan, the furthest place members of this band would ever reach. In 1950, the new Xinjiang government also disbanded this group. Reverend Mark Ma Ke and about half the members had already left Xinjiang and the band mostly for health and personal reasons long before the communists took over Xinjiang. The remaining members of this band, numbering less than a dozen, shared a similar fate to that of the members of the Northwest Spiritual Ministry Band mentioned above. All told, the Spiritual Band mission movement lasted just about ten years and numbered merely a few dozen people in total, with perhaps some copycats in different parts of China, and all eventually disappeared. However, their mission model laid the foundation to shape the mission spirituality and orientation of the Protestant community in China.

PROTESTANT TRADITIONS FROM 1949 TO 1980

After the missionaries left China in the early 1950s, the Chinese Protestant communities entered into a new sociopolitical reality where all religions were under the strong control of the communist authority. Protestant churches were nationalized under the pretext of the Three-Self Patriotic Movement (TSPM). All denominations were allowed to operate independently; the Anglicans were still able to hold their last General Synod in China in 1956, and the Methodists were ordaining pastors as late as 1957. By 1958 all had to join the TSPM and conduct united services.[6] The TSPM, a political organization on paper that held de facto ecclesiastical authority, approved and held ordinations under its name, such as in Yunnan Province in 1957. By the

---

6. One of the best accounts of this period is Chee Nan-pin's *The Search for the Identity of the Chinese Christian Church: Ecclesiological Responses of the Chinese Church in 1949–1958 to the Political Changes* (Hong Kong: WEC International, 2016).

mid-1960s, there was only one public form of Protestantism in China: churches that operated under the auspices of the TSPM. Usually these churches followed a simplified form of service order resembling their former denominational tradition, or they combined several denominational elements into a simple liturgical rubric. There was little theological consideration because these church services were operating in survival mode, trying to adapt to the new socialist China that was hostile to Christianity. Bible schools and seminaries from different denominational backgrounds were forced to merge into a few united theological schools that offered courses in different theological traditions. By 1966, even these simple forms of Protestant services were suppressed, giving way to the Cultural Revolution.

During the next fifteen years of increasing religious constraint, Chinese Protestant churches essentially had to stop all official contact with churches in the West. The National Christian Council of China (NCC) had already withdrawn its membership from the World Council of Churches in the early 1950s, terminating contacts with churches abroad, and the NCC was disbanded to give way to the TSPM. Theological developments in the West, such as the emergence of evangelicalism, liturgical reform, the ecumenical movement, liberation theology, and feminist theology—popular since the 1960s—had no effect on Protestants in China. Chinese Protestants were cut off from the rest of the worldwide church, save for a few links with Protestants in the Soviet Bloc,[7] and a few well-orchestrated visits of foreign church leaders who were regarded as friendly to the Chinese regime.[8]

As for those who refused to join the TSPM, they retreated to the private sphere and held on to their faith in secret. Many met at home to conduct simple forms of worship, usually modeled

7. For example, Bishop Ding Guangxun (K. H. Ting) led a Protestant delegation to visit the Reformed Church in Hungary in 1956. He was awarded with an honorary doctorate in theology from the Reformed Seminary of the Hungarian Reform Church for his support of the Soviet military suppression of the Hungarian Uprising of 1956.

8. One example is Bishop Ronald Hall (1895–1975) of Hong Kong, who supported the Chinese communist revolution, was connected closely with TSPM leaders, and was invited to visit China in 1956. See "History of the Province," Hong Kong Sheng Kung Hui, 2019, https://tinyurl.com/yy4hdnmh.

after the gatherings of the Local Church. Learned laity took over pastoral roles, and liturgies were usually not performed. Since Bibles were often confiscated by the authorities, and the Bible was no longer printed after 1956, believers began the practice of reciting and memorizing key verses. Devotional hymns with simple tunes were popular as they were easy to memorize. Many Protestants were forced to make difficult choices as they were confronted with the increasing social trends of communism that regarded Christianity as the opium of the people. For example, in the mid-1950s, a top student at the Shanghai Music Conservatory majoring in vocal performance refused to sing the *Internationale* because the second stanza of the version used in China reads, "There is no such thing as a Savior in this world." As a devoted Protestant raised in a family of several generations of believers, she believed that this song was against her faith. She was openly criticized in an assembly in front of the whole school population. She was also expelled, despite the school's original plan to send her for graduate studies in the USSR endorsed by the Russian faculty, who saw the potential for a successful career as an opera singer in her. She was arrested, charged as an anti-revolutionary element, and sent to a farming labor-reform camp for about twenty years. While in the camp, she led many to faith in Christ and effectively built a Protestant community there, including even some prison guards.[9] This type of story, of which hers is one among many, shows another facet of the Protestant experience in China during this seemingly suppressive period where few visible signs of Protestantism were observed.

---

9. This lady is Yang Xinhui (1925–2014), the sister of my mother-in-law. In 1979, when Yang was released from the labor camp after more than twenty years of imprisonment, she recounted her experiences in the camp as well as of the Protestant communities that she had established during those years. These communities have since developed into many ACCs, now numbering more than twenty thousand.

PROTESTANT TRADITIONS FROM 1980 TO THE PRESENT

Post-Denominational Church (TSPM/CCC): Practices and Theology

Since the formation of the China Christian Council, along with the reconstituted TSPM in 1980, the CCC has been issuing ecclesiastical regulations to govern the TSPM/CCC churches. The CCC assumes that it holds the ecclesiastical authority to govern Protestant churches in China, and it has proclaimed that Protestantism in China has entered a new postdenominational era. There has not been any clear theological exposition on post-denominationalism other than claiming that it is biblical. Some Protestant circles in the West praised the situation as a new ecclesiastical contribution from the Chinese Protestant community. So far, the TSPM/CCC has expressed this new ecclesiastical creation as being the authentic expression of Protestantism by the Chinese through the brilliant leadership of the Communist Party of China. It has gotten rid of the Western imperialistic sin of division in Christianity.

This postdenominational China Christian Council established ministerial offices at the national level (bishop, reverend, elder, deacon, etc.), issued church regulations, claimed ministerial authority (such as the power to approve episcopal appointments), and authorized the various provincial councils to approve the ordination of clergy, among other authoritative moves. In short, the CCC ecclesial polity resembles a Reformed ecclesial orientation, with perhaps the addition of the honorary episcopal office (with no defined office, authority, faculty, function, or jurisdiction). Many ecclesial issues of this CCC postdenominational polity need to be articulated. First, the whole TSPM/CCC follows the government's administrative divisions and structures with its corresponding geographic jurisdictions, ranks, and authority; such civil administrative division disregards the actual Protestant population distribution in different provinces. For example, the Province of Henan has several million Protestants, whereas the Qinghai Province has perhaps less than ten thousand. However, both provincial councils enjoy similar authority and privileges with similar resources allocated from the CCC. Furthermore, the episcopal office, although established on paper, has no theological definition of its role as far its jurisdiction is concerned and lacks clarity as to whether a provincial council is like a diocese under episcopal authority or whether the clergy need to be under the authority of the bishop. Finally, CCC demands that the most essential qualification for candidates of any ministerial office, even candidates applying for seminary training, is the political loyalty and support to the Communist Party of China—a political rather than religious requirement that makes one wonder about the very nature of this council. The inclusion of ordaining clergy and the possible consecration of bishops as ministerial offices under the CCC's regulation, along with the self-assumed authority of the councils on many ecclesiastical matters, suggests a strong denominationalism modeled after the mainline denominational mode with a diocesan or conference-level ecclesial authoritative structure. This basically denies other ecclesial models, such as the congregational-based free church ecclesiology, or a nonclerical ecclesial model like the Quakers or the Brethren. Also the pro-government political stance of the council not only denies any dissenting political views within its rank but also seriously weakens its ecclesial function as a prophetic voice in society.

As for the worship order, the CCC's liturgical manual reads much like a Presbyterian-based United Church service handbook. The official hymn book contains mostly familiar Western hymns (translated into Chinese) from mainline denominations introduced by missionaries during the past century, with only a few written by Chinese. Eucharist and baptism formulations are rather undefined and tend to depend on who performs the rites. Vestments are nonstandardized with many local freely adopted styles, often with little theological connotation. At one time, I taught an introductory course on liturgy to clergy in northern China; some of the clergy showed me their stoles, some of which were yellow in color. I asked them for the theological and liturgical rationale in using this color, and most replied that it looks good to have a change from just red or white (the Reformed tradition). These clergy often choose color for aesthetics rather than with a theological or liturgical reason in mind. One replied that the Chinese word *yellow* (*Huang*) sounded identical to the Chinese word for *emperor* (*Huang*). In imperial China only the emperor could wear clothing and use utensils in yellow; it was reserved for imperial usage, so the yellow stole represented Jesus our king or the emperor of the universe. Furthermore, a student also added that yellow looked like gold, and gold is precious. The whole class clapped their hands for these brilliant answers. So much for creative theological indigenization. None knew that the yellow stole was in fact used, serendipitously, for a liturgical feast day—Christ the King—which is not celebrated in China among the Protestants.

In practice, the churches within this postdenominational TSPM/CCC operate in different regions in China, especially in urban areas, and follow various forms of church tradition, mostly resembling their former denominational practices and church orders. It seems that as long as the term *tradition* rather than *denomination* is used, each church can use whatever form of liturgy from whatever denomination it pleases. In some places, such as in Shanghai, the TSPM/CCC even consecrate bishops with the Anglican liturgy following the apostolic tradition so that the bishops are recognized by the Anglican Communion,[10] whereas in Guangzhou the Seventh-Day Adventists still observe their Sabbath on Saturdays and sing Adventist hymns. Clergy from the former Presbyterian Conference (or Presbytery) in Fujian wear Presbyterian liturgical robes and stoles, while in former Baptist and Free Church areas pastors reject all forms of clerical robes. In formerly Anglican areas, many churches still follow the liturgical calendar and conduct services with the Book of Common Prayer (some in simplified form) with full vestments. In formerly Lutheran areas, ministers tend to

10. There has been only one episcopal consecration under CCC. It took place in Shanghai in the early 1980s and included co-consecrators who were not valid bishops according to the apostolic tradition, such as a Baptist pastor and a Presbyterian minister who had no episcopal tradition to speak of. However, there were more than three valid bishops (all Anglican) present to serve as co-consecrators to ensure that those two new bishops would be validly consecrated in the apostolic tradition. They were called Bishops of Shanghai but with no clear ecclesiastical authority or jurisdiction.

wear white liturgical robes and celebrate the Eucharist with a transubstantiation Eucharistic prayer, whereas the church in a neighboring district, due to its Free Church background, might conduct the Eucharist with the remembrance Eucharistic prayer. As mentioned earlier, the Local Church, the True Jesus Church, and some communities following the Jesus Family traditions all kept their own ecclesial traditions and their own hymn notes. In places where the Protestant communities were established after 1949 with no denominational precedent, it all depended on the local Protestant leaders to decide, some rather creatively, the local form of church order and liturgy.

The visible liturgical rubrics mentioned above are found mostly in urban communities where Protestant activities are more sophisticated and have greater exposure to the outside world, along with church buildings dating back to the old days where specific liturgies were performed. However, the majority of Protestant populations live in rural areas, and a large number meet in households under the auspices of the TSPM/CCC or ACC. They usually follow this common program: prayer, hymn singing, Bible reading, teaching, sharing testimonies, prayer again, and hymn singing. In some gatherings, there may be a time to recite the Lord's Prayer and even the Apostles' Creed. The hymnody and preaching seem to be the main focus of these services, and the preaching can last anywhere from forty-five minutes to several hours. Most of the leaders of the rural Protestants communities are laity and are often those who started the actual groups.

The case of a church in Louping County, under the administration of Qujin Municipality of Yunnan Province, exemplifies these rural congregations. There was no record of Christian presence in this remote area until early 1980, when a young lady, Tien Ying, was converted through a relative who came to visit. All she had at the beginning was a Bible and some simple devotional materials. She went to the municipal capital Qujin City, about one hundred kilometers away, and bought some hymnodies and cassette tapes of Sunday sermons from the church in Qujin City. She then started a small gathering in her home and began to share her newfound faith with her relatives and friends. After a few years, the number of people attending grew to a few dozen, and they started to rent a place for their Sunday meetings. Some would travel to neighboring towns or cities with churches and attend Sunday worship there. They came back and recited whatever they had learned from the preaching. Eventually the local municipal Christian Council became aware of this new community and arranged for a pastor there to hold regular services and perform baptisms. At first, the local (county) authority did not understand the nature of this group, labeled it an evil cult, and threatened to shut it down. Eventually, in the late 1990s, the group obtained temporary registration as a Protestant gathering point. Tien, with only primary school education, went to the provincial capital to attend a short training course run by the Provincial Christian Council. With this training certificate, she was ordained as an elder by the Municipality Christian Council and became the de facto pastor.

By the beginning of this century, this small church in Louping had about one hundred attendees and several gathering points in surrounding townships within the county, all started by and under the spiritual guidance of Tien's Louping Church.[11] A few years ago they even bought a plot of land and built a five-story church with a training center and a sanctuary that has the capacity to seat five hundred. Elder Tien has been looking for youth in the church in hope that some of them may attend the Bible school and eventually become pastors shepherding the church. Meanwhile, Tien still performs most of the pastoral duties and has not received a cent for the past thirty-five years. Instead, she and her family donated all of their savings to build the Louping church. One can hear stories like this one all over China, especially in the rural areas. Most of these churches owe their existence to humble and dedicated believers with no knowledge of denominationalism or liturgical tradition.

In summary, there has been a wide range of diversity in church traditions within the postdenominationalism of the TSPM/CCC, from all the major mainland denominations in China in the past, to the indigenous groups developed by the Chinese Protestants, to many new ecclesial forms emerging

11. All churches in TSPM/CCC are basically named after the geographic location, be it county, city, or district. If there is more than one church in a city, it is named after the district in which the church is located.

through Chinese pastors. Such diversity in ecclesial practices has been fully accepted within the communion of the TSPM/CCC as long as these churches follow the political leadership of the Chinese authorities and use the term *tradition* instead of *denomination*. It seems that political rather than ecclesiological principles define church practices in the TSPM/CCC.

The ACCs and Their Many Manifestations

Protestant groups that are not part of the TSPM/CCC networks are usually not fully registered and often exist in the gray area commonly known as house churches. Theologically speaking, many of these groups cannot be considered churches as they usually meet only some of the essential theological criteria of a church, namely, teaching authority, ministerial office, polity, and sacraments such as baptism and Eucharist. These criteria define church membership, ecclesiastical structure, and ecclesial self-understanding. Most important, the presence of these essential criteria enables a community to preserve its self-defined teaching, enable its functionality, provide stable governance, differentiate its uniqueness vis-à-vis other social communities, and perpetuate its existence. Many of the ACCs may not perform initiation rites such as baptism, and they often function more like a fellowship of believers than an established church due to the absence of some of the criteria mentioned above. Theologically speaking, some of these ACCs are ecclesial communities or fellowships instead of a church in a theological sense.

In the early 1980s, there were several major ACC networks, mostly based in Henan, that eventually developed branches all over China. These networks are known as the Six Family networks, with some individual networks numbering more than a million followers (most of whom are peasants). All of the networks have clear doctrinal positions, organizational structure, training facilities, and secure communication networks through which they can avoid the close monitoring of the civil authority. Theologically they are conservative and emphasize mission and evangelism. They believe in the separation of church and state and maintain respect for but not submission to any civil authorities, but they are certainly not against them. Some are charismatic, and most embrace a Reformed, or Calvinist, theological orientation. Most of their core members were converted sometime during the Cultural Revolution, and they almost all recount miraculous experiences as the foundation of their faith. These networks began to grow long before the reappearance of the TSPM/CCC, and all enjoyed a huge growth period in the 1980s and 1990s. They have been mostly rurally based but now also have a significant portion of their members in urban areas due to increased urbanization in China and the migration of rural labor to urban areas. The heads of these networks have evidently been able to communicate among themselves and discuss issues of common interest; together they may perhaps be the largest nonregistered Protestant alliance in China.

Alongside these rurally based Protestant groups that constituted the majority of the ACC population from 1980 until the 1990s, there are also new types of ACCs emerging. The first of these is the emergence of the new urban house churches riding on China's urbanization. China has gone through a rapid urbanization process, perhaps the largest in human civilization, designed to transform more than eight hundred million citizens from a rural into an urban lifestyle within a few decades: from 15 percent of the population in 1980 to 50 percent in 2010, and about 60 percent in 2018. Currently there are more than fifteen cities that have a population of over ten million, and at least fifty with more than 2 million,[12] that draw tens of millions from rural areas to urban settings. With such a high concentration of the population in urban areas and only a few TSPM/CCC churches in urban centers, some ACCs are beginning to emerge to cater to the needs of the young professionals coming from across the entire nation to urban areas seeking job opportunities. Some TSPM/CCC pastors who found too many constraints within the TSPM/CCC systems have started their independent urban ACCs. Other ACCs began as a group of believers from the same origin who came to a new city and started their own gathering that eventually evolved into a church. There may be some who found Christianity on university campuses, usually concentrated

12. Rolando Wee, "The Largest Cities in China," World Atlas, updated June 28, 2018, https://tinyurl.com/yxsxmfqm.

in urban areas, and later stayed and settled in that city, beginning their own ACCs. They can also be the fruit of church-planting work carried out by large ACCs networks that target people from their own province currently working as migrant workers in that city. There are also those that are developed by foreign missionaries in China, such as the Koreans, which are by far the largest group of foreign missionaries in China. There are also increasing numbers of urban ACCs started by overseas returnees who found the Protestant faith while abroad and did theological training before returning to start their own church in China; many of these Protestant returnees are well connected with the political and commercial elite in China.[13]

The common denominators among these new urban ACCs are a high level of independence, strong local support, and leadership through local pastors. Many who attend these ACCs are highly educated professionals and accustomed to the use of advanced, high-tech gadgets and technological innovations like online chats, social media, and interactive presentations. Quite a large number of these urban independent churches have their own constitution, church polity, website, and sophisticated operations resembling a typical independent congregation found in the West. Many even operate their own training centers or seminaries, even with international accreditation,[14] and develop among themselves intra- and interregional networks. Further, almost all of these ACCs are operating in plain view of the authorities, making little attempt to hide. These independent ACCs liaise with the authorities but do not submit to its governance. These types of ACCs are becoming the dominant types of ACCs, gradually replacing the older, more traditional, rural house church networks as the new representation of the ACCs

---

13. For example, the son-in-law of the former Premier of China, Wen Jiabao, accepted Christian faith while he was studying in the US and subsequently finished his seminary training, also in the US. He is a pastor running an ACC in Beijing.

14. Although nonregistered and illegal in the eyes of the Chinese authority, some of the Bible schools and seminaries operated by these churches have received accreditations from theological institutions, such as the Asian Theological Association (ATA), reflecting that the quality of their training is at par with established standards. Their names are withheld for confidentiality reasons.

in China, especially to the overseas Protestant organizations and mission agencies.[15]

Although the Constitution of China states that any religion in the country should not be under the dominion of foreign forces, there are some denominations that have been established in China with support from abroad. For example, it is known that Southern Baptist missionaries have worked in China for many years under various labels, such as foreign language teachers. In fact, I have encountered many ACCs who identified themselves as Baptist congregations, receiving supervision and support from Baptist missionaries and Baptist mission boards outside of China. Many Korean churches note in their publications that they operate churches in China under the names of their denomination or congregation. Sometimes the Korean missionaries may start a new church through their evangelistic efforts; however, there are also some who simply acquire an existing ACC through an initial payment followed by continuous financial support and place that ACC under their banner. International mission agencies such as OMF (Overseas Missionary Fellowship, formerly the China Inland Mission, or CIM) have many missionary workers clandestinely in China and have also established many new congregations by partnering with local pastors. Some of these congregations even called themselves CIM churches and ordained their pastors under this name, thus resurrecting an old ecclesial tradition and establishing a de facto new denomination.

There are also ACCs taking theological or spiritual guidance from overseas that still operate their own ecclesial communities. I came across a Bible school run by a megachurch in an Asian country that had more than 150 mainland graduates, most of whom had already started congregations modeled after this charismatic megachurch, which featured contemporary music and dance and praying in tongues. At times, these graduates would return to that Bible school for refresher training, and senior pastors from this megachurch would in turn visit the graduates and their congregations in mainland China. The relationship is a spiritual one, not financial or administrative. This

---

15. For example, most of the invitees from the Chinese house churches to the Cape Town Lausanne Conference in 2014 were from this ecclesial category.

model of ACCs with international connections is on the rise as more contemporary ecclesial forms are replicated in China.

Finally, there is the missional form of the ACC. In the mid-1990s, a Protestant preacher named Zhao Ximen from Xinjiang, who was associated with the Northwest Spiritual Band as well as the Back to Jerusalem Band back in the 1940s and 1950s, went to settle with some ACCs in Henan. He shared the old vision of these bands with the ACCs in Henan. Some ACCs rekindled this vision and began to mobilize their members for cross-cultural evangelization, particularly to the northwestern part of China with its predominantly Muslim population, and called it the Back to Jerusalem Movement. With the increased attention drawn to Muslims in the West after Huntington's thesis on the clash of civilizations, heightened by the 9/11 incident, many Western mission organizations started to take notice of the Back to Jerusalem Movement promoted by these ACCs. In the past fifteen years, there have been many international conferences, consultations, and joint efforts between ACCs and mission agencies from abroad to actualize this vision.

As Chinese are increasingly being accepted into Muslim countries due to the increasing commercial ties between China and countries in the Muslim world, ACCs believe that this is the era for global missions for the Chinese. ACC leaders are convinced that since many ACC members have years of experience in clandestine ecclesial operations, Chinese ACC members would be suitable for mission work in restrictive environments not unlike these Muslim countries. Currently, there are more than thirty mission institutions both in China and abroad that are training ACC members to engage in cross-cultural missions, primarily focused on the Muslim population. By 2018, at least a thousand Chinese missionaries from ACCs had been sent to Muslim-dominated countries to conduct mission work. The public did not know of their clandestine mission endeavors until two were killed in Pakistan by ISIS in 2017.[16] With the increased outflow of Chinese citizens, accentuated by China's new global

---

16. See the comprehensive report on this incident by the BBC in Kevin Ponniah, M. Ilyas Khan, Yashan Zhao, and Muhammad Kazim, "Risky Road: China's Missionaries Follow Beijing West in Quetta," BBC, September 4, 2017, https://tinyurl.com/y3zvh9ro.

"Belt Road Initiative" (BRI) to connect over sixty countries in Eurasia into a gigantic economic entity headed by China, the number of Chinese missionaries is on the rise. The impact of the ACC missionaries may be felt soon as more Chinese in general are found in different parts of the world, not only for commercial trade, education, and immigration, but now also for mission. ACCs are not only confined to China but also may bear global significance.

Other Forms of Protestant Manifestation

In addition to the TSPM/CCC churches and ACCs, there are some other unique and largely invisible groups of Protestants in China. Since the ruling party in China is the Chinese Communist Party, which has adopted atheism as the party's orthodox ideology, the ninety million party members who mostly serve in public institutions are not allowed to join any religion. The same prohibition on joining a religion also applies to those who belong to party and government institutions, such as military personnel, government and party officials, and even administrators in educational institutions. They cannot openly admit their religious beliefs nor openly attend religious activities until after retirement, or they could face severe consequences for their careers. Many of these people who have embraced the Protestant faith have not been baptized and carefully avoid participating in public religious activities. I know of a high-ranking military official who attends church on Sundays but does not wear his uniform or use his official vehicle; he has not been baptized and would not take part in this rite until after he retires. Some intellectuals even openly identify themselves as "cultural Christians," prepared to admit that they admire some of the moral and social teachings of Christianity but would not be willing to say that they are "Christian" in the sense of receiving initiation rites like baptism, openly affirming Christian doctrines, or participating in public Christian worship activities. Many of them hold important positions in political, military, and intellectual arenas and have great influence. They sometimes help the church, such as by using their authority or resources to facilitate church activities or applications. They are not Christian in an ecclesiastical sense, yet they perpetuate Christian influence.

Most of the campuses among the three thousand–plus colleges and universities in China have some form of Protestant fellowship, and some are even found at the Party's Academy and at military colleges.[17] Individual believers operate many of these campus fellowships, and they may be faculty members, foreign teachers, or even students. Some groups are supported by missionaries from abroad who specialize in campus ministry. These fellowships are elusive, as most operate in a semiclandestine manner through word of mouth and in dormitories, coffee shops, or offices. Often, entrepreneurial believers run bookstores or coffee shops on campus, with names such as Canaan Book Store or Manna Coffee Shop, and hold regular meetings to discuss matters of faith. Authorities often turn a blind eye as long as the gathering is not too influential or has too high a profile in public. Many people have been converted on campus, and school administrations have repeatedly cracked down on this form of Protestant existence but with little success. These campus fellowships are theologically not churches, as membership is unstable and highly transient, and no sacraments are performed; however, it is a form of Protestant community with high impact on its surrounding population. However, since 2017, university authorities have received strict orders to clamp down on all religious activities on campus, particularly Christianity, as part of a nationwide ideological campaign to curb Western influences on Chinese society. Protestant activities on campus are now becoming less visible but not necessarily less vibrant.

There is also a type of Protestant community that embraces Christianity as a major part of their ethnic identity. There are fifty-five officially recognized ethnic minority groups in China, with perhaps hundreds of subgroups. Some of these groups, such as the Miao, Lahu, Wa, Lisu, and Jingpo, had been exposed to Protestant missionary work and already had a large Protestant influence before 1949. Missionaries not only created written forms of their languages but also introduced modern education,

17. Rev. Dr. Bob Fu, now an advocate in the US for religious freedom in China and running the China Aid Organization, was a faculty member at the Party's Academy in Beijing when he became a Christian.

medicine, and other technologies.[18] Conversion to Protestantism among these people was often communal rather than individual, and it was not uncommon for entire villages to become Protestant in response to the activities and preaching of missionaries. There were, however, substantial differences in conversions according to the local socioeconomic conditions of those communities and the extent to which the missionaries helped them through escalating their social status, especially vis-à-vis the predominant Han Chinese, and improving their economic conditions.

The Chinese government has a separate policy with regard to religion for the ethnic minority groups, granting them much more tolerance in religious beliefs and practices than to the Han Chinese. These minorities are potentially restive, and in some cases, religion is already entrenched in their ethnic identity. Hence the policy is designed in part to avoid social instability among these minorities. Religion is now generally regarded as part of their cultural heritage and often not subjected to religious governance by the civil authorities. Consequently, Protestantism was able to develop rather rapidly among some of the minority groups in China, such as the Big Flower Miao (a subbranch of Miao in Yunnan and Guizhou), Lisu, Jingpo, and Lahu. Currently more than 50 percent of all the Lisu in China, numbering about half a million, are Protestants. But other minority groups previously without a viable Protestant population now also have increasing numbers of converts, such as the Khampa Tibetans in Yunnan, among whom a dozen Protestant communities have started since the beginning of this century. This Protestant trend, in the form of ethnic identity, is one of the many diverse forms of Protestantism in China.

18. Christian missionaries developed phonetic writing systems for many of the national minorities in China, especially during the first half of the twentieth century, followed by having the Bible translated into their new scripts. These groups previously had no written language; even if they had, it would be in some form of religious-liturgical script known only to the priest or shamans.

SIGNS OF INTERDENOMINATIONAL DYNAMICS:
RECONCILIATION

Among the diverse ecclesial groups in China, the TSPM/CCC and the ACCs are perhaps the largest two; however, they are seemingly antithetical to each other and thus hinder ecclesial unity. There has been no specific mention of reconciliation between the TSPM/CCC and the ACC on either side. It seems that both sides are still bitter and resentful toward each other. However, during the past decade, there have been some signs of hope for such reconciliation. One of the most important factors is the emergence of church leaders of a younger age. Currently most TSPM/CCC leaders are in their forties and fifties, whereas ten years ago most were in their seventies and even eighties. There is a similar phenomenon within the ACC leadership. Unlike their predecessors, the younger generation has virtually no experience of the bitter rivalry between TSPM and house church leaders during the 1950s until the late 1980s. They have been brought up, especially in terms of spiritual formation, during the 1980s and 1990s, when attention was focused on the pastoral needs of the rapidly growing churches. Therefore, their memories of past resentment between the two factions are not intense, which may give them more freedom to approach their rivals for pragmatic cooperation.[19]

There are many signs that this reconciliation is occurring. For instance, some ACCs exist in gray areas: they are not officially aligned with the TSPM/CCC, yet they have certain pastoral links with TSPM/CCC and are not antagonistic toward the TSPM/CCC. In recent years, a team of TSPM/CCC pastors at a provincial capital told me that not only did they have to take care of their TSPM/CCC churches and household gathering points, but they are also at times called upon by ACCs to provide pastoral assistance at weddings, funerals, and baptisms.[20] It is interesting to note that in this region some ACC members seek

19. Memory is an important element in reconciliation. See Jacques Matthey, "Mission as Ministry of Reconciliation," Preparatory Paper No. 10, WCC Conference on World Mission and Evangelism, Athens, Greece, May 9–16, 2005, section 42–46.

20. Personal interview conducted in March 2012. Name and location withheld for security reasons.

baptism by TSPM/CCC pastors so that when the civil authority checks on them, they can claim that they are legitimate TSPM/CCC members. Also, the TSPM/CCC churches recognize ACC baptism and grant these ACC members TSPM/CCC memberships. With such an arrangement, ACC members can have weddings and funerals openly conducted in TSPM/CCC facilities, which are lacking in ACC for obvious reasons. This arrangement implies a mutual recognition of sacraments—an important theological step toward ecclesiastical unity.[21] Such mutual recognition is, at least for now, not officially admitted openly by either side but in fact is in practice in some areas.

Another sign of reconciliation is the open protection extended by some TSPM/CCC leaders of ACC churches. Rev. Joseph Guo Yuse, who was a prominent leader of the Zhejiang Christian Council and the senior pastor of one of the megachurches in China, has shared one of his experiences. There are many ACCs near Hangzhou (the provincial capital of Zhejiang Province) that often hold large evangelistic rallies, all of which are illegal. The government learned about one of the rallies, and the Public Security Bureau arrested the organizers and wanted to check their backgrounds. They called Rev. Guo to verify whether the organizers had been officially sanctioned by the TSPM/CCC. If so, they would let these people go, and if not, they would be charged and prosecuted. Rev. Guo visited them in the detention center and told the government that these people were of the same spiritual family as his, and so the government released them. The ACC leaders, previously antagonistic toward the TSPM/CCC, were very touched by Rev. Guo's help and his willingness to take a personal risk for the ACCs. Eventually they developed a working relationship without submitting to each other, and both sides became aware that their main enemy was not each other but the strong antireligious forces in the government.[22]

---

21. It is significant to note that mutual recognition is an important element in ecclesial unity. See Faith and Order Commission, *Baptism, Eucharist, Ministry* (Geneva: World Council of Churches, 1983).

22. Rev. Joseph Guo Yuse made this presentation at the First Conference on Religious Dynamics and Religious Issues in China, Renmin (People's) University, Beijing, April 19–20, 2011. This is a by-invitation only and closed-door meeting. The

Rev. W., a former TSPM/CCC pastor, instigated a third group that exists between the TSPM/CCC and the ACC.[23] He could not accept the TSPM/CCC's restrictive orders limiting evangelism,[24] so he and his coworkers, along with many followers, split away from the TSPM/CCC and formed their own ecclesial support network. They have now extended into several provinces and run a few training centers that primarily facilitate evangelism, church planting, and pastoral training. When they run training programs, pastors from both ACC and TSPM/CCC also participate. This third network identifies itself as neither TSPM/CCC nor ACC but a Uniting Church Network. The government, too, considers them as a distinct group and has been liaising with them about independent registration without a requirement to join the TSPM/CCC. This new ecclesial identity provides a neutral ground for the TSPM/CCC and ACC to cooperate for greater unity in forms of uniting ministry, such as training.

The ACCs and the TSPM/CCC share similar theological and pastoral challenges. As one traces the teachings of the TSPM/CCC and the ACCs from the 1980s throughout the 1990s, sermons primarily focused on perseverance of faith, suffering and the cross, and the grace and hope of God interspersed with many testimonies on the power and grace of God, including miracles and healings. From the 1990s to the present, preaching has focused on witnessing in a changing society, evangelism and mission, family and marriage, resisting materialism, and Christian moral living to confront the rapid change of social moral standards in the context of China's present economic development. It seems that both camps now face similar challenges from China's current embrace of secularism and materialism.

---

presentations were not published as some of them contain classified data. Permission had been obtained from Rev. Guo to quote the content of his oral presentation.

23. Personal interview conducted on April 29, 2012. Name and location withheld for security reasons.

24. Different provincial governments exercise various degrees of restriction on religious propagation. This particular province is extremely harsh on Christians, and the leaders of this provincial TSPM/CCC are well known for their zealous imposing of the government's wishes on the church. Many TSPM/CCC churches have split off and formed their own ecclesial communities.

Theological resources are limited for both camps due to the challenging history of Christianity in China. Theological resources are few, and the needs are overwhelming. Since Protestant churches in China were isolated from the global Christian community for almost half a century, theological developments in the West such as neo-orthodoxy, evangelicalism, feminist theology, ecotheology, missions and social justice, process theology, liberation theology, contextualization, and others are not familiar to Protestants in China. Furthermore, most of those who survived the hardship of persecution and refused to join the TSPM come from fundamentalist backgrounds. Therefore the ACCs tend to embrace this theological position with a strong emphasis on the Bible. While the TSPM/ CCC incorporates both fundamentalism and some strains of liberalism within its theological teachings, one can find Bishop K. H. Ting's teaching on justification by love alongside many TSPM/CCC's publications on literal interpretations of the Bible. The majority of the Protestant community in China, be it TSPM/CCC or ACC, is theologically conservative, some extremely so, so there are very few in-depth theological discussions about the relationship between Protestant faith and Chinese culture and society.

Despite the many ecclesial manifestations one finds in China, they are more diverse in ecclesial form than theology, since the majority of the Chinese Protestant community generally embraces a theologically conservative stance. However, it is very encouraging to notice the increasing ecclesial options available, as well as the increasing dialogues and instances of cooperation between different ecclesial factions. Protestantism, by definition, is constituted by diverse understandings of the Christian faith within a common biblical framework. The Protestant community in China seems to embody such a vision in its own profound way—from traditional, mainline denominational expression to contemporary worship models; from indigenous, laity-centered local churches to missiological communities such as the spiritual bands; and from highly involved lay leaders in rural churches to nonbaptized, cultural Christians who never step inside a church building. These ecclesial diversities transcend the dichotomy of the TSPM/CCC and the ACCs and point toward the vision of Chinese Protestantism in the days to come—a church that includes the solemn liturgical tradition of mainline denominations, the missiological zeal of the Free Churches, the communal spirit of Chinese society, the pietistic devotion of Chinese religiosity, and the vibrant dynamics of charismatics.

4.

Geographical

With 9.7 million square kilometers of land, China is the third-largest country in the world, with geographic diversities ranging from cold taiga to fertile plains, from frozen plateaus to subtropical rain forests, and from snowcapped mountains to stony deserts. Economically, politically, and culturally, there is an approximate division between the central and coastal plains, which have mild climates inhabited by the majority of the population, the Han ethnic group,[1] and the peripheral or border regions of steppes, plateaus, deserts, and high mountains, whose sparse population primarily consists of minority groups such as the Mongolians, Tibetans, and Uyghurs. These are the official national minorities, and they have different languages and cultural customs.[2] The majority of the wealth, population, and economies are concentrated within the central and coastal plains. This is where the mass media's general impression of contempo-

1. In ordinary usage, the term *Chinese* usually refers to the largest ethnic group in China, the Han people. Han people compose 90 percent of the current population in China.

2. There are also other ethnic groups, fifty-five in total, as designated by the authority in 1956, such as the Tibetan, the Mongolian, or the Manchu. However, the Chinese government usually uses the term *Chinese* to denote the citizens of the People's Republic of China, which includes ethnic groups other than the Han. This book uses the term *Chinese* in the conventional usage to designate the Han people instead of the political usage of Chinese citizens by the Chinese government. Every Chinese citizen must file his or her ethnic identity under one of the fifty-six ethnic nationality groups.

rary China is portrayed: bustling city life with high-rise build-ings and traffic jams juxtaposed with rivers, lakes, temples, and rice paddy fields. The peripheral areas, however, are pictured with ethnic minorities in exotic dress and beautiful natural scenes of grassland, deserts, and snowcapped mountains. These two viewpoints mark the traditional demarcation line between the Chinese world and the non-Chinese world—or more pre-cisely, the Han world versus the non-Han world.

Traditionally, the Han Chinese live in these central and coastal plains, with natural geographical barriers, such as moun-tain ranges, plateaus, and deserts, and man-made barriers, such as the Great Wall, blocking them off from other non-Han peo-ple. Even when the peripheral areas were under the sovereignty of various Chinese emperors, these areas were regarded more as vassal states with autonomous administration than as provinces directly under the central government's administration. Chinese in coastal and central areas considered the peripheral areas fron-tiers, and not part of China proper culturally, because these areas are inhabited mostly by non-Hans. Since 1949, the government has tried to integrate these peripheral areas with the central and coastal regions of China, often by investing heavily in social welfare schemes, infrastructures, subsidies, and the migration of skillful Han workers to these areas in order to bridge the huge socioeconomic gaps between these two regions. In the 1990s, the government also initiated a ten-year "Go West" campaign to invest heavily in boosting the economy of these areas. As a result, the social and economic differences between these two regions have been much reduced. Despite all these efforts, how-ever, there are still clear gaps between the two regions, mainly due to their geophysical differences, such as close access to sea-ports for global trade or higher farming production yields due to milder climates. This favors the economic development of the central and coastal plains.

As Christianity was introduced into these two major areas, it faced different challenges and eventually developed unique ecclesial manifestations. Within these two major regions, there are diverse sociocultural circumstances that shape each local region in different ways. For example, the local government of a Muslim-dominated region would have a different attitude toward Christianity than a government ruling a region where polytheistic-animistic religions are practiced. This chapter first looks at the central and coastal plains, where the majority of the Chinese are living, and discusses the Christian faith of this region's two socioeconomic categories: rural and urban. The second part of this chapter focuses on the peripheral areas and looks at the churches of the national minorities and their unique characteristics.

THE CENTRAL AND COASTAL REGION

Since the mid-1950s the Chinese government has adopted a Soviet-style planned economy, and every citizen is thus a part of the national production machinery. The government has also devised a household registration system to govern where its citizens can live, how they produce within the national scheme, and most important, what kind of opportunities they will have. Household registration is divided into two categories: rural population and urban population.[3] If a household is categorized as rural, that family and their children can only live in the villages tilling farms as determined by the government. The children can only attend the local school, and the family has access only to the local medical facilities. Their entire life is linked with farming. In very exceptional cases, if their children could get into a university and manage to secure a job in the urban areas, they might change their registration category to urban, provided they could join the limited urban population quota. Children in households classified as urban can attend schools in the cities, which are usually of a much higher educational quality than those in the villages. Their lifestyles are sustained by the amenities and facilities provided by the cities, which are quantitatively and qualitatively better than those offered in the rural areas. The government's plan is meant to use the resources of the rural areas to support the cities, where the political centers are located and the political elite live. As a result, the rural and urban areas are two rad-

---

3. Official names are Rural Production Population and Non-Rural Production Population. For simplification, they are usually referred to as Rural Population and Urban Population.

ically different worlds with virtually no crossover. Rural people are regarded as uneducated, unskilled, and to some extent uncivilized simpletons in the eyes of urban citizens.

In 1980, 85 percent of China's population was in the rural category, and 15 percent was urban. In the 1980s, China launched the Reform and Open policy, followed by a huge urbanization program. By 2018, almost 60 percent of the 1.4 billion population was classified as urban, that is, living in cities or newly developed urban zones. However, there was still about 40 percent of the population—six hundred million people, or about twice the population of the US—living in rural areas. Out of these six hundred million, perhaps as many as two hundred million—the majority being able-bodied workers from eighteen to forty-five years old—were migrant workers who had built the new cities and skyscrapers, worked in the assembly lines to run the factory of the world, and constructed the new railways, airports, and superhighways speeding up China's economic flow, along with performing the low-pay, low-end menial jobs that served the emerging, middle-class, urban rich. Although many rural people live in urban areas as migrant workers, because of the Household Registration system, they and their children cannot access social services in the cities and have to pay a huge premium in order to attend local urban schools or to receive medical services in the city. They are also barred from many good jobs that are only available to registered urban dwellers. Today, the discrimination against the rural population is still part of China's social reality, and this gulf between the rural and urban populations provides a disturbing background necessary to understanding the Protestant communities in the central and coastal regions of China.

Christian Communities in Rural Areas

Before 1980, rural life in China was relatively stable, as every peasant able to work was assigned to production brigades under the commune system. The collective or the commune provided all education, medical, elderly care, and other social welfare services, however basic. The price of all commodities was fixed by the state and kept artificially low. All farming produce belonged to the state, and there was no private ownership or private trade of any kind. Peasants were allowed to keep a fixed amount of rations to feed their family and then had to sell the rest of their produce to the state at an extremely low price. With so little cash in hand, they could only buy basic household goods, and most of these goods, such as soap, matches, and watches, were also rationed. Travel was not allowed, except for official purposes with permits issued by local authorities. Children continued their parents' lifestyle as they were registered rurally and therefore cut off from the urban system. The government, however, would subsidize the peasants if the harvest was not ideal so that no one would starve. In essence, everyone lived at a similar subsistence level with rudimentary social services. Everyone was poor by world standards, with GDP at less than USD $200 per person per year in the late 1970s. Yet few complained; they could make no comparison since China was closed to the rest of the world.

Since 1980, China has carried out the Reform and Open policy, which privatized farm production from collectives to households (you keep whatever you can produce after fulfilling the government's quota) and allowed for the possibility of a gray market to sell privately produced farm products. There was also the gradual cessation of all communally based social services such as medical and education facilities, as few would contribute to the collective pool to run these concerns. Such socioeconomic change also led to a large surplus of farming labor. This in turn fed the increasing demand for low-skill jobs available in new construction sites and factories in coastal areas and also in the huge infrastructure projects invested in by the government. Soon there were tens of millions of peasants, many of whom had never traveled out of their villages, becoming migrant workers. During the 1980s and 1990s, the rural areas lost their former social cohesiveness, and many peasants felt that they had lost the basic living security they had once enjoyed. They struggled with the new economic adjustments, trying to cope with the newly privatized and expensive medical system and living in fear of an uncertain future as the former social safety network had vanished. Their faith in the government diminished, and they turned to other, however intangible, belief systems. Very soon traditional folk religions reemerged, and religions such as Christianity became popular among the rural populations. The government called this period a time of crisis of confidence or a spiritual vacuum, and it named the religious upsurge as Religious Fever.

In the 1980s, virtually all reports on Chinese Protestant communities noted that the majority of Chinese Protestants were concentrated in the rural areas of the central and coastal provinces such as Henan, Anhui, Jiangsu, and Shandong as many of these rural Protestant communities experienced phenomenal growth in both the TSPM/CCC and ACC networks. These rural Protestant communities shared four similar characteristics: they were mostly female, elderly, poorly educated (primary school or lower), and new converts. These four features became the hallmark of Chinese Protestantism from the early 1980s until the year 2000, as Christianity in China experienced a major upsurge of membership when converts from the rural population swelled the ranks. The social factors contributing to such religious growth are rather obvious. As the peasants saw their social support systems disappear, they were desperate to cling onto anything that could promise them a cure for illnesses, a better income, and a faith amid an uncertain future. When they heard testimonies from Protestants of their God healing the sick, casting out demons, transforming people's characters, and usually providing them with good fortune,[4] these peasants were drawn to transfer their religious allegiance from traditional Chinese folk religious practices, or even socialist ideology, to Protestantism. They hoped for a better and more powerful force than their former deities, one that could address their immediate concerns. Many of them could echo the Mount Carmel experience of a powerful encounter between this new God and the deities of their past. Once people experienced this new religious reality, they would immediately introduce it to their relatives and friends. Such natural sharing of positive religious experiences constituted the primary means of faith transmission and

4. More than once I have heard testimonies from Protestant peasants about experiencing this new God in their bumper harvests despite the lack of fertilizers and having a much higher yield of rice than their non-Christian neighbors.

was the reason for the rapid growth of the Christian population in China during this period.

In fact, it was very common for any visitors to the rural churches in China in the late 1980s to see lines of people after the service asking for prayers for their particular illnesses, as most of them could not afford to get proper medical treatment when the former commune-based medical care system collapsed. Some claimed to be possessed by demons, but on closer examination, these were mostly cases of mental illness. Some had been urged by their Protestant friends to try this God with the firm conviction that it would work and cost nothing. Many embraced this new religion after experiencing something positive. It was not uncommon for some to bring their sick chicken, or even pigs, and ask a preacher to lay hands on them so they would be healed.[5] In fact, most of the reported growth in rural Protestant communities during this period could be attributed to some kind of miracle, sign, or wonder. The massive migration of young people from the rural areas to work in the newly built factories in coastal areas, as well as to various urban areas as construction workers for the new national program, meant that the housewives, the very old, and the very young stayed in their home villages. Thus the population profile of the rural church was shaped with a high proportion of women and the elderly.

The story of Madam Chen Shaoying, a retired teacher from Cigong Township, embodies the typical experience of a rural Protestant convert. Cigong, a cluster of villages and hamlets thirty kilometers from the Yangshan County Seat of the Qingyuan Municipality in the northern part of Guangdong Province and neighboring Hunan Province, is one of the most remote and poor rural counties of the province of Guangdong. It had no record of any previous Protestant presence. In 1991, while visiting her daughter who had just had surgery at the county hospital, Chen befriended a visitor who was a distant relative of a patient in the bed next to Chen's daughter. This visitor was a believer, shared the gospel with the Chens, and prayed

5. I have encountered these requests. Despite the lack of biblical reference to pray for healing for animals, the pastor was obliged to offer such prayers, and this often resulted in phenomena that could not be explained by veterinary medicine and were theologically interpreted as miracles.

for the recovery of Chen's daughter. The Chens accepted Jesus and began to share this new faith with their friends and neighbors after they returned to Cigong. Soon, many began to gather at the Chens' home. Madam Chen eventually found a Protestant church in the municipality of Qingyuan almost a hundred kilometers from her home and brought back some Bibles, hymn books, cassette tapes of sermons, and booklets on basic Christian doctrines. By 1992, there were seventy followers gathering at her home, and a year later more than 150 people were meeting at five different homes. Most joined when they experienced healings or other miracles after praying to this new God: Jesus. The local authority had no idea how to deal with this new group: was it a cult or a genuine religion? Also the registration of a religious group requires a certain number of confirmed believers as well as a trained religious leader; both requirements were lacking for this group as none had been baptized. As a result, the local authorities harassed these groups and tried to shut them down. The believers went into hiding, and by 1994, their number had increased to more than 250. While they were in hiding, a nurse from the county hospital at Cigong who visited her mother, a believer, was converted when she experienced a deep sense of peace after being prayed over by the believers. She brought her new faith along with a Bible with a few pages missing back to the county seat and shared this new faith with her colleagues and friends. Within a year she had almost one hundred followers in Yangshan County and regularly received spiritual support from Chen's group in Cigong.

These new groups faced a chicken-and-egg dilemma: without an ordained minister (there were none in that municipality at that time), there could not be initiation of new believers as recognized church members because only an ordained minister could conduct baptism. Without a sufficient number of recognized members, the group could not register, and without registration, they could not call for or hire a trained religious leader, that is, a preacher or pastor. Such dilemmas were common in rural areas where Protestantism had grown the fastest during the 1980s and 1990s, especially in areas with no previous Protestant presence. Each Protestant group had to resolve such dilemmas in their own ingenious way. In this case, in December 1995, these believers chartered two buses to transport sixty people to the church in Qingyuan for the Christmas service. For the majority, this was the first time that they had traveled outside of Yangshan County. For most of them, it was the first time they had ever attended a church service or even entered a church building. Fifty out of the sixty were female, middle-aged, semiliterate peasants. In that service, there was an ordained minister who had been invited from another city for this special Christmas service.[6] At the service, he baptized all sixty of them, and they each received a baptismal certificate issued by the church confirming them as bona fide members. Now Cigong had forty baptized church members, and Yangshan had twenty. Madam Chen, the nurse from Yangshan, and a few other newly baptized members immediately enrolled in an intensive three-week theological course for lay leaders run by the Qingyuan church. Upon completing the program, they each received a certificate that qualified them as lay preachers—legally accepted by the authority as trained religious leaders. Both groups then filed their registration applications, and in 1998, Cigong Church got its registration certificate as Protestant Meeting Point Number 001, the first in that county. Soon Yangshan Church, too, got its registration, certificate Number 002. By the turn of the century, Cigong Church had close to one thousand followers and Yangshan more than five hundred. Now both have their own church buildings and their own ordained, seminary-trained pastors. The genesis of the Cigong and Yangshan churches is a typical story that was repeated in most rural Protestant communities, in both the TSPM/CCC and ACC networks in China, with perhaps some local variations. Cigong and Yangshan started as ACCs and later moved into the TSPM/CCC structure; however, many groups have remained as ACCs.

Since 2005, the government has carried out major reform programs to elevate rural income and lessen the economic gap

6. Religious regulation requires that the church needs to apply for permission from the local Religious Affairs Bureau to invite clergy from outside its region to conduct religious services. Such a request was hard to gain but would usually be granted if the invitee was accepted by the local authority. In this case, the Qingyuan Church invited an ordained minister from Hong Kong who had received honorary citizenship from the Qingyuan Municipality for his socioeconomic contributions to that region.

between the rural and urban populations. These reforms have included abolishing farmland tax, providing free education, establishing basic health insurance, subsidizing household electrical appliances, and providing tax breaks for small rural enterprises. As a result, rural living has become more attractive, with fewer peasants leaving the rural areas for economic reasons. In addition, many rural areas have been rezoned as urban areas, especially those adjacent to sprawling urban developments in which many migrant workers settle as they become used to urban living. Many children of these rural migrant workers, born in the cities, would find it hard to adjust back to life in the rural villages. Though these migrant workers would have had to pay a premium to continue to live in the cities and would typically exist at the bottom of the economic food chain, they and their children do have increased opportunities for upward mobility. All these socioeconomic changes have transformed the rural areas, which now contain less than half of the total population, as rural areas are catching up with urban living amenities.

The impact on rural churches is correspondingly drastic. With the improvement in health and social welfare services, the signs and miracles that propelled the high conversion rate in the 1980s and 1990s have almost completely disappeared, and the rural conversion rate has dropped correspondingly. The rural Protestant population is aging as more young people migrate to urban areas with better economic opportunities. Even many young, aspiring pastors from rural Protestant communities are leaving their pastorates to join urban congregations in areas with higher salaries, better working conditions, and more opportunities for upward mobility. Furthermore, as many developed rural regions are rezoned into urban areas, formerly rural churches are now integrated into urban churches. Overall, rural Protestant populations are declining, and empty pews in rural churches are common, as people, especially those of a working age, settle in urban centers. The rural Protestant community, once the centrality of the Chinese Protestant community, is now gradually moving toward its periphery.

Similar to the Protestants, the majority of Catholics reside in the rural areas. Most of the Catholics in China are concentrated in the provinces of Hebei, Shaanxi, Shanxi, Inner Mongolia, and Jiangsu, which have large rural populations. Rural Catholics tend to cluster in Catholic villages, as many of these Catholic villages carry a history of more than a century resulting from communal conversion, which was common in the eighteenth and nineteenth century in China. These Catholic villages often form natural parishes, with the church being the center of communal focus. With the liberalization of religious policy since the 1980s, the Catholics, parallel to the Protestants, have actively rebuilt their churches and reestablished their religious activities, centering on major feast days of the liturgical calendars.

Differing from their Protestant brethren however, there was no major surge in Catholic population from 1980 to the present, no massive conversion reported during the Cultural Revolution, nor any significant sightings of miracles or signs reported among believers. Instead they enjoyed steady growth, slightly above population growth. Their growth is attributed more to the familial transmission of the Catholic faith than from the religious conversion that is commonly found among Protestants. The difference in growth rate between these two communities seems to be mainly caused by ecclesiastical differences in religious personnel. The sacrament-based Catholic Church activities very much depend on the availability of a priest, of which there are few—the demanding requirements, including being male and making a vow of celibacy, limit its number. In the Protestant church, any untrained laity of either gender, married or not, can take up a pastoral role. This gave rise to literally tens of thousands lay pastors. Also the Catholics, with only several hundred priests surviving the Cultural Revolution in the 1980s and several million Catholics to care for, could only provide minimum pastoral service, mostly in sacramental form, to their flock in order to maintain the most basic form of Catholic faith. It is not uncommon for some rural parishes to have just one annual visit of a priest to celebrate Eucharist with them. The limitation of pastoral service was also aggravated by the demarcation line drawn between the Patriotic and the underground factions, often using precious resources to fight against each other rather than to work with each other.

Living in the very same sociopolitical context, rural Catholics experience the same contemporary challenges as Protestants, such as the massive migration of the rural young population to urban areas leaving behind empty pews in churches filled with elderly, women, and children; the economic pull for priests from rural areas toward the urban pastorate; and the urbanization of rural areas. All these socioeconomic changes are pushing the rural Catholic communities toward uncharted territory.

Christian Communities in Urban Areas

In 1985, only 15 percent of the total Chinese population lived in urban areas; as of 2018, about 60 percent of the population lives in a city. In less than thirty-five years, China has experienced the largest urbanization process in the history of human civilization, transforming more than seven hundred million people, almost the entire population of Europe, from rural to urban living. At its current rate of social development, China will have two-thirds of its population urbanized by 2020. Now the majority of China's population is urban instead of rural, with most people concentrated in the central and coastal regions. These social changes affected Protestantism in China as the centrality of Chinese Protestantism moved from rural to urban centers.

Several factors contribute to the differences between rural and urban Protestant communities. First, the urban population is usually better educated than the rural population, and therefore they receive more indoctrination in communism than their rural counterparts. Since the state officially endorses atheism, those who have received more education are less likely to have had any religious influence, especially from the folk religion popular among the less-educated peasants. As the bulk of the new urban converts are intellectuals and skilled workers, they transfer their ideological allegiance from Marxism-Leninism to Christianity. Thus the main competing organizations to Protestant community are the Communist Party and the Communist Youth League. Therefore, the growth of Christianity in urban areas poses a direct sociopolitical threat to the ruling Party and generates fears among the Party leadership. The Party responds to this threat by imposing administrative measures targeting the growth of Protestantism, such as a reluctance to grant permits to

Protestant groups to exist legally; the denial of applications for more services or religious activities to the registered groups; limitation of foreign contacts with these groups; and bans on religious propagation in public spaces, such as education institutes, hospitals, parks, shopping malls, and even internet virtual space easily accessed by the urban population. As a result, Protestant communities in urban areas face stronger administrative constraints than their rural brethren.

Second, for those who live in urban areas, faith issues are often more intellectual than pragmatic in nature. The Marxist scientific worldview, from which many of these converts come, does not make for an easy ideological transition to Christianity. The existence of God and faith, and intangible subjects such as the soul and heaven, are often hotly debated topics among new believers and seekers. The evangelical approach to urban people often relies more on apologetics than on the powerful spiritual encounters used by their counterparts in rural areas. Many urban converts make an individual decision after a lengthy intellectual struggle. While the rural Protestant community experienced a sudden outburst of growth during the 1980s and 1990s as miracles helped draw in a large group of followers, urban Protestantism grows steadily, tagging alongside the general growth of urban population.

Third, urban areas in China are densely populated, and real estate is at a premium. Usually only churches established before 1949 own property and are mostly registered with the government. These historical churches are able to build or rebuild a church in a city. Even so, the government often takes church property, which is usually located in city centers and valued as prime commercial real estate, and in return gives the church a larger piece of land on the outskirts or in a new urban zone. In some instances, the government sells the church a piece of land in newly developed urban zones so that a new church can be built; however, the government still tightly controls the number of churches and church buildings. Even with initiatives for new church buildings, the number of urban churches is far too insufficient to cater to the increasing number of urban Protestants. The churches in the cities are often overflowing, but this phenomenon reflects more the severe lack of church space than the piety of Chinese Protestants. With church buildings in the urban landscape few and far between, and with ever-expanding city areas rendering intracity travel a time-consuming effort, many church activities are conducted in home gatherings where a group of believers live in close proximity. Some churches even rent offices or flats to conduct their pastoral services. This type of situation is typical for TSPM/CCC churches in any major city. The rural situation is different, as land is easily available, and local village authorities easily approve most building constructions proposed in rural areas.

The ACCs may not have a church building simply because they are not registered. In the past, they could usually meet in homes or apartments. Now, with the increasing number of urban believers, most urban ACCs have to rent apartments, office buildings, or even hotel conference halls, factories, warehouses, and convention centers to hold their meetings. The government exhibits a high degree of tolerance for these groups so long as neighbors do not complain, at least until 2017. As a new religious regulation has been in effect since February 2018, there are increasing reports of urban ACC meetings being closed down, and the reasons given are usually fire regulations or rental disputes rather than religious reasons. Most urban ACCs are forced to break down into small groups gathering back at believers' households. As for rural ACCs, since the typical village house courtyard is quite spacious and can easily hold up to one hundred people, they do not have too many difficulties conducting their activities without a formal church building.

Fourth, there is a higher socioeconomic cost for urban converts than for rural converts. Rural citizens, believers or otherwise, mostly earn a living by farming. Except for the few village cadres who are usually Party members and whose income comes from the government, the religious affiliation of ordinary peasants does not normally affect their farm production or income.[7] However, an urban convert's abandonment of the atheism officially endorsed by the state is a religious decision with political implications. For example, if he or she is a Party member, or employed by the state in education, banking, state-owned

7. Cadres are government officials and also Party members. In fact, almost all Chinese civil servants are Party members.

enterprises, health-care systems, government services, or other state employment, he or she has to hide this religious conviction or face discrimination, demotion, and perhaps even dismissal from employment. Party members must recant religious faith or lose their membership, which carries with it the loss of government employment and the privileges of being a Party member. For a person in a senior government or Party position, the consequences of choosing Christianity may not just be personal but also affect the whole unit under his or her supervision. I know of a very senior ranking officer of the PLA Navy who is a believer. He cannot become a formal Christian by baptism as such an act would not only cost him his job, but also many of the subordinates under his command would suffer negative consequences. He is, ecclesiastically speaking, not a Christian, as he has not undergone the initiation rite of baptism; however, he is a follower of Jesus. There are many such followers among the intellectuals or working in government service, the military, the police force (security apparatus), and the Party who are not part of the visible Protestant communities, especially in urban areas, but remain part of the mystical body of Christ. These individuals are frequently referred to as "cultural Christians," "hidden Christians," or "anonymous Christians."

Fifth, China's cities are much more open to foreigners and foreign influences than in the rural areas. Along with foreign cultural influences, various Protestant denominations have also been introduced to China in urban areas where a foreigner can take up residence and deepen the influence of Christianity. The Korean style of prayer, Singaporean charismatic songs and worship styles, Taiwanese praise group dances, US Vineyard songs, Australian Hillsong hymns, or even Taizé chanting are rather popular in both TSPM/CCC and ACC urban communities simply because of the easy access to these worship modes offered by foreign missionaries who can easily stay in the cities under various guises. In addition, educated urban Protestants can readily absorb these new styles, for they tend to be more open to new ideas and have foreign language skills that their rural counterparts usually lack. As a result, one can easily find many contemporary worship styles in China's urban Protestant communities.

Finally, there is a type of Protestant gathering found mostly in urban areas in China: businesspeople fellowships. Since China adopted the Reform and Open policy in 1980, there has been a gradual emergence of a business class. Business activity predominantly takes places in urban areas. At the moment, businesspeople in China enjoy a rather prestigious and powerful social status, and more and more people are joining their ranks. Businesspeople are increasingly being invited to join the ranks of the political elite, such as becoming members of the People's Congress or the People's Political Consultative Conference. Some are even invited to join the Chinese Communist Party![8] At the same time, there are increasing numbers of Chinese businesspeople embracing the Christian faith, mostly due to the witness of fellow Protestant business colleagues, and especially from expatriate business partners from Hong Kong, Taiwan, and overseas Chinese Protestants. Because of the status and growth of business in China, usually local officials turn a blind eye to these Christian fellowships as long as they do not challenge the government's authority. The Full Gospel Business Fellowship has now established many chapters in China. These believers often do not attend church services on Sunday because they are traveling or attending to their growing business enterprises spreading all over the country and overseas. Also, many seem to find the Sunday sermons preached in their local churches irrelevant to their daily life.[9] Most resort to their own fellowships, often held in hotel halls, private clubs, or exclusive dining rooms in fancy restaurants under various pretexts such as gourmet fine dining, wine tasting, or birthday parties. Many of them are not baptized and, theologically speaking, not church members. Their gatherings are not part of any church (although some of them may be affiliated with a church), and there are no sacraments. This kind of ecclesial community is common in urban China and is part of the Chinese Protestant landscape.

8. One may wonder how Karl Marx might react if he was living in China now, hearing that businesspeople, the capitalists, are invited to join the Chinese Communist Party. Who then would fight for the right of the workers and the proletarians exploited by the capitalist Party members?

9. A Christian businesswoman told me that one Sunday she heard the preacher denouncing money as the source of all evil, and earning money means loving the world, not God. She felt even more disgusted after the service when the preacher asked her to donate money for the church building fund because she was wealthy.

Other than the characters of the urban Protestant communities generally found in China, there is also a unique urban ecclesial form from a particular urban center, Wenzhou, in eastern China, that may shape the Chinese Protestant community especially in terms of global mission. Wenzhou is a municipality in the northern part of Zhejiang Province with slightly more than ten million residents: about 6.5 million locals and 3.5 millions migrant workers from other areas. There are also 1.5 million Wenzhou natives living in different parts of China and half a million in more than 160 countries in the world.[10] The Wenzhouese speak an ancient dialect that few outside of the Wenzhou region can comprehend. There are also several major subdialects within the Wenzhou region that clearly identify the locality of the speaker. In fact, the Wenzhouese identify and cluster themselves more by their subdialects and subregions than by the geopolitical entity of Wenzhou.

Since the hilly regions of Wenzhou have little farmland to adequately sustain the livelihood of the population, traditionally Wenzhouese work as itinerant merchants and go wherever there is a business opportunity. The Wenzhou people are entrepreneurs by tradition and led China's economic reform by establishing the first batch of private enterprises in China in the late 1970s before the government allowed private commercial activity. Each male individual in the Wenzhou community has to prove himself worthy by starting his own business. Currently Wenzhou is the city with the highest income per capita among all the municipalities in China. The Wenzhouese are perhaps the richest private citizens in China, as there is at least one trillion RMB (RMB 6.2 = USD $1) in liquidity available in Wenzhou looking for investment opportunities. It also has the highest percentage of merchants in their population as virtually every family has someone engaged in business or private enterprise.

10. Mr. Yang Shangming, deputy director of the Liaison Office of the Wenzhou municipal government, supplied the figures about the population profile of Wenzhou. Mr. Yang is the expert on this topic as he keeps track of all the Wenzhouese not only in China but also their whereabouts all over the world. Personal interviews, November 24–26, 2005. There are no reliable published data on this subject due to the dynamic nature of the Wenzhouese in their movements. The basic data were supplied by Mr. Yang and updated by me through many other sources. All figures are estimates only.

Wenzhou businesses are all interconnected via family or clanship networks. It is common to find a household of five that may run four different companies that are all related in terms of the production supply chain. More than 95 percent of GDP in Wenzhou is from the private sector, whereas the national average is merely around 60 percent.

Out of the 8.5 million Wenzhouese, 1.5 million are scattered across all parts of China doing business, from the rich coastal provinces like Jiangsu to the harsh plateaus like Tibet. In virtually every city, county, and town in China, one can find at least one shop operated by Wenzhouese. In many townships in remote frontier areas, the only merchant from the outside would most likely be a Wenzhouese. There are another five hundred thousand, not counting the two hundred thousand who have already obtained citizenship or residency in their host country, doing business in more than 160 countries all over the world, from Morocco to Montenegro, from Algeria to Zimbabwe.

Significant to our discussion, Wenzhou has the highest percentage of Protestants among all municipalities in China with an official figure of one million out of the 8.5 million Wenzhouese,[11] about 12 percent of the total Wenzhou population. Reliable sources suggest there are currently at least 1.75 million Wenzhou Protestants (including those under the ACCs not counted in the official figures) among these 8.5 million Wenzhouese, or about 20 percent of the Wenzhouese population. Visitors to this region can find church buildings in every village across the whole region, and many villages have more than one church building. In addition, most of the church members are merchants, and some are successful entrepreneurs with busi-

---

11. Rev. Matthew Deng Fucun, president of Zhejiang Christian Council, gave the figure of 770,000 on March 24, 2006. This figure did not include the unregistered ones, as well as those Wenzhou Christians who are not living in Wenzhou—about 27 percent of the Wenzhouese! I interviewed several Wenzhou church leaders in April 2011 in Zhejiang Theological Seminary while giving lectures to these church leaders, and they all suggested that there are well over one million Christians within the registered churches and at least another half million within the nonregistered sector. Since all these leaders are from the registered churches, they may have a rather conservative figure on the nonregistered sector. The actual figure could be higher, and the Protestant population would certainly have increased since 2011.

nesses all over China and in many parts of the world. Sometimes these Wenzhou believers are called "Boss Christians."

The Wenzhou Protestants have proudly called Wenzhou the Jerusalem of China, and they feel that their material and spiritual blessings are not coincidental but rather a divine plan for them to be the chosen people that revive China and eventually bless the world. Churches in Wenzhou have long supported many churches in rural and poor regions in different parts of China by channeling funds and sending missionaries. They have also established many training centers, mostly not registered, to train pastors and missionaries. The students are not only from Wenzhou but also from all over China. Wenzhou churches often serve as the beacon of Protestant faith in China as they have kept building monumental buildings with multiple Gothic arches and Roman domes topped with big crosses.[12] These crosses often become local landmarks, visible from afar as an open sign of the presence and the power of Protestant faith in an atheistic society where any display of religion in public has been discouraged.

Such bold assertions of Protestant faith in a communist regime have faced some setbacks. In 2014, the Party Secretary Xia Baolong of Zhejiang Province inspected the Wenzhou Municipality and saw the Christian crosses dotted all over the landscape. As a protégé of Xi Jinping, who seems to be a political hardliner, Xia ordered the local authorities to remove all the crosses publicly appearing on the church buildings. The Wenzhou Municipality dragged its feet, and Xia fired a few local officers, ordering the provincial government to pass a provisional building regulation legitimizing his campaign and expanding it into a province-wide program. The situation became violent as the government had to deploy riot squads and thousands of military police to

---

12. I asked local church leaders about the theological message and symbolic significance of these types of church buildings—typically with multiple domes, arches, and tall crosses—that the local believers want to convey. All of them had the same answer: (1) it looks Western, and therefore people would not associate it with local folk religion but rather a foreign religion such as Christianity; (2) the more arches and domes, the more ecclesial elements it contains, and therefore the more "churchy" it becomes; and (3) the cross on the church increases the overall height of the church building, and the higher building—preferably higher than the church of the neighboring village—symbolizes the more blessings they have received from God! Indeed, it is a Wenzhou form of indigenized theology.

remove crosses from more than three thousand churches, both Catholic and Protestant, in the province. Despite protests from registered churches and overseas groups and international media attention, this campaign lasted until the end of 2016, when virtually all crosses on church buildings in Zhejiang had been torn down.[13] Many church members were injured trying to protect their cross. Some pastors who publicly voiced their dissenting views, including the officially recognized chairperson of the Zhejiang Christian Council, Rev. Joseph Gu Yuse, were arrested, stripped of their church positions, indicted on various trumped-up charges, and incarcerated.[14] Some church buildings, including one that could seat more than 1,500 people, were demolished. The national TSPM/CCC was silent on this matter despite repeated pleas from the Wenzhou Protestants. The provincial TSPM/CCC, after firing dissenting pastors including Rev. Gu, the former chairman of the church council, issued statements of theological justification and Scripture quotations urging believers to obey the government and be good citizens. As a result, many Wenzhou believers—laity and clergy alike—left the TSPM/CCC and joined the ACCs or started their own ACC. The TSPM/CCC lost credibility, as many Chinese Protestants felt that the official church had not fought for their rights and had even colluded with the secular forces to persecute believers. The whole campaign led the Wenzhou believers to focus less on tangible projects such as large church buildings, which had consumed huge amounts of resources in the past, and more on intangible works like mission and evangelism. They began to internalize the cross as a metaphor for the Christian faith rather than an external display of faith. The experience of the Wenzhou Protestants in this cross-removal campaign challenged the whole Chinese Protestant community to rethink the church-state relationship and led to greater mistrust of the government and the TSPM/CCC.

There are about 1.5 million Wenzhouese working as mer-

13. In 2018, similar cross-removal campaigns appeared in other provinces, such as Henan. By September 2018, the local authority had removed crosses from four thousand churches in Henan.
14. He was released in December 2017 without charge but stripped from all church position.

chants all over China, and at least 20 percent are Protestants. These Wenzhou Protestant merchants frequently establish Protestant gathering points (house churches) among themselves in new places where there is a lack of Christian presence. Almost all of their gatherings are unregistered, but local authorities generally ignore the religious activities of these merchants. For example, Wenzhou Protestants established perhaps the first government-sanctioned Protestant meeting point in Lhasa, Tibet, beginning in the late 1990s, with almost a thousand gathering every Sunday just a few blocks away from the Potala Palace. Furthermore, most Wenzhouese combine their business goals with missiological aims: to share the gospel in places where they have business ventures, especially newly developed markets in remote places.[15] Their model of combining business and mission has been in practice in China for more than two decades, introducing commercial goods and the gospel to the farthest corners of China. Their missiological impetus primarily stems from Wenzhou Protestants' belief that they are a chosen and blessed people. As many of them share their faith with local inhabitants in areas where no missionary had ever been before, they also help the new converts to start their own gatherings, which gradually evolve into self-sustaining faith communities. Some Wenzhou merchants, in order to spread the gospel and establish churches,[16] deliberately set their business in areas without previous Christian presence. Many new Protestant communities, especially those in remote corners of the country, owe their existence to these Wenzhou merchant-cum-missionaries. Wherever one spots a Wenzhou business operation, there is a good chance there is a Protestant gathering nearby. At least one out of five Wenzhou people are believers, and through their commercial activities, they have already helped expand the Protestant influence in every imaginable corner of China.

The impact of the Wenzhou Protestants is beginning to be

15. See Kim-kwong Chan, and Tetsunao Yammamori, *Holistic Entrepreneurship in China* (Pasadena: William Carey International University Press, 2002), 65–72.

16. I met some of these Wenzhou merchants living in sensitive regions (border areas, military zones) in 2005, 2011, and 2014. They can, as merchants, have access to these places. They have successfully established viable Protestant communities there among the local populations; some are of national minority groups with no Christian churches. For security reasons, names, locations, and interview dates are omitted.

felt in other parts of the world. With at least half a million Wenzhouese working as merchants all over the world, there are perhaps one hundred thousand Wenzhou Protestant merchant-cum-missionaries currently carrying the good news of affordable Chinese products as well as the good news of salvation to over 160 nations and regions of the world. They are also the founders of many new Chinese congregations in Europe, Africa, and the Middle East, including the first Chinese church in Bucharest, Romania, in the late 1990s and the first Chinese church in Egypt (Cairo) in 2008. They operate the largest Protestant church network in Italy, the Chinese church in Prato, which numbers more than a thousand in their congregation on Sundays. They also operate perhaps the largest Protestant congregation in Rome in a former casino next to the Rome train station, which they bought and converted into a church where hundreds gather every Sunday.[17] Through their global commercial activities and their strong evangelistic zeal, they are able to proselytize in places hard to access through conventional mission channels, especially in countries that have forbidden any missionary activity or are inconvenient for missionaries from the West. These countries are often open to Wenzhou merchants much as they were to their European counterparts—the Moravian Brethren—several hundred years ago. As China increases her global presence and influence, the Chinese Protestant communities, through the Wenzhou Protestant merchants, may have a significant role in shaping global Christianity by spreading the gospel to hard-to-access places.

The Catholics in urban areas have strongholds at major coastal cities with strong foreign influence such as Shanghai, Qingdao, and Tianjin. With rapid urbanization, many professional and skilled laborers are flocking to these metropolitan areas, swelling the population many times over in twenty years. This new urban population, uprooted from their home and situated in a

---

17. The largest reported Protestant congregation in Italy by Western media is the Baptist Church in Rome, with two hundred attending on Sundays. In 2016, the Wenzhouese Church, with several hundred members in Rome and more than a thousand in Prato, plus at least another twenty-five other sister churches all over Italy, was perhaps the largest Protestant network group in Italy, but this has not been recorded or reported by any English or Italian media.

new social environment, is open to various economic and ideological ideas. Catholicism in urban areas is experiencing rather similar challenges to those that the Protestants are facing, such as high sociopolitical cost of being a believer and lack of space for religious activities.

Unlike Protestantism, where the impression, rationality, and modernism appeals to new Chinese converts, many of the new Catholic converts are drawn to Catholicism by the mystical dimension of the serenity of a cathedral, the pietistic devotion to a tangible subject (Eucharist), the spiritual uplifting of liturgical services, the visible union to the two thousand–year continuum of Christian faith, and the link to the rich European culture and civilization.[18] The tension between Patriotic faction and underground faction in urban areas remains intense. Unlike the rural areas where pro-Rome fractions often have their own public venues or even parishes in the open, their counterparts in urban areas are more secret in nature and operate often in a clandestine manner.

PERIPHERAL REGIONS

Ten percent of China's population is made up of national minorities (non-Han) scattered throughout the peripheral regions, land that constitutes more than half of China. The population in these regions is a mixture of Han and national minorities. The ideological preferences among the Hans in the peripheral regions are similar to the Hans in the central and coastal regions, as a majority of them are recent migrants to the peripheral regions. They are either sent by the government to these areas as administrators or technicians, or they came as merchants seeking commercial opportunities. They serve as the Hans' sociocultural extension into the national minority population. This Han population is mostly agnostic or atheist, especially the educated migrants, such as technicians or government officials. Some may have embraced religions such as Chris-

18. Unlike most of the Protestant missionaries to China, who were from the English-speaking world, the majority of Catholic missionaries were from countries such as Italy, Germany, Spain, and France.

tianity, Buddhism, or Daoism. In contrast to the Hans, ethnic minorities are usually religious, and religion is one of their main ethnic characteristics. The majority of these ethnic minorities have embraced Islam, such as the Hui (Sinicized Arabs or central Asians), Kazakhs, and the Uyghurs, in total about thirty million. The second-largest religious groups are the Tibetans and the Mongolians, who have mostly embraced Tantric Buddhism and number more than ten million. The remaining groups believe in folk religion or polytheistic animism, with a few embracing shamanism in the northeastern part of China adjacent to Siberia.

In Xinjiang and Tibet, the two largest peripheral regions in China,[19] the predominant religions are Tibetan Buddhism and Islam, and both religions often identify with specific ethnic minority groups. These two religious groups fiercely defend their status quo in order to gain political concessions. As the majority of Protestants and Catholics in these regions are Hans, they have virtually no political power, and they are at the mercy of the Muslims or Tibetan Buddhists, who dominate the local government posts. If one of these ethnic minority people were found to have embraced another faith such as Christianity (Protestantism or Catholicism), this individual would face the danger of being cut off from his/her community. In order to please these minority groups for social stability, the government has actually issued orders to Christians not to convert Muslims or Tibetan Buddhists, for such conversions may trigger social unrest and upset the delicate dynamics of ethnic harmony. A gain of a Christian convert from one of these groups may result in bloody riots, as these religious groups may claim that the government is trying to diminish their cultural heritage by allowing Christians to Sinicize their people. Because of such political favoritism against Christianity, Christianity has made the least progress in these regions, and new converts often keep their new faith in secret. However, there are reports of some conversions from Tantric Buddhism to the Protestant faith, and about a dozen churches have formed in Tibetan-dominated regions. There are also several villages that have converted to Catholicism in Yunnan, bordering Tibet. Even so, these numbers are

19. They are not provinces. Instead they are officially ethnic autonomous regions, and they are granted special autonomy and enjoy the status of a province.

insignificant when compared to the millions of Tibetans and Mongolians in the population.[20]

Christian believers who live in Muslim- and Tibetan Buddhism–dominated areas often feel that they live in a suppressed regime and are the objects of discrimination. In spite of the negative religious environment for Christianity, many of these Protestants do still carry a strong desire to share the good news with others. Some even adhere to the strong eschatological conviction of preaching the gospel all the way back to Jerusalem through the Muslim regions of central Asia and the Middle East as a prerequisite for the second coming. Driven by this missiological vision, these believers consider themselves to be anchors in the global relay race of the mission movement. This eschatological hope sustains them, as many are descendants of the Spiritual Bands. Through decades of hardship, they have sought the opportunity to share the gospel with their Muslim or Tibetan Buddhist neighbors. Their missiological vision, which began in the peripheral regions of China aimed at particular ethnic minority groups, is now being shared among all Chinese Protestants as the major mission movement of the Chinese church.

Most of the smaller ethnic minority groups have their own traditional religions that tend to resemble polytheistic animism, especially those living in the southwestern part of China bordering southeast Asian countries. They are often discriminated against by the Hans and considered uncivilized, uneducated, backward, and even barbaric, such as the Wa people, who still practiced cannibalism until as recently as the 1950s. These groups often exist as poor subsistence farmers in the mountains. Most have no written language, and almost all have little access to education, which is only available in Chinese. The Chinese government has attempted to raise the standard of living of these peoples, devising written languages for them and providing many subsidies and various incentives. However, there is still a clear cultural and economic gulf between the Hans and the national minorities. In addition, many of these ethnic groups are scattered between different neighboring countries, and their

---

20. I documented the formation of these Tibetan churches in Yunnan with the first one, started in 1999. Kim-kwong Chan, "The Tibetan-Protestant Community in China," *News and Views: Bulletin of Hong Kong Christian Council* (Fall 2004): 9–11.

ethnic identities are more binding than a political adherence to their country of residency, where they usually remain as minorities.

Missionaries, predominantly Protestants, have labored among these groups both in China and in neighboring countries since the beginning of the last century. Catholic missions to these minorities are few, and their impact is relatively smaller when compared to the Protestants'. Therefore, the following descriptions of Christian influence among the national minorities are, unless specified, mostly regarding Protestantism. Missionaries have created written languages for some of these groups, along with Bible translations and hymns in the native tongues. Ethnic groups such as the Lisu, Miao, Yi, Dai, Lahu, Wa, and Jingpo have been beneficiaries of these attempts. With written forms of their own languages, these groups are able to receive education from missionaries and learn modern skills such as personal hygiene, as missionaries introduced them to modern medicine.[21] As a result, these peoples feel that this new religion could not only give them a new God but also a higher level of civilization with a better sense of self-esteem that could elevate their socioeconomic and cultural position. As they have been allowed to practice Christianity since the 1980s, some of these groups have embraced the gospel for decades and experienced revivals, with a corresponding rapid increase in converts. For example, the Lisus have already suggested that Protestantism will soon be part of

21. Many of these heroic medical missionaries sacrificed their lives while helping their patients. For example, one of the medical missionaries at the Methodist hospital at Jiaotong, Yunnan, Dr. Lillian Mary Grandin (1876–1924), the first female medical doctor of Jersey, contracted typhus while serving her patients. She died and was buried in Jiaotong along with many of her colleagues. For more information on her, see La Vingtaine de la Ville, "Lilian Mary Grandin (1876–1924)," Vingtaine.org, https://tinyurl.com/yy4pk726. The Jersey government commemorated this fine daughter of Jersey by issuing a set of stamps of her mission work in China at her centennial in 1976. However, the Chinese authority prohibits the commemoration of missionaries as China still regards them as imperialistic invaders. Even the reestablishing of Dr. Grandin's tomb, desecrated and destroyed by the Red Guard during the Cultural Revolution, took years of negotiation and was finally rebuilt at the original burial site at the hill called Mount Phoenix, which is just a few kilometers from the original mission hospital. It was dedicated with an open-air commemorative service that I had the honor to officiate on Easter Sunday of 2005, with hundreds of Christians from all over Jiaotong gathering at the site.

their ethnic identity as more than half of them, totaling about half a million in China, are already believers.

In some instances, the local government has even encouraged these people to embrace the Protestant faith, hoping that if these people accept this religion, they would become better citizens and thus make the government's administration of civic affairs easier. For example, it is very common among these ethnic minorities for them to spend a huge amount of their income on alcohol, gambling, drugs such as opium or heroin, and animistic sacrifices. Such expenditure on these items has kept these national minority populations in an impoverished state and has been an important socioeconomic issue for the government; the authorities have attempted to elevate the economic status of these national minority populations, trying to bridge the economic gap between the Hans and the national minorities. Once these national minorities embrace Christianity, they tend to stop these lavish spending habits because Christianity, as taught by the missionaries, prohibits alcohol, drugs, smoking, gambling, and animist sacrifice. Almost all national minorities experience economic improvement once they become Christians; they naturally attribute such economic gains as a blessing from this new God they have accepted.

There are also government cadres who feel that converting these people to Christianity is a political-ideological advancement of these people from polytheism to monotheism, a necessary step toward the ultimate goal of Marxist-socialist ideological evolution: atheism. Therefore, they feel that Christianity would pave the way for these polytheistic national minorities to eventually embrace communism. Consequently, unlike the governments in Han-dominant areas, local governments of peripheral regions with large populations of national minorities do not discourage the growth of Christianity. As a result, Christianity, especially in the form of Protestantism, has grown rapidly in recent years among some of these groups. Christianization, or total conversion, of some national minority groups in China is not an impossibility.

Many of the national minority groups that welcome Protestantism feel they are the chosen people. Certainly the Israelites' experience in the Old Testament as the chosen people of God is an attractive theme among people groups such as the Miaos and the Lisus. The Lisus are so grateful in their self-perception as God's specially chosen people that they feel that it is their honor and privilege to send missionaries to evangelize other minority groups. During the past several years, they have successfully converted some of the Tibetans, Pumis, Musous, Marimashas, and the Dulongs. The Miaos, whose ancestors were defeated by the Hans several thousand years ago and who had to retreat into the mountains in Yunnan and Guizhou, also have an oral tradition that they will be one day be saved by a savior with a sacred book. The missionaries' message of Jesus and the Bible fit well with this ancient belief; therefore many Miaos are embracing this new religion, thinking it brings the salvation of their ethnic tribe. Currently more than 30 percent of the Big Flower Miao (the largest Miao subgroup) in Yunnan are believers, and the number is increasing. The Miaos have already established their own mission movement to evangelize and plant churches among their own as well as other branches of the Miao who speak different dialects. These Miao believers are one of the most zealous mission groups among the Chinese Protestant communities; some of them have already engaged in cross-cultural mission by working among other national minorities in the northwestern part of China.

As for other national minority groups that have long embraced the official religions, such as Theravada Buddhism for the Dai and Hani peoples, there is a strong resistance from Buddhist ethnic minorities to this Protestant advancement, for they feel it is a threat to their cultural and religious identity. Often local authorities, composed of ethnic minority leaders, seek measures to curb the growth of the Christian church. It is not uncommon to hear of churches and believers' households being burned to the ground by their Buddhist neighbors while local authorities stand by and watch. This is a price that many believers in ethnic minorities have to pay in order to embrace Christianity.

Although there is one strong and centralized government, China is so diverse in geocultural differences that the country seems to be a cohesive political concept that has difficulty translating policy into a unified national reality. The central and coastal regions are very different from the peripheral regions in terms of habitation, culture, and livelihoods. Within the central and coastal plains, there are also significant differences between the rural and urban areas. Different national minorities in the peripheral regions shape the local situation based on their cultural and religious preferences. All these diversities render Chinese Christianity a mosaic of different faith communities, each with their own distinctiveness—the Wenzhou Boss Christians worship in a lavishly built Gothic cathedral-style church, *sine crucis*, while a newly established Tibetan Protestant community gathers in a straw hut on the top of a mountain. Some urban professionals sing and pray in a rented apartment in Shenzhen; a group of Chinese Protestant businesspeople have a Bible study and gourmet dinner in a private dining room of a five star hotel in Beijing; a group of Catholics conduct a Taizé prayer meeting on the campus of one of the more than thirty universities in Shanghai; and a Catholic parish in rural Hebei holds a Palm Sunday procession accompanied by gongs, cymbals, and firecrackers. These daily realities of Chinese Christianity defy stereotypes. Perhaps the very few common denominators they all share are flexibility in their ecclesial expressions, zeal in evangelization, earnestness in mission, resilience in trials, and loyalty to their Lord Jesus Christ, even at a high cost. These characteristics are, however, hallmarks of many Christian communities in different ages and places. After all, any Chinese Christianity community is still part of the mystical body of Christ with unique traits that mark them as different, not from other Christian communities, but from their non-Christian neighbors.

5.

Biographical

There are many Chinese Christians who have helped to shape Christianity in China in different ways, such as writing, witnessing, and serving. To highlight any individual does injustice to others, as each individual is an essential part of this community of faith. However, there are some individuals that highlight the unique shape of contemporary Christianity in China. In the mosaic depiction of Chinese Christianity, these serve as major design lines shaping the contours and patterns of this complex picture. In recent years there have been biographies and testimonies published of various Chinese Christian figures, such as Bishop K. H. Ting, Wang Mingdao, Watchman Nee, T. C. Chao, Grace Ho and Mecca Zhao, Yang Xinhui, Archbishop Dominic Tang, and many more. This chapter focuses on several Protestants who are not well known outside of their community due to lack of documentation, especially in English, or who are deemed too ordinary to be recorded and published. It will also include a prominent Chinese Catholic whose life epitomizes the complex experience of Catholics living under Chinese communist rule.[1] They come from different backgrounds, and

---

1. Due to the numerical dominance of Protestantism in contemporary Chinese Christianity, the emphasis on this chapter is on Protestantism: three Protestant cases versus one Catholic case. Also because the number of Orthodox in China is very small and documentation of their faith experience is scarce, their stories are not included here.

each represents unique spiritual characteristics shaping the spiritual contour of the Chinese Christian community. This chapter focuses on their understanding of Christian faith and how they developed their unique spiritual characteristics in the sociopolitical environment in which they live, as well as the impact of their spirituality in their communities.

BROTHER LI, THE FIRST BELIEVER OF MUJIA VILLAGE: SIMPLE, PRACTICAL, AND GRATEFUL

Millions of Chinese turned to Christianity in rural areas for the simple reason that they believed that this Christian faith would give them a better life than their previous religion and traditions could. One such individual is Mr. Li, a peasant from the Lahu national minority group with merely two years of primary education, who lived in a small hamlet in Yunnan Province in the southwestern part of China. After describing the general socioreligious background of this region, this section will highlight the conversion experience of Mr. Li based on my extensive interviews with him in June 2000 and subsequent visits in 2005 and 2015.

Baipidezai (a hamlet) is located in the Mujia village under the administration of the Shanyuan Township of the Lancang Lahu Autonomous County under the Simao Prefecture of Yunnan Province.[2] In June 2000, more than 70 percent of the population of Lancang County was Lahu. The Lahu people, a recognized national minority group, had one of the lowest literacy rates in the province; in the year 2000, more than 80 percent of the Lahu living in this county had less than three years of primary school education, whereas the provincial average was around 60 percent. Lancang was also one of the poorest counties in the province and survived mainly on government subsidies. The Baipidezai hamlet had fifty-four families with a total of 207 people—all Lahus. The hamlet is located on a mountain

---

2. In 2007, Simao Prefecture changed its name back to Pu'er City, its name prior to 1950, to capitalize on the increasing popularity of Pu'er tea produced in the Simao region.

slope within a day's walking distance from Myanmar and at least three days of travel from Pu'er City, the nearest urban center.

In the past, all the villagers believed in the Lahu traditional folk religion of animism and polytheism, composed of a pantheon of ghosts and deities in a hierarchical order that governs virtually every sphere of life in Lahu cosmology. Their religious activities are centered on livestock sacrifices under the guidance of local shamans called *muba*.[3] Whenever someone is sick, the family invites the *muba* to hold a divination ritual. If the cause of the disease is attributed to a powerful ghost or deity, the family has to slaughter large livestock (a cow or pig); if a minor ghost is the cause, they only need to sacrifice small livestock, such as a chicken. If the sacrifice is a small one, the sacrificial animal is then eaten by the family members and the shaman. Where a large animal is sacrificed, there would be a feast for the whole village. The afflicted family has to continue offering sacrificial animals until the patient is healed.[4] This practice has become one of the main financial burdens among the Lahus and a major contributing factor to their poverty. Since opium and heroin are readily available in this region (which is just next to the infamous Golden Triangle), these drugs have been a cure-all medicine along with sacrificial animals for generations, especially when the Lahus have been too poor to afford proper medical services. In fact, opium was a traditional gift among the Lahus on important occasions or to honor guests, a common practice banned only in recent years. Most of the adults have taken opium and heroin, and many are addicts. Drug addiction has been and still is

3. *Muba,* or *moba,* depending on the linguistic branch of Lahu, is the shaman or the priest of the local village. This position is handed down through hereditary succession. There is also the *sheba,* that is, the "black" witch who can also exorcise ghosts for healing purposes. See Simao National Minorities Affairs Bureau Editing Committee, *The Study on Traditional Culture of Lahu in Simao* (Kunming: Yunnan People's Press, 1993), 15–20.

4. Lahus rarely have meat in their daily diet simply because it is too expensive. Meat is consumed only on festival days or after a healing sacrifice. Being trained as a nutritionist, I would suggest the possible healing effect is caused by the supplementary high-quality protein intake from eating sacrificial animals. Continued intake of a protein-rich diet would surely improve the general health status, especially the boosting of the immune system, as from my observation many Lahus in that region could be classified as malnourished.

a major socioeconomic problem in this region, especially among the non-Christian population. Some of the villagers had relatives living in Xiadade village, about one day's walk away. As they visited their relatives, they noticed that this village had some Lahus who believed in a new religion called Protestantism. These Protestant Lahus had healthier bodies, better income, more chickens and pigs (an economic indicator of prosperity), good hygiene, and did not practice livestock sacrifice—a custom termed "feudal superstition" by the communist government. Also, none of the Protestants took opium or heroin. Some Baipidezai villagers decided to invite the Protestants to share their new religion so that they themselves could enjoy this new elevated living standard. In 1998, the church at Xiadade sent a preacher to teach the gospel to the villagers at Baipidezai. Very soon, more than ten families converted. These believers met at the home of Mr. Li, whose family members were the very first group of believers. In 2000, there were twenty-three families totaling eighty-five people, or 40 percent of the village population, who belonged to this new Baipidezai church. In 2005, they were able to build their own church building that could house about 120 people. By 2015, most of the households of this village had been converted, and they have also shared their faith with the surrounding villages.

The following contains some abstracts from the interview with Mr. Li, the leader of this new Protestant community. This interview took place in June 2000 at his home, which was also used as the meeting place for the believers.[5]

At first, I asked Mr. Li how he accepted this Christian faith, what his understanding of this new religion was, and what he had experienced after his conversion. These questions were meant to obtain the perception of Christianity vis-à-vis the former Lahu religion from the newly converted Lahu Christian as expressed by Mr. Li, the leader of this faith community. Mr. Li said that one day he had knelt in front of the cross (in fact a Christian poster with a cross on it), and the preacher from the nearby village held his hand to pray for him. After praying, this

5. The conversation was conducted in Lahu and interpreted from Lahu into Putonghua by Madam Zhang Caixian, chief of the County Ethnic Minority Affairs Bureau.

preacher asked if he wanted to join this religion, and he replied yes. The preacher then took him out to the river at the edge of the village and baptized him. With the help of the preacher, he then burned his altar table at home, which every Lahu family has in order to worship Lahu deities. After he renounced his old faith and joined this new religion, he had better health, a higher harvest yield, and more livestock in his possession, as no sacrificial animal was required by this new religion. He also emphasized that this new God, whom he referred to by using the Lahu name for the Supreme God (*Ngo Sha*),[6] would protect him and provide him with good health and prosperity in life. When I asked who Jesus is and what the meaning of the cross is, the two most essential elements of Christian faith, he said that Jesus is God. He used a Lahu term for a deity just a rank lower than *Ngo Sha* in the Lahu cosmological hierarchy, and the cross was a teaching that he humbly admitted he has not yet learned as it was meant only for advanced Christians.

The interview suggested that Mr. Li has benefited from physical and material well-being after his religious conversion, an experience that echoes that of many Christian converts in rural China, be it Han or national minority people. Also the form of initiation rites is baptism by immersion in public, a rather dramatic performance richly endowed with religious symbols that is particularly appealing to the rural population. As for the metaphysics of faith, such as Christology, he could at least distinguish the seniority of the Father over the Son within the Godhead, as the metaphor of the Father-Son hierarchical relationship was within his intellectual comprehension. The teaching of the cross, Christian soteriology, is a bit too complicated for Mr. Li, a new convert with minimum education. Also for Mr. Li, this abstract doctrine bears little consequence for good health and good harvest. However, I have seen Christian posters with the cross at the center in most rural Christian households all over China.

I then asked about the communal witness of this new Christian community, that is, if there were any differences from non-Christian neighbors and also their common religious activities.

---

6. *Ngo Sha* is the name of the God of Creation in Lahu cosmology. There are different names given to other deities.

Mr. Li said that in contrast to the non-Christian villagers, the Christians did not steal each other's rice or grains. They did not commit adultery. They did not take poison (alcohol, opium, and tobacco). Most of the Christians were drug addicts before, but after they converted to Christianity, they stopped their drug addictions. So far, all of them have remained drug free, a phenomenon that amazed even the government cadres, who are all atheists. They also help each other by working in each other's fields, so that everyone can prosper economically. Mr. Li did not elaborate if they would render help to the non-Christians. Also he emphasized that they would all meet on Sunday, not in the morning as most Christians do in other parts of China, but instead in the evening after they have finished their labor in the field. They would sing hymns and listen to the sermon from different local preachers who came from nearby Christian communities with messages that would encourage them to work hard and not to be lazy. After the sermon, the preachers would usually teach them some scientific agricultural methods. Each family has a Lahu Bible and a Lahu hymnal that they would take to the meeting.[7] All Christians were economically better off after they converted to Christianity, and they regarded such economic prosperity as having come from the God of this new religion. As per Li's words, this new Christian community seemed to gel together as a mutually supportive unit centered on Christian faith and shared values in the context of a vastly non-Christian environment. Furthermore, their abstinence from drugs and alcohol, along with intense laboring in the field, bears an obvious contribution of new wealth to these Christian households. Their newfound prosperity has enhanced the superiority of Christianity against the traditional Lahu religion and further attracts new converts from among their neighbors.

I also asked about Li's personal Christian devotion, such as his prayer life. He said that there are twelve commandments that he has to obey, but he could not memorize them all.[8] He just

7. American missionaries developed a Latinized Lahu language in the 1920s and later translated the Bible as well as some hymns to become the Lahu hymnal. The China Christian Council reprinted the Lahu Bible and hymnal in the 1990s and distributed them among the Lahus free of charge or just for a token fee.

8. There are various forms of the commandments handed down by missionaries,

remembers the three "do nots": do not take opium, do not drink alcohol, and do not smoke tobacco. As for daily devotion, he says a prayer before his meals three times a day. He recited this fluently for me:

> Today's food is not easy to come by. God (*Ngo Sha*) gives it to us. After we eat it, we will not be sick. God protects us so that we can have the next meal. He protects us so that everything is prosperous, and we have peace. All our family members, from young to old, need protection from God. After we finish this meal, we will have the next one. All our pigs will be healthy. We will have plenty of chickens and cows. God protects us so that we can live better than before. We work hard, and we eat from the fruit of our labor. All our maize and grain will not be eaten by rats or cows. In harvest time, we will have a bumper harvest. The first bowl of rice is offered to God, and we eat the second bowl. After we eat, our blood and flesh [Lahu expression for the physical body] will not be sick. Lead our family members to live in peace. Amen.

I finally asked Mr. Li if he would like to sing his favorite hymn, as Lahus love to sing and dance. He took out his Lahu hymnal and sang all four verses of "How Great Thou Art" by Carl Boberg in Lahu, translated by some US missionaries back in the in the 1930s. I joined him in Chinese, as this is also a favorite hymn among Chinese Christians. The several county officials who had accompanied me for this visit and all happened to be well-educated Lahu and Party members were astonished that I could sing this Lahu hymn. One of them immediately offered a theological explanation for this ecclesial phenomenon: surely the *Ngo Sha* (Supreme God) of this foreign religion empowers his believers, especially *muba* Chan (referring to me, a pastor, therefore also a shaman of the Christian religion), so that whoever follows this religion would be possessed by the same singing spirit of Mr. Li and sing the same song through the same spirit.

who formulated them in the 1930s and 1940s for new believers in accordance with their mostly fundamentalist practices in relation to the local situation. In this particular case, it includes not taking poisons (alcohol, tobacco, and opium), regularly washing the face and hands, and wearing clean clothes before going to church services. I would speculate that their common witness of better health after conversion may be partly attributed to this hygienic practice of washing as a religious requirement—cleanliness is holiness!

Perhaps the ability to sing "How Great Thou Art" may become the new litmus test by the local county officials to check genuine religious connection between a true believer and this foreign *Ngo Sha*, a consequence certainly not intended by Boberg when he composed this song in 1885.

Mr. Li's faith in this Christian God is simple, practical, loyal, and grateful. Theological debates are not important to him. His faith is based on pragmatic reasoning: the economic uplift he experienced since he committed himself to this new *Ngo Sha*. He has also experienced better health; whether this is due to constant washing (thus less bacterial growth and infection), higher hepatic function from alcohol abstention, or a better diet from a higher income is beside the point. For Mr. Li, this new God helps him enjoy a better life in the present, whether or not there is an afterlife. He holds on to his new religion and gratefully shares it with many others. Others see the remarkable changes in Li's life and join him. They follow their twelve commandments and exhibit high moral values: hard work ethic, honesty, and no drugs. For Mr. Li and many millions of Chinese Protestants—and probably many Chinese Catholics as well—in the rural areas, their spirituality is simple, concrete, and practical: if you obey the commandments and are faithful to God, you are blessed on earth. For them, God is a real divine entity whose reality and faithfulness one can experience in daily life. The daily bread (or bowl of rice, congee, dumplings, or noodles) that God provides every day demonstrates his providence, which is all that matters to Mr. Li and many others like him. Faith is a concrete reality and an authentic experience. All other theological issues are for advanced Christians, such as educated believers living in urban areas.

WANG ZHIMING (1907–1973):
FAITHFUL UNTO DEATH

At the Great West Door of Westminster Abbey, there are ten statues that were unveiled in 1998 by Her Majesty Queen Elizabeth II to commemorate ten Christian martyrs who died in the name of Christ in the twentieth century. Among them are well-known Christian figures such as the Polish Franciscan St. Maximilian Kolbe, the American civil rights activist Rev. Dr. Martin Luther King Jr., the Salvadoran Catholic Bishop St. Oscar Romero, and the German anti-Nazi theologian Rev. Dr. Dietrich Bonhoeffer. The tenth statue is of a Chinese pastor named Wang Zhiming, who was virtually unknown in China, both in public and in church circles. In fact, the members of the Wang family themselves did not know about this honor until at least a couple of years later.[9] Even today one cannot openly commemorate Rev. Wang Zhiming in China. Wang represents hundreds if not thousands of Chinese Christians in contemporary times who were faithful to their calling unto death for Christ and his church.[10] Many have been largely forgotten even by their contemporaries; however, their faithfulness has not been neglected by church historians and certainly will not be forgotten by the God for whom they laid down their life.

At the turn of the twentieth century, a Methodist missionary, Samuel Pollard, went to Zhaotong City in the northeast part of Yunnan Province and met some Miao minorities. He then called for colleagues to establish a mission center at the village of Shimenkan, located at the top of a mountain with a vibrant Miao community (it was formerly part of Yunnan Province and rezoned to Guizhou Province in 1950), to develop the written Miao script, to translate the Bible into Miao script, and to operate schools and clinics for the Miaos. One of the schools, a primary school, even has a swimming pool—the first primary school in history of China to have a swimming pool for

9. Rev. Dr. Philip Wickeri was instrumental in recommending Wang for this Martyr Project of Westminster Abbey, perhaps even against the wishes of the church leaders in TSPM/CCC. I helped to supplement the biography of Wang during the application process. In 2002, when I met one of Wang's sons and told him about his father being honored by this Martyr Project, he was utterly surprised to hear of his father's monument in Westminster Abbey.

10. There are just too many of these cases in China since the founding of the People's Republic of China in 1949. An earlier one was the Chinese Jesuit Father Beda Chang of Shanghai, who was tortured to death by the authority on November 11, 1951. A recent case was the wife of a pastor, Madam Ding Cuimei, who protested against the government's forceful demolishing of a church building legally built on ground owned by the church; she was buried alive by the government's demolition team on April 14, 2016. Her husband was also buried and barely survived the incident. See Ava Collins, "Henan Church Wins Rights to Land Where Pastor's Wife Was Killed," China Aid, April 27, 2016, https://tinyurl.com/y4wxnagc.

the students! Based in Shimenkan, the missionaries reached the Miao people, who were scattered throughout various pockets of Miao communities in Yunnan and the neighboring Guizhou Province. In 1906, Pollard and his colleagues established another Miao mission center at Sapunshan village in Wuding County in Yunnan Province. This was where Wang was born a year later. There is no record of his family background or his youth.[11] Apparently, he encountered Christianity very early on in his life and may have belonged to the first group of Miao converts in Wuding County. He attended the local Christian school operated by Arthur G. Nicholls, a colleague of Samuel Pollard. He was a bright student and served the school as a teacher for ten years. He later became an evangelist. In 1944, the head of the church council of Sapushan, then Arthur G. Nicholls, left Wuding, and the church council elected Wang to be the new head of the council overseeing all ethnic churches in the county (other than the Miao churches, there were also churches run by the Black Yi, White Yi, Lisu, and Dai). In 1949, Wang became the superintendent not only over the various national minority churches of Wuding but also the churches of the three neighboring counties: Luquan, Fumin, and Yuanmou. In 1951, at the age of forty-four, he received his ordination,[12] becoming the first ordained minister of the Miao people and perhaps one of the most educated Miao at the time.

Wang was a strong supporter of the new Chinese regime. He signed the very first Protestant Three-Self Manifesto to strive for the independence of the Chinese church from the foreign missionaries and joined the Three-Self Patriotic Movement. He also became one of the few representatives of the Miao people in various regional and national events, including receiving an

11. There are few written records on Wang. I had to piece together Wang's biography from many different sources and interviews with several of his family members, eyewitnesses, and oral history passed down by Wang's contemporaries. One of the most comprehensive published accounts on Wang's death is the article by Lisa Ravenhill, "Researching a Yunnan Revival," Asian Center for Pentecostal Theology, January 17, 2016, https://tinyurl.com/y5kp3pxj.

12. In general the missionaries in China were reluctant to ordain locals, citing the lack of qualified local candidates. In 1951, almost all missionaries were forced to leave China, and there was no choice but to ordain Wang. By then, he was already a well-known church leader overseeing thousands of believers from at least five different national minority groups spreading across four counties.

audience with Chairman Mao Zedong himself. The government named him a Model Worker. In 1952, the government launched the Land Reform Campaign to seize land from the landlords and redistribute it to the peasants. During this campaign, Wang refused to denounce the landlords and the former missionaries. He also encouraged Miao Christians not to take part in these denunciation meetings. He said that since his hands had baptized many, he should not allow them to commit sins, which in this case meant joining in these denunciation meetings that often focused on trumped-up charges motivated by personal vendettas. Later the government forced church leaders to sign away all church properties and stop church activities unless there was prior government approval. Wang was sent to work on the farms to receive political reeducation through labor. The government established cultural centers in various national minority communities with large Christian populations to promote atheistic and scientific ideas, hoping to replace church activities. At times the government even paid Christians to join these cultural events. Some Miao church leaders recanted their faith and encouraged many to follow suit. Meanwhile, other Miao believers began to meet Wang secretly. He clandestinely ministered to them and even baptized many against the government's orders.

In 1966, Mao Zedong launched the Great Proletarian Cultural Revolution and rallied the Red Guards to destroy anything that hindered the progress of socialism. The authorities in Wuding County attacked religion as they believed, as Marx had written, that religion was the opium of the people. They particularly focused on Christianity. Wang's former colleagues, those who renounced their faith, reported Wang's secret ministry to the authorities, and Wang was dragged to many open struggle sessions—massive rallies that used verbal, psychological, and physical violence to force people to confess their political crimes and to adhere to the current political policy. These were aimed at making Wang recant his faith. Because of his influential status among the Miao Christians, his recantation might have decimated the Miao Christian community. He stood firm despite suffering much physical and verbal abuse during those meetings. Moreover, Wang remained active in his ministry, for which he was arrested on May 10, 1969 while on his way to baptize some believers.

Wang was sentenced to five years in prison with no contact with his family. There were five charges against him: (1) being a lackey of the foreign imperialists and an incorrigible spy; (2) using spiritual opium to poison people's minds; (3) consistently undermining the government's religious policy; (4) leading a group of gangsters to ambush the Communist Red Army when they were passing through Lufeng County in the 1930s and killing seven communist soldiers (even though Wang was in the neighboring Wuding County at the time of the ambush and could have had nothing to do with the incident); and (5) being a counterrevolutionary. Eventually twenty more church leaders were also arrested in Wuding County, but the government still could not stamp out Christian activities. The authorities decided, at the end of Wang's sentence, to execute him to make an example for those who refused to obey the government.

On December 28, 1973, the county authority informed Wang's family that they would execute Wang the following morning and allow the family to say farewell. It was against the norm at that time, as the family of the condemned counterrevolutionary would usually have no opportunity to say farewell and often would receive no information of the execution. They would usually be told to collect the body after the execution and often needed to pay for the bullets used. However, in this case the authorities made an exception to express their leniency, citing their revolutionary humanitarianism to this counterrevolutionary element by allowing the family members to meet Wang for a few minutes on that evening.[13] The family members immediately departed and walked for several hours to the county jail. Wang spoke his last words at this final meeting with his family members.

Wang was in shackles around his ankles, and he looked frail.

---

13. During the Cultural Revolution, counterrevolutionary elements were regarded as the class enemy of the proletariat undermining the people's revolution. The authority would show no mercy to them and would deprive them of all rights, even the most basic human rights, and subjected them to all kinds of cruelties. A good account on this period is Frank Dikötter's *The Cultural Revolution: A People's History 1962–1976* (New York: Bloomsbury, 2017).

There were prison guards around who forbade them to communicate in the Miao language; instead they had to talk in Chinese so that the Han prison guards could follow the conversation. Mrs. Wang asked Wang Zhiming to say his last word as the head of the Wang household. Wang said, "I haven't been able to reform my thinking. And since I cannot be changed, I am responsible. I deserve whatever is about to happen to me." His family members interpreted that Wang was trying to say that he had kept his faith and was willing to accept the consequence.

He followed, "But all of you are not to follow me. You must listen to the words from above. Do what the above tells you—repent and become new people." At the Cultural Revolution, the term *above* referred to the latest revolutionary directives from Beijing or Chairman Mao. Those who had fully embraced the revolutionary thoughts of Chairman Mao Zedong were referred to as "New Persons." Wang was, in fact, using the common language popular during the Cultural Revolution so as not to raise the suspicion of the prison guards yet also to convey the subtext of a spiritual message to his family. His family members immediately picked up this message: God alone is their authority, and they must obey him.

He then said his last words: "You should work hard to ensure you have enough food to eat and clothes to wear," and "Don't get sick. Pay attention to your personal hygiene and stay healthy." These words were familiar to the Miao Christians, as they had been repeatedly preached by missionaries as well as by Wang himself to the Miao Christians. These words were general instructions for good Christian living—diligence, wholehearted purity, and holiness. His oldest son told Wang that they would listen to the directives from above, but he also asked about what would happen if he was not coming back and who would take care of the children. His son was referring to the many Miao Christians who would be without a shepherd should Wang be killed. Wang took three of six boiled eggs from his wife, who had brought them over to Wang for his last meal, and left the other three with them. They understood the cryptic message—the Trinity—God the Father, the Son, and the Holy

Spirit—would be with Wang and with them all. They would not be alone.

Then a prison guard came to announce that their visiting time was up. He also told the Wang family about the execution, which would be carried out the next day after a public trial at the stadium just outside the county seat. There were two other criminals in the same trial whose sentences were reeducation through labor. This type of public trial was meant to be a political tool to educate the public in the form of a mass rally. The show trial was organized by the government and attended by about ten thousand people. Many of the attendees were Miao Christians forced to attend by authorities in order to frighten them into submission. Wang Zhiming's family was told to squat down on the ground with their hands on their heads. Militia encircled them, with rifles pointed at them, so they could not make any attempts to disrupt the trial. All the government leaders of Wuding County sat on the stage, and before them was Wang Zhiming with the other two criminals on either side of him. Wang's hands and legs were tied with rope, and around his neck hung a large wooden signboard listing his alleged crimes. Blood flowed from one corner of his mouth where a guard had used his bayonet to slash out his tongue just before he was placed on a truck for an open rally from the prison to the stadium; it was a common measure to silence the condemned in public trial.

A former Miao pastor called Old Long (Long is the last name of this pastor, meaning "Dragon," a common last name among the Miao), who had openly renounced his faith and joined the Party, stood up on the stage to accuse Wang of his crimes and to demand his execution. The chief prosecutor then concluded, "Wang Zhiming is to be sentenced to death. His execution will be carried out immediately." Such trials were all staged and more of a public announcement than a trial in the legal sense. Soldiers then lifted Wang Zhiming up on the stage so that everyone could see him, and the crowd began to roar. Some shouted, "Long live Chairman Mao!," which was the standard slogan on all occasions during the Cultural Revolution. However, a group of Christian Miao women, seemingly oblivious to any possible consequences, rushed up to the stage where Old Long was still sitting and cried out, "Backslider! Devil! Your evil crime is

against the gospel of Jesus Christ. We dare you to come down!"
The crowd was thrown into chaos.[14]

Wang Zhiming was led away and pushed onto a truck with
the other two prisoners. Another truck containing armed militia
drove behind. These two trucks went through the main streets
in the county seat to parade the prisoners for half an hour before
arriving at the site of an abandoned old airport just outside the
county seat. Wang Zhiming was taken down from the truck and
was shot. This happened mid-morning on December 29, 1973.

Later, the family collected Wang's body on a cart for their
long journey back home to their Miao village, about five hours'
walking distance from the county seat. Their family said that
Wang Zhiming appeared so peaceful that it was hard to believe
he was dead. Along the country road, not only Miao believers
but also old and new friends of the Wang family, as well as
strangers, paid their final respects to Pastor Wang. Some came
up to the cart and stroked his body. The family arrived home
just as the sun was setting. Village officials and militia guarded
the house where Wang's body was lying and kept away anyone
who might want to visit. After midnight, when the guards were
sleeping, fellow Christians took great risks to creep into the
house to pay their last respects to Wang and pray with the family. The next morning, the family buried Wang, but the authorities forbade them to erect a gravestone or to hold any memorial
activity during the funeral, as Wang was labeled as a political criminal. Any attempt to honor a counterrevolutionary was
regarded as a political challenge toward the authorities. However, the government did not charge the family for the bullets
that took Wang's life.

Seventeen years later, in 1980, the government admitted mis-
judgment on Wang's case and exonerated him posthumously.
They compensated the family with RMB 1,300 (in 1980
exchange rate about USD $250) and allowed them to put a
monument at his hitherto unmarked grave. When Wang was
arrested in 1969, there were fewer than three thousand Protestants in Wuding; now there are more than thirty thousand.
There are just a handful of Catholics in Wuding County, then

14. Ravenhill's "Researching a Yunnan Revival" records some of the witnesses'
accounts of this incident.

and now. Two of his four sons have since been serving many ACCs, building up a new generation of believers. Perhaps Tertullian's saying, "The blood of the martyrs is the seed of the church," said in 197 CE, was still valid in 1973 CE. Wang had not written any articles, published any books, left behind any sermons, or initiated any church movements. All he left were a few cryptic sentences the day before he went to be with his Lord. His life exemplified one of the spiritual markings of Christian community in China: faithfulness to the Lord even unto death. Today, the statue of this humble and simple pastor from a virtually forgotten corner in China is standing alongside well-known church giants such as Martin Luther King Jr. or Dietrich Bonhoeffer above the Great West Door, welcoming all into Westminster Abbey.

LIU XIAOMIN: HEAVENLY TUNE

Despite the diversity among Protestant communities in China—churches under the government-sanctioned Christian Councils, the ACCs, urban intellectual believers, or rural peasant Protestants—there is a collection of hymns that articulates a deep spiritual yearning common among almost all Chinese Protestants. Called the *Canaan Hymns,* this collection consists of more than 1,500 hymns written and composed by a single Chinese Protestant, Ms. Lui Xiaomin, from a rural county in Henan Province. Her songs were officially banned from the TSPM/CCC churches. Neither were they allowed to be officially published. Even so, most Protestants in China are familiar with her songs, and most have a copy of *Canaan Hymns* and sing the hymns openly even in TSPM/CCC church services. *Canaan Hymns* is perhaps the most popular—and pirated—hymnal in China despite the fact that it officially does not exist. Furthermore, the songwriter was not formally educated beyond the eighth grade and has no formal training whatsoever in music. Yet her songs touch the soul of tens of millions of Chinese Protestants and move many to tears. These hymns even travel across confessional boundaries, as I have also come across some Chinese Catholics who have sung the *Canaan Hymns.*

Lui Xiaomin (popularly known as Xiaomin) was born in a village in Henan in the early 1970s. Her parents were illiterate peasants of the Hui minority, Sinicized Arabs who mostly embraced Islam, yet they did not seem to observe Islamic practice. Her family was so poor that her parents almost gave her away when she was two years old. While in school, because of her sinus infections, she was often very dizzy and nauseous, which eventually led to her leaving school to help at home with farming and household chores. After one of her aunts shared the Christian faith with Xiaomin, she began attending church services in her village against her family's wishes. During the first few church gatherings she attended, she was convicted that God would eventually heal her illness, guide her, and use her in the future. At the end of 1990, Xiaomin began singing original songs she composed. Her brother was astonished by her musical gift, as he knew that his sister had never studied music. He wrote down the notations and words for her songs and passed them to some believers; however, he did not tell them that it was composed by Xiaomin. Her songs were loved, and she later composed more songs that believers in that village began to sing in their church. As her songs gained popularity, Xiaomin's role as the composer came to light. Those who knew her were shocked, as the Xiaomin they knew was a shy and timid young girl. As she heard the congregation singing her early hymns, she was very moved by the feeling that God had chosen her, a peasant girl with no education. This was the beginning of her hymnology career. According to Xiaomin, her inspiration for her hymns came from the Holy Spirit during her prayer and quiet time. She began with words and themes and then moved toward verses and melodies. After her brother gave her a tape recorder, Xiaomin would compose by singing into the recorder whatever melody and words came to her heart. Friends would then put the melody in musical notation and write down the words. Sometimes she was moved to sing something from her heart at a meeting, and others present would write down this new song.[15]

The lyrics of Xiaomin's hymns are simple and short, and the tunes are traditional Chinese peasant music popular in central

15. Most of the information on her is taken from her testimony at Xiao Min, "Lord, What Am I?," CCLW, January 2004, https://tinyurl.com/y4kqptn2.

China. Most of these hymns do not have a title, and often the first or last sentence becomes the title. I have attempted to translate her hymns, but no translation can convey the full sense of the original lyrics. Also, translation cannot fully capture the Chinese country folk style in which these tunes are sung, nor the significance of that particular musical style to the Chinese people, especially those from rural China. Despite these issues, it is hoped that through these translations, readers can at least catch a glimpse of Xiaomin's spiritual aspiration through her hymns as well as the spiritual yearning of many Chinese believers touched by them. I have selected some of the most popular ones, discuss their background, and relate them to the spiritual experiences of the Chinese Protestants.

The following hymn, "Oh Lord I Praise You,"[16] is one of Xiaomin's earliest. It was sung in the church of her village when no one knew that it was composed by her:

Oh Lord I praise you because you have chosen me
In the vast sea of people you have searched for me
Oh Lord I love you as you have loved me
Your love has filled the universe, the whole world.
Your Love has redeemed many.
Your Love has encouraged us to live
Who will not bow to you, and who will not praise you with songs?
Oh Our Great God, Our Great God in Heaven
It is you that have lifted us out from dust
Lift us up high above dust
Words cannot express your loving kindness and mercy; songs fail to
    praise your righteousness
Who will not thank you and praise you in this vast land?

This hymn expresses her profound gratitude for being God's chosen one and a deep sense of unworthiness. Many Chinese Protestants would echo such emotions as they feel that the Chinese Protestant church has been a very weak community in China, yet God has empowered it to become a strong group with tens of millions of fellow believers.

16. Each Canaan Hymn has a designated number and a title. The titles are usually the words from the first verse. This one is Canaan Hymn # 5. This site provides both the text and the notation: https://www.zanmeishi.com/tab/15797.html.

Another early composition, "Oh Lord May You Hold on to Our Hands,"[17] was inspired by the weather. While walking to a church gathering in the midst of a storm, Xiaomin prayed, "Lord, may you guide our hands as we travel in storms." Considering the words of her prayer as encouragement from God, Xiaomin composed the following hymn:

> Oh Lord, may you hold on to our hands as we travel in storms
> Oh Lord, may you carry our hearts to fly all over the world
> May your soldiers depart from here; your troops arise from here
> May the torch of your Gospel be carried to all four corners of the earth
> Go go go, we follow you; run run run we follow you
> One day China will arise; one day China will arise
> Break through the closed door, and crush down the mighty fortress
> The flag of the Gospel will fly over China
> The Church needs to be united, be united.

This hymn depicts the desires of Chinese Protestants in the early 1990s amid uncertainty and persecution—especially the intense governmental persecution of the ACCs, of which Xiaomin was a member. Even in her very early compositions such as this one, she already showed a strong belief in evangelism despite persecution, a deep love for her country, and a desire for church unity—themes that have constantly reappeared in her later works.

In 1992, she and many other believers were arrested, sentenced, and placed in the county jail. During a visit from her family, she learned that her parents were very worried, and her father's health was declining. She was told that if she would renounce her faith, the authorities would release her, and she could rejoin her parents. She replied that she would rather stay in jail for the rest of her life than to recant her faith. She believed that God would have mercy on her and would comfort her parents. In jail, she and her fellow Christian cellmates prayed, fasted, and sang hymns to others. Many nonbelievers turned to God through her hymns. One day, after hearing the screams of fellow believers tortured by the jailers, she was unable to sleep. Some words came into her heart: "Longing for freedom, for peace, for

17. *Canaan Hymn* # 8, https://www.zanmeishi.com/tab/15800.html.

God's love to fill this world. The dark corner needs light. The place with conflict needs peace. I want to be the messenger of love. I felt that God has chosen me and spared my life so that I can share the Gospel to those who need it." That night, she dedicated her life to serving God.

After Xiaomin was released from jail, she became an evangelist, preacher, and composer of hymns. Her hymns have been copied, distributed, and sung by tens of millions of Chinese Christians (some Catholics also sing the *Canaan Hymns*) as these songs seem to echo the deep spiritual yearnings of the Chinese Christians beyond what their own words could describe. It is not uncommon to see people weep while they sing the *Canaan Hymns*, as the words of the hymns touch the desires of their soul. Their folk melodies capture many hearts in China, and their simple words echo their intense devotion to Christ. The following is an example written out of Xiaomin's loneliness as she embarked on her journey as a minister of the gospel. Her christocentric devotion in times of loneliness has reverberated in the hearts of many others as illustrated by this hymn of hers, "The Best Friend":[18]

O Lord you are my soul mate
O Lord you are my dearest partner
Everyday my heart longs for you
I long to see your face
In every stage of my life
At every step of my journey
Your hand has always been holding me
To bring me close to you
To guide me where to go
So that I would not enter into the death zone
Oh how deep and wide is your love
My heart is in awe
What more do I want when I have my Lord?
My heart is linked with my Lord's
I have sworn that I would follow the Lord
I will change not.

18. Canaan Hymn # 34, https://www.zanmeishi.com/tab/15826.html.

Other than devotion to Christ, one of the main features of
Xiaomin's hymns is the burning desire for China to be for
Christ. She has written many songs inspiring fellow Christians
to evangelize China despite the adverse conditions. These
hymns are instrumental in rallying an evangelistic movement
among the Chinese believers, for both China and global missions. Conspicuously, the theme of evangelizing China is not
very present in the hymnody of the TSPM/CCC. This hymn,
"China Belongs to God,"[19] is one of Xiaomin's more popular
hymns centered on evangelization of China, and she was moved
by the Spirit to sing it during a church meeting:

> Even if I have only one drop of blood left, one drop of sweat left
> I will pour it all over China
> Even if I have one last breath left, one last bit of strength left
> I will give it all to China
> Harken to the voice from Mother that travels through the straits
> Chinese are Children of God
> China, O China, come to have rest
> God has already found you
> You are no longer struggling astray
> China belongs to God.

At that church meeting, the whole congregation rose in an
uproar immediately after she finished this hymn. They were
waving hands and shouting, saying, "China belongs to God!
China fears you! From kings to ordinary people, from ministers
to soldiers, all have to know you!"

The following hymn, "5 a.m. in China," has inspired a nationwide prayer movement, across the whole spectrum of Chinese
Protestant community, to pray for China at 5:00 a.m. every
morning:[20]

> There are prayers from China at five o'clock in the morning
> May God grant us revival and peace, give us victory in unity
> At five o'clock in the morning, there comes the sound of praise
> Everyone offers their genuine love: one heart, one spirit for China
> There are prayers from China at five o'clock in the morning

19. Canaan Hymn # 551, https://www.zanmeishi.com/tab/16343.html.
20. Canaan Hymn # 268, https://www.zanmeishi.com/tab/16060.html.

Flying through mountains and rivers, melting the frozen hearts
No more bondage and no more war
Bless China, change her fate, for another bumper harvest.

The "Chinese Heart"[21] is another China-related hymn from Xiaomin, and it is so popular that most Chinese Christians have memorized it. Although Xiaomin has a great love for the souls in China, she is not exclusively ethnocentric; she always reminds others to love people beyond their own race, as illustrated in the last verse of this hymn, "Chinese Heart":

We are far apart from each other by ten thousand rivers and thousands
*   of mountains; the Chinese Heart gathers us as one*
Joining our hearts together, we work hard to promote the Gospel
God loves China and loves us even more
He searches for people like us here and there
Time never stops for a minute or a second
The flame to proclaim the Gospel has ignited in our heart
Make haste and march on
Under the shadow of the moonlight, and the gazing from the stars above
To light a new lamp for the hut in the dark
Bring peace to the fifty-six nationality groups
We all have a sincere Chinese heart
To love our people, our kinsmen, and everyone on this earth.

Xiaomin's hymn "Fellow Traveller,"[22] or literally "The one that travels on the same road," may perhaps be the most well-known hymn in China, even among Chinese Protestants in diaspora.

Because we are travelling on the same journey
We can have similar experiences
Because we are travelling on the same journey
We have the same desires
Taste the same bitterness, share the same sufferings
Only fellow travellers are the dearest
Shed the same tears and enjoy the same joyfulness
Only fellow travellers are the most genuine
Thank God that we can meet on this path of Truth

21. Canaan Hymn # 143, https://www.zanmeishi.com/tab/15926.html.
22. Canaan Hymn # 40, https://www.zanmeishi.com/tab/15832.html.

And we become fellow travellers
In our heart we sing the same hymns
To praise this wonderful salvation
We unite as one spirit and we understand each other
Fellow travellers must be united in one heart
A beautiful hope
An eternal Kingdom
Forever belongs to us.

This hymn stirs up deep spiritual emotions from each Chinese believer due to their long isolation from the global Christian community, the struggle to keep their faith in their small ecclesial circles, constant harassment and suppression by the government, and even discrimination from their own family members and neighbors. They feel that their deep sense of loneliness and sorrow can only be comforted by God himself and can only be shared with fellow believers who have experienced a similar spiritual pilgrimage. This hymn best illustrates the spiritual journey of Chinese Christians as well as the intense spiritual bond that connects Chinese believers. In so doing, it highlights the strength upon which the Chinese church has drawn to withstand adversity and succeed despite sociopolitical challenges. Because of the way in which this hymn responds to the particular isolation experienced by Chinese Christians, it is popular in the remote countryside, in vibrant urban centers, and among Chinese Christians living outside of China.

Xiaomin, in her unique way, symbolizes the spiritual aspirations of the Chinese Protestant community. With simple words and folk tunes, her *Canaan Hymns* express their devotion to God, passion for evangelization, gratefulness for being the chosen ones, love for their nation, and treasuring of the spiritual bonds among followers of Christ. Xiaomin attributes all her achievements to God, the giver of all grace and gifts.

A MAN OF ALL SEASONS: BISHOP ALOYSIUS JIN
LUXIAN, SJ (1916–2013)

Bishop Aloysius Jin's ninety-seven years of life ran parallel with the political turmoil of China during the past century: fighting among the war lords in Republican China; the emergence of nationalism; Western domination, especially in Shanghai; the Sino-Japanese War; the civil war between communists and nationalists; the Cold War; the many communist political campaigns against religion and old traditions; the Cultural Revolution; the Reform and Open period; and the new capitalism in China. As a Catholic priest, he was incarcerated for twenty-seven years along with Cardinal Ignatius Kung Pin-mei (Gong Pinmei) and many other Chinese Catholics charged as counter-revolutionaries and treated as enemies of the people. He received independent consecration as an illicit bishop of Shanghai, held a senior position in the Catholic Patriotic Association, yet later received recognition from Rome as the coadjutor bishop in full communion with the pope, serving alongside the underground bishop Joseph Fan Zhongliang, SJ, of Shanghai. He almost singlehandedly rebuilt the Shanghai Diocese as one of the most well-established dioceses in China, along with one of the best Catholic seminaries—Sheshan Seminary, which has produced more than four hundred priests during the past thirty years. He successfully introduced mass in Chinese in line with the teaching of Vatican II and openly prayed for the pope—against the Chinese government's explicit order—through the reprint and distribution of the *Missale Romanum* when mass was celebrated in Latin in China. He was a Jesuit, yet many of his cofriars accused him of being a traitor to the faith. The Jesuit Society expelled him for many years yet later reintegrated him back to the Society. He received dignitaries such as Bill Clinton, Angela Merkel, and Mother Teresa, and he befriended many theologians who were ahead of their time, such as Henri de Lubac, Pierre Teilhard de Chardin, and Hans Küng. He was perhaps the most interviewed bishop in China by the foreign press, and he published a memoir in English.[23] He had access to senior Chinese leaders pressing for more freedom for the church, and at the same time he kept communication with the pope through intermediaries.

Bishop Jin was perhaps the most influential Catholic prelate in China, and he was called the Yellow Pope by a biographer.[24] Yet to many he was and still is an enigma.[25] Caught in the tension between Beijing and Rome, some in the Catholic community regarded him as a communist spy working for the Chinese authorities against the church, and many in the Chinese government had doubts whether Jin was really serving the interest of the Vatican to sabotage China's desire for an independent Catholic Church. His dramatic, controversial, and tragic life illustrates the complex experiences that many Catholics in China have gone through. I highlight some important moments in Jin's life that trapped him in dilemmas, explore their contexts, and study the means through which Jin survived. His life encapsulates the fateful journey of the Catholic Church in contemporary China: torn between the Vatican and China, split into competing factions, living in a hostile political environment, yet managing not only to survive but also prosper.

Born to a Catholic family in a Catholic village on the outskirts of Shanghai (now Pudong, the financial center of Shanghai), Jin had an older sister and a younger brother. Since his father received a Catholic education from the missionaries, including learning French and English, his father was able to land a good job as a trader, thanks to his knowledge of foreign languages. In Jin's teenage years, his family went broke because his father made some bad business deals. Jin was very smart and attended the Catholic school run by the French Jesuits. At that time, the Catholic Church in China was divided up by different mission religious orders; Shanghai was given to the Jesuit's Paris province. As the city of Shanghai was carved up into many for-

23. Jin Luxian, *The Memoirs of Jin Luxian: Learning and Relearning*, vol. 1, trans. William Hanbury-Tenison (Hong Kong: Hong Kong University Press, 2012).

24. Dorian Malvoic, *Le Pape Jaune: Mgr. Jin Luxian, Soldat de Dieu en Chine Communiste* (Paris: Perrin, 2006).

25. Didi Christen Tatlow, "Farewell to an Enigmatic Bishop," *New York Times*, April 29, 2013, https://tinyurl.com/y2wm9d8b.

eign concessions, the Catholic Church in Shanghai, along with most of the parishes and institutions, were located in the French Concession, not under Chinese sovereignty. Consequently, the Shanghai Catholic schools would celebrate Bastille Day rather than the Chinese national day. The Catholic Church, at least in Shanghai, was a de facto French enclave that had been extended into China. It is not surprising to note that Chinese officials thus interpreted the Catholic Church as part of the foreign colonial occupation in China—a stigma that the Catholic Church in China has carried ever since.

Jin joined the Jesuit order and studied philosophy and theology under the French missionaries. At the beginning of the Sino-Japanese War (1937–1945), his studies were not affected, because France was not at war with Japan, and the French Concession was spared. However, when the war extended to the Pacific, the Japanese took over the concession areas and placed all the non-Axis foreigners in internment camps. The Catholic schools were somehow spared because there were many German, Austrian, and Italian Catholic missionaries whose countries were allies of Japan. Japan even sent a Japanese Jesuit to supervise some of these schools, and he was rather protective of the Catholic Church. In 1942, as Japan gained major advances in the China war theatre, increasing the Japanese-occupied territories, the European Catholic missionaries assessed that Japan would be the new ruler of China and planned to enhance the relation with Japan. Jin's superior asked him to study Japanese in preparation for him to be the liaison to the soon-to-be Japanese Empire of Occupied China. It was perhaps the first time that Jin began to reflect on his fidelity to the church vis-à-vis his national identity, a church that was advancing the political interest of the foreigner at the expense of his national interest. He did not express his thoughts to his French superior, however; instead he determined to do rather poorly in his Japanese language studies, as he felt uncomfortable serving the Japanese who were invading his country. Eventually his superior terminated Jin's Japanese course. Jin's experience reflected the Chinese Catholic Church's image before 1949 as an extension of foreign political power in China and the dilemma many Chinese Catholics faced as they were caught between the Chinese national aspiration and foreign political interests of the church. Trying to obey his foreign superior and not deny his patriotism, Jin did what he could: he took up a passive resistance to the command of his superior, a method that he would later employ when he was placed in a similarly tough position.

After the Second World War, some missionaries spotted Jin's academic talent and sent him for further studies in Europe, beginning in France and later in Rome, where he completed his doctorate in theology at the prestigious Pontifical Gregoriana University. He also brushed up his language skills, becoming fluent not only in French and Latin but also in English and German. Many of his classmates became prominent church leaders, such as the theologian Karl Rahner and the former Primate of France Albert Decourtray, who, among many others, later helped Jin to restore relations with the Holy See.

When he finished his studies in early 1950, Chinese communists had taken over China, and the Soviet Union began to consolidate the Eastern Bloc. Communist influence was expanding across Europe, as the Italian Communist Party was gaining popularity and challenging the traditional authority of the Catholic Church. Pope Pius XII ordered the Italian Catholics to resist the communists, regarding communism as an evil that denied God. Jin was ordered back to China to prepare the Chinese Catholic Church to fight this holy war against communism, while many of his coreligious fled China. Jin also noted that almost all the prelates of the Chinese Catholic Church were foreign nationals, and very few were Chinese. As more foreign missionaries, many being bishops, were expelled, the vacant posts were handed to Chinese often at the last minute, usually as acting heads executing orders for their foreign superiors who could not be in China. Many of these foreign missionaries believed that they would return to China as they thought that communism would soon end. At the same time the Chinese Catholic Church, under orders from Rome, was in a bitter confrontation with the new Chinese government. Chinese priests who took up these new posts from the foreign missionaries became the enemy of the state, targeted by the new government, which regarded these Chinese priests as agents serving foreign political interests.

By 1955, Jin was the acting head of the Sheshen Seminary,

the acting superior general of the Jesuit Society in China, the acting ordinary of the Haizhou Diocese, and the acting head of the Jesuit Commission of China since the former Jesuit superior, Fernard Lacretelle, was arrested and later expelled. Even though Jin was the acting head, the major decisions were still made by the foreign missionaries, be it those still remaining in China or those who had already left. Jin knew that the Chinese government, in order to crush the Catholic resistance, would first target people like him. He was fully aware of his predicament and had prepared for the worst as a martyr for God. Like most Chinese Catholics in the 1950s, he was caught between loyalty to the Church, with a strong political stance against the new Chinese government, and the patriotic sentiment of supporting the newly established communist China. Few Chinese Catholics would dare to openly embrace the new regime, for they would be labeled as apostates and excommunicated. Such tension is still the hallmark of the difference between the underground church and the official church.

In mid-1955, Jin and several hundred Chinese Catholics were arrested as counterrevolutionaries in a political campaign attempting to root out antigovernment elements. He spent four years in solitary confinement, and fourteen more years in different prison camps. He was released in 1973 after serving eighteen years of jail time. However, part of his sentencing was nine more years labeled as a counterrevolutionary. This was a special form of punishment to deny one's rights as a citizen: one would have no job or right to travel and usually be kept working in a labor camp while being treated as a political criminal under constant supervision. He spent another nine years in various labor camps. In 1979, three years prior to his scheduled release, China began to embark on the new Reform and Open policy and needed various technical expertise. Jin was transferred to a camp where many intellectuals were held. The purpose of these prisoners was to provide translation for the government, especially of scientific and technological nature, to help China catch up with the world. Jin's foreign language skills were appreciated, and he did translation work for the last three years of his total twenty-seven in incarceration. He was promoted to section head of his translation unit, and this promotion was later used as evidence to prove his compromised stance with the communists in betraying the Church and the Catholic faith. At that time, anyone who cooperated with the government was regarded by some, especially those who had followed Rome's directive since the 1950s, as a "Judas" or traitor, a theological position that is still held by many in the underground faction.

He was released in 1982 at the time when the government began to allow the church to operate in the open, yet the church in China was in ruin due to almost two decades of systematic destruction. Jin was again facing a dilemma: to help rebuild the church by cooperating with the authorities and face accusation from many colleagues as a traitor, or to operate clandestinely against the authorities like many of his cofriars, such as Father Vincent Chu (Zhu Hongshen) SJ, who were willing to be arrested and even martyred. This very same choice has faced Chinese Catholics for decades, be it in the 1950s, 1980s, or even today. Jin chose to rebuild the Diocese of Shanghai and the Sheshen Seminary. Many of his Jesuit cofriars accused him of collaborating with the communists and raised suspicions that he had betrayed other coreligious while he was in prison. The Jesuit Society expelled Jin based on these accusations.[26] This abandonment by the Jesuit Society was perhaps the most painful blow that Jin had felt, even much more than the long incarceration; Jin identified the society as his spiritual mother whom he could trust for her understanding, and he longed for her comfort. He was utterly shattered when he heard the news of his expulsion; he felt he had been misunderstood, unjustly accused, and wrongly forsaken by his spiritual mother, the Jesuit Society.[27]

Jin's decision to work with the authority for the rebuilding of the church was probably due to his reflections while in prison. At first he fully trusted his Jesuit superior, Fernand Lacretelle, who was arrested and later expelled from China. After leaving China, Lacretelle told everyone that he had not betrayed anybody while he was suffering under the hands of the Chinese communists. Jin and others regarded him as a saint and followed

---

26. Laszlo Ladany, SJ (1914–1990), the former author editor of the *China News Analysis*, showed these accusations and alleged evidence to me in 1984.

27. Jin Luxian, *Memoirs of Jin Luxian*, chap. 5, sec. 9.

his order to resist the Chinese government. When Jin was arrested, the authority showed him eight hundred pages of Lacretelle's handwritten confessions detailing many of the Chinese Catholics' antigovernment activities leading to many of their eventual arrests, as well as his confessional tapes.[28] Jin felt betrayed and questioned the orders of Lacretelle to Jin and others, which led them toward a suicidal mission. He then began to question the motives of these missionaries and gradually came to the conclusion that these foreign missionaries, no matter how religious they were, did have a different political perspective than that of the Chinese. He then felt that Chinese Catholics needed to have their own independent judgment on political and religious matters and not simply follow orders from others, serving as a pawn and sacrificing in the international political arena.[29]

As a priest, Jin felt that pastoral needs should be the top priority for Catholics, such as reopening the churches, restoring liturgical life, and retraining priests, as all of this had been suspended for more than a decade. For Jin, such pastoral needs superseded the political struggle against the Chinese communist regime, which, unlike in the 1950s, by the 1980s was already firmly established as a major world power. He then wrote hundreds of letters to his friends overseas for help; soon money and all sorts of materials, such as books and missals, began to pour in, and he rebuilt the Shanghai Diocese, which has become today one of the most vibrant Catholic communities in China. He managed to pray for the pope during mass against the government's explicit order; he accepted the independent consecration as an illicit bishop against Rome's standing order; and he promoted Vatican II's liturgical reform by celebrating mass in Chinese. Holding mass in Chinese came against resistance from most of the Chinese clergy in the early 1980s, as Vatican II's reform on vernacular mass was not known by most of the Chinese Catholics. He soon became one of the most controversial Catholic prelates in China, as he seemed to act rather

---

28. Those who would simply accuse Jin suggested Jin was a liar; either the whole confession story of Lacretelle was Jin's fabrication, or those confessional materials were fake. It was the word of Jin versus the word of Lacretelle.

29. Jin Luxian, *Memoirs of Jin Luxian*, chap. 4, sec. 5.

paradoxically while treading a fine line between patriotic duty to China and fidelity to the Vatican; the pastoral needs of the faithful against the rules of canon law; and the autonomy of the Chinese Catholic Church and communion with the universal church. Constantly under pressure from all sides, one can easily take either side all the way, such as the illicit bishop of Beijing Michael Fu Tieshan (1931–2007), who openly defied orders from Rome, or many underground bishops such as Bishop Peter Joseph Fan Xueyan (1907–1992) of Baoding, who vigorously resisted the government and was repeatedly incarcerated. However, Jin developed a *modus vivendi* trying to satisfy all sides and creating an open space in China for the Catholics to operate. His own words in an interview in 2010 give us a glimpse of his inner world: "It is very complicated here, and I have had to be, how do you say, both a serpent and a dove. I am both a serpent and a dove. The government thinks I'm too close to the Vatican, and the Vatican thinks I'm too close to the government. I'm a slippery fish squashed between government control and Vatican demands."[30]

Eventually his pastoral achievement won him great respect from all walks. Superior General Kolvenbach later reintegrated him back into the Society of Jesuits, and his episcopal status was also ratified in full communion with the Holy See. He was also cooperating with the underground bishops of Shanghai to coappoint their successor, a significant symbol marking the beginning of cooperation between the open and the underground factions in the Chinese Catholic Church, the deescalation of the conflict between these two groups,[31] and the establishing of a *modus vivendi* for other dioceses in China as a reference.

In the introduction to Jin's memoirs, Anthony Clark describes Jin as a politician, protector, and prisoner.[32] Jin was indeed an accomplished politician who not only navigated the complex power corridors of Beijing and the Vatican but also maintained

30. Gerard O'Connell, "Shanghai's Bishop Aloysius Jin Luxian Is Dead," *Vatican Insider World News*, April 27, 2013, https://tinyurl.com/y3ge27k3.

31. For more on the conflicts, see Kim-kwong Chan, "Open and Underground Catholic Communities in China," *Settimana News*, February 22, 2018, https://tinyurl.com/y6mdaa9r.

32. Introduction to Jin Luxian, *Memoirs of Jin Luxian*.

a working relation with both diametrically opposite powers. He was a protector that sheltered the Shanghai Catholic community under his wing and facilitated its growth in a hostile environment. He was a prisoner for literally more than a quarter of a century in various prisons and labor camps in China and metaphorically for most of his life, entrapped among the bitter confrontation between the Chinese authority and the Church hierarchy. Perhaps he was just a simple pastor who constantly placed the interest of his flock above all others, be it the government's regulation or the Vatican's order. His desire was simply to discharge his pastoral duty to the best of his ability for the glory of God as reflected in the motto "*Oportet illum crescere, me autem minui*" (John 3:30), which he decided on as his ecclesiastical heraldry. Bishop Aloysius Jin Luxian, SJ, seemed to constantly struggle with his various identities, responsibilities, and conscience. Despite the historical and confessional differences, perhaps Robert Whittington's description of Sir Thomas Moore could indeed be a fitting portrait of Jin: "Moore is a man of an angel's wit and singular learning. I know not his fellow. For where is the man of that gentleness, lowliness and affability? And, as time requireth, a man of marvelous mirth and pastimes, and sometime of as sad gravity. A man for all seasons."[33]

The first three individuals described in this chapter were chosen for how they represent the main spiritual markers among Christian communities in China, be it Protestant or Catholic: simplicity, costliness, and extraordinariness. For Brother Li, the gospel works in his life in simple ways. The gospel addresses his relevant needs and transforms his health, economy, and morality. Through his transformed life Mr. Li demonstrates, often without words, the power of the gospel in concrete realities that one can see, feel, touch, and experience. Millions of these often anonymous and humble believers like Mr. Li constitute the bulk of the Chinese Protestant community. The transformative testimonies of these ordinary believers give credibility to the Christian faith in the present atheistic society that China claims to be.

As exemplified by Pastor Wang Zhiming, Chinese Christians

---

33. Marvin O'Connell, "A Man for All Seasons: An Historian's Demur," Catholic Education Resource Center, 2002, https://tinyurl.com/y4nrsgla.

often pay a high price for their faith. Christian faith cost Wang and also many other Protestants and Catholics alike years in jail and eventually their life. His final words resonate with tens of thousands of Christian martyrs throughout the ages who held firmly to their conviction that the Christian faith transcends one's soul, from the temporal world into the horizon of eternity. Wang epitomizes the many Chinese Christians whose faith was purified through many years of trials and suffering. It is this purified faith that has sustained the Chinese church even in her darkest hour.

Sister Lui Xiaomin's powerful hymns, as well as her story, represent the extraordinary spirit of Chinese Christianity, especially the Protestant community, as there was no designated liturgical rubric to follow. She has the unique gift of tapping into the deep psyche of Chinese believers and converting spiritual aspirations into folk songs with simple words. Her *Canaan Hymns* encourage the disheartened, uplift the depressed, and bring hope to the hopeless. Xiaomin has constantly reminded others that it is the Holy Spirit, and not her, that is the real composer of these hymns. She considers herself an instrument of God, and the focus is on him rather than on her. Such a humble yet profound attitude captures the most basic tenet of the Christian faith: God is the creator of all, and we are his creatures and instruments. The story of Xiaomin and the extraordinary popularity of her hymns embody the unique experiences of the Protestant community in contemporary China. Despite several decades of harsh suppression, with virtually no theological or pastoral resources, it has grown into a huge community of more than sixty million in 2018. The unexpected and astonishing growth of Xiaomin's musical ministry points to the extraordinary growth and success of Christianity in China.

The final person, Bishop Aloysius Jin Luxian, represents particularly the Chinese Catholics who had been caught between many historical and political forces: communism and Catholicism, Chinese patriotism and Western imperialism, God and Caesar. Yet Jin performed a very sophisticated balancing act that enabled him to not only survive many hostile forces but also reestablish the Shanghai Diocese. This diocese transcends the internal factions as an authentic expression of Catholic faith in a metropolitan city that embraces both socialism and capitalism: an ecclesial orientation that the Catholic Church in China is heading toward.

6.

Theological

Since the reemergence of Christianity in China in the late 1970s, its mere ecclesial presence has amazed Christendom. Most church observers could hardly imagine the resilience of the tiny Chinese Christian community (Catholic, Orthodox, and Protestant) that survived three decades of powerful suppression by Chinese Communist authorities, as most thought that Christianity had ceased to exist in China after the infamous Great Proletarian Cultural Revolution, where all religion was eradicated by force. This chapter mostly focuses on the theological implications of the Chinese Protestant community, since Protestants make up the bulk of the current Chinese Christian population. There is a separate section discussing the Catholic Church in China exclusively. I will not examine the Orthodox situation due to a lack of documentation, as well as the tiny size of this community and its limited impact on both China and Christendom.

The Protestant community in China surprised the Christian community not only by its miraculous survival under harsh suppression but also by its amazing, rapid expansion under an unfavorable environment in the past few decades. It has become one of the fastest-growing churches in the world despite the limited resources at its disposal, postdenominational practices, strong national sentiment despite harsh governmental control, and diverse ecclesial expressions within a similar sociopolitical milieu. Indeed, the Protestant church in China has evolved from a group of barely surviving remnants to a complex and dynamic community that finds itself increasingly important both in Chinese society and in the global Protestant community. As a minority in an antireligious political environment, the struggle of the Chinese Protestant community for a relevant ecclesial identity can indeed be an inspiration to many. Some have even speculated that Chinese Christians will soon be the largest single block of Christians in any nation and that Chinese missionaries will become the largest missionary team in the days to come. There is even hope that the large number of Chinese Christians may one day transform China into a Christian nation, reshaping the global geopolitical order. The ecclesial phenomenon of the Chinese churches provides a fertile ground for all sorts of ecclesiological as well as sociopolitical speculations, just as many have made different conjectures about the possible role of China in global affairs in the twenty-first century. This final chapter focuses on the major ecclesiological periods of modern Chinese Protestantism, the distinctive ways in which churches grow in China, the Chinese Catholic Church's impact on the universal church, the implications for Chinese Christians constituting the largest group of Christians worldwide, and the major challenges facing Christianity in China.

MAJOR ECCLESIAL PERIODS OF MODERN CHINESE PROTESTANTISM

Three biblical motifs help distinguish the major moments in the ecclesial journey of the church in China from 1980 until the present. These motifs symbolize both the self-understanding of the Protestant church based on its main church life activities and spiritual emphases, and the notion of its role vis-à-vis society at large. I will elaborate on these three periods through the lens of these biblical motifs.

The Cross

The first period, from 1979 to about 1990, can be symbolized by the cross. As the church reemerged after the Cultural Revolution, during which religions were totally suppressed by force, few would dream that even such a possibility could occur. Believers hesitated to claim their identity publicly, fearing possible political backlash. As the government showed more determination to uphold their new policy of freedom of religious belief, more Christians, both Protestants and Catholics, began to attend newly reopened churches. Protestants quickly reestablished various meetings and gatherings enabling believers to hold fellowships, Bible studies, prayer, and worship. As they compared notes, most believers shared similar experiences of suffering and hardships they had endured during the Cultural Revolution. Because of the overwhelming number of testimonies of persecution and their various experiences of God's deliverances, the theme of suffering became the most preached topic in the Protestant church, with various expositions. Christian sufferings, symbolized by the cross, echoed the spiritual aspiration of most Chinese Protestants during this period of ecclesial reemergence. Believers would identify their sufferings with the suffering of Jesus on the cross, from which they drew encouragement and comfort to soothe the pains and loss of persecution. Through this spiritual identification with Christ, the sufferer, they drew spiritual meaning from their suffering, which was not in vain but purified their faith and paved the way for the revival of the church in China.

The popularity of teaching on suffering was intensified by two other factors: a lack of religious resources and some of the local authorities' continued suppression. During this early phase of ecclesial reemergence, religious resources were scarce; hand-copied hymns and biblical texts were not uncommon. It was a period of great spiritual hunger for any available spiritual material, especially for the Bible, as there had been no Bible printed since 1956. Most copies of the Bible were burned during the Cultural Revolution, and it was a severe crime at that time if one was found to have kept a copy. In 1980, the TSPM/CCC in

Shanghai reprinted the New Testament, and the complete Bible a few months later, in traditional characters using templates from the old edition printed in the 1950s.[1] However, even the tens of thousands of copies printed were far insufficient to satisfy the millions of Protestants coming out of the shadows. Many tried to smuggle Bibles into China or even secretly print them in underground presses; they were severely punished if caught. At that time, even though the government allowed Christians to reconvene in the open, believers still had to pay a high cost just trying to obtain the most basic Christian literature, the Bible. Also, despite the central government's clear directive to allow Christians to have religious activities in the open, many local authorities still acted conservatively on religious policy and, consciously or otherwise, continued to suppress various Protestant groups. These authorities had long experienced many sudden reversals of political decisions during the Cultural Revolution, and they expected the central government to retract such a liberal policy on religion at any moment. Consequently the general political stance contributed to the continued harassment of believers and sustained the teachings on suffering among Protestants until around the early 1990s, when many local authorities gradually shifted to more liberal social policies.

Rebuilding the Temple

The second period, from 1990 to about the year 2000, can best be illustrated by the Old Testament motif of rebuilding the temple, as recorded in Nehemiah. As the government's Reform and Open policy continued, Chinese society entered an era of prosperity that brought with it new socioeconomic challenges. The Christians, after a decade of observing the government's genuineness in carrying out the Reform and Open policy for real socioeconomic change, were confident enough to invest in a phase of rapid expansion—mainly in quantity rather than quality. Thousands of new churches were built during this ten-year

1. This first batch of reprinted New Testaments and complete Bibles was printed by the People's Liberation Army Press, as no other printing press had the resources or facilities to undertake this task. Personal interview with the late Dr. Han Wenzao, Chairperson of TSPM, in Shanghai, 1991.

period, alongside the refurbishing of old churches. This rapid church-building phase also coincided with the general building boom in China, as the Chinese population was able to cash in on the economic boom from improvements in livelihood—especially in housing, which had been stagnant since the 1960s. Newly built or refurbished churches rapidly sprang up all over the country, often with gothic battlements and turrets and topped by a big red cross.

The Amity Foundation, supported by the United Bible Society, was established as one of the first NGOs in China. One of its subsidiaries, Amity Press, began to print Bibles and hymnodies in massive numbers. The national TSPM/CCC and many of the regional TSPM/CCCs also ramped up their production capacity to produce basic Protestant religious materials such as hymnals, liturgical orders, devotional and formational literature, decorative materials with Christian symbols and Bible verses, and sermon tapes. Production of basic Catholic materials such as missals, rosary beads, and religious medals and pictures were also in high gear. There was such a huge market for these materials that many underground printing presses and factories emerged in order to pirate the popular Christian materials and try to satisfy the growing demand. Some even pirated the latest Christian literature that had been smuggled in from Hong Kong or Taiwan, which was not generally available in the officially sanctioned religious organizations.[2]

As the few pastors who had survived the years of persecution were overwhelmed by the upsurge of new believers flocking to the newly opened churches, there was an urgent need for anyone who could preach at the pulpit or lead Bible studies. Many short-term, intensive programs ranging from several weeks to

2. In 2005 I was visiting a provincial Bible school in northeastern China. I noticed that some of the students had a multivolume edition of the Chinese-Greek interlinear New Testament, as well as a Greek-Chinese lexicon, which had been published very recently in Taiwan and carried a rather high price tag. As I examined these and some Chinese theological textbooks more closely, I observed that they were all pirated copies. A faculty member showed me a catalogue and told me about the existence of a very well-established underground supplier of theological textbooks by some entrepreneurial Wenzhou Christians. The faculty member said that everyone in his field knew about these underground presses, yet nobody would openly talk about them.

several months were established to train lay preachers (*Yi Gong*, "voluntary workers") in basic Christian doctrines and biblical knowledge. Some Bible schools and seminaries began to reopen after decades of devastation, many with virtually no textbooks or dedicated faculty members. These institutes ran one- and two-year programs and trained the first batch of formally trained pastors since the late 1980s and 1990s. Their objective was to train, as deeply and as quickly as possible, a large number of lay preachers and pastors to fill the urgent pastoral needs and to consolidate the quickly growing Protestant community.

Protestants and Catholics alike focused most of their energy on consolidating the church's position by building churches as a visible presence in society and by initiating an ever-increasing number of new believers who would flock to any church that opened its doors. When facing such a massive demand, quantity, not quality, was the key. Publications of homilies were popular. Sermons, rather than testimonies, dominated Protestant worship services and household gatherings. Church building projects became the largest expenditure item for most of the TSPM/CCC churches. Fundraising campaigns were in high gear. The atmosphere somewhat resembled the rebuilding of the second temple recorded in Nehemiah, as this biblical motif—rebuilding the temple—became one of the most popular themes among the Protestants, be it from the pulpit, in church publications, or at fundraising campaigns. In contrast to the physical church buildings of the TSPM/CCC, ACCs considered their role in rebuilding the temple as the establishing of a spiritual temple. Their primary focuses were faith formation and evangelism, which led to a major phase of church planting all over China. Having massive numbers of lay preachers became the norm in church leadership, especially in rural areas where there were simply not enough professional pastors to shepherd the ever-growing flock. The church was now in an expansion phase that went beyond the survival mode of the previous decade.

Golden Lampstand

Ever since the year 2000, China has experienced an unprecedented period of social and economic prosperity. Internationally, China is enjoying an ever-increasing importance in global affairs. Domestically, China is shifting into a diverse society with a quickly growing middle class, which is supported by increasing wealth. Within this sociopolitical context, the church in China has become more dynamic than in the previous two decades, particularly as church leadership becomes younger, more energetic, and more sophisticated. Believers no longer long for quantity but instead demand quality when it comes to pastoral services and Christian resources. The most popular types of Bibles are no longer the simple standard editions but versions with commentaries or leather-bound gift editions. Various forms of worship, new hymns, theological classes, internet discussion groups, and media chat groups are slowly replacing long sermons as the popular forms of Protestant activities. Pastors, too, often feel inadequate and seek to upgrade their training with emphasis on pastoral skills and specializations, such as church administration or pastoral counseling.

During this period, the church has worked to become an authentic element of Chinese society that can make contributions to China. The church is no longer focused merely on its own survival needs but also the needs of a society reeling from rapid social changes. Churches have begun to experiment with social services such as orphanages, medical clinics, and elder hostels, and providing community services or scholarships. Furthermore, the church has started to stress the theme of holiness, urging believers not to follow the world's moral standards, particularly as traditional Chinese social values of modesty quickly fade, giving way to consumerism, individualism, and materialism. The church wants to be part of Chinese society in an authentic way and at the same time remain rooted in the transcendent realm. During this time, many church leaders use the biblical motif of the golden lampstand as an ecclesial symbol for the Chinese Protestant community, as the church is built after the design of God to give spiritual light to the dark world and to remind the world of the divine glory through the holiness of believers (Rev 11:3–4).[3] The Chinese church, much like the golden lampstand, would like to shine forth the glory of God in China through its good deeds and moral teachings.

The cross, the rebuilding of the temple, and the golden lampstand represent the three different stages of the modern ecclesial journey of the Chinese Protestant church. It has gone from surviving to consolidating, and it is now in the outreach phase. It has experienced the pain of suffering, the exaltation of rebuilding, and now the challenge of taking root in Chinese society at a time when China is facing tremendous social challenges, ranging from income polarity, an aging population, extreme consumerism, and the disintegration of traditional marriage and family systems to ecological conservation. Historically and internationally, Protestant churches have been involved in leading social changes with their values of justice and compassion, such as during the American civil rights movement or the British abolition of slavery. Chinese Protestants now have opportunities to help shape Chinese society. The pilgrimage of Chinese Protestants is still unfolding as they travel as the people of God and bear witness to God's grace in China.

CHURCH GROWTH—CHINESE STYLE?

A cursory search of "church growth principles" on Google results in hundreds of articles and links to topics such as "Nine Biblical principles," "Twenty-two successful principles," and "Twelve principles that work." Every set of principles suggests that they are common rules extrapolated from case studies of churches that have experienced fast growth rates. These methods, presented as principles, imply that if one diligently applies these methods to an ecclesial community, one may expect similar results of growth to the cases from which the methods are derived. Many megachurches also run church-growth institutes

3. Hymn #127, "I Love the Chinese Protestant Church," in the national *Hymnody* (TSPM/CCC) has used this motif to describe the Chinese church. This hymn became one of the most popular hymns sung in TSPM/CCC churches across the whole nation during major church events, such as anniversaries or dedications of new church buildings; it expresses the ecclesial aspirations of the Chinese Protestants.

to teach others to achieve growth like theirs by following their principles. With the popular notion of church growth in mind, I first will discuss some of the popular church-growth principles and check their applications vis-à-vis the phenomenal growth of the Chinese Protestant community over the past four decades. I will then discuss church-growth methods perhaps unique to the Chinese church.

One of the most commonly used methods among evangelical circles in the US and UK has been "saturated evangelism," which begins with region-wide media coverage and culminates in massive rallies, such as the popular campaigns associated with the Billy Graham crusades during the 1980s and 1990s. Due to the regulatory restrictions faced by Protestants in China, Chinese churches are unable to employ typical church-growth methods, as no religion in China can use the public domain to promote religion. Also, the massive financial resources needed to support such campaigns are often simply beyond the reach of believers in China. In fact, massive evangelistic promotions and public open rallies have not been commonly observed in China during the past few decades.

Another popular method is small-group or cell-group ministries with a high number of pastors or lay pastors, which enable an intimate and intensive degree of pastoral care between pastors and believers. There are many cell groups in China if one places the ACCs within this category; however, ACCs were not created this way out of intention but out of necessity for survival's sake. Also, almost all lay leaders in China are not professionally trained. It would be a luxury for an average congregation in China to adopt a small-cell group method that has to be led by a team of professional pastors or trained lay leaders.

As for the currently popular one-stop-service megachurch model, it would hardly be possible with the simple high congregation member–to-pastor ratio in China, from one pastor to several hundred in rich urban areas to one pastor to several thousands in poor rural regions. Such low availability of pastors renders the high staff numbers of a typical megachurch impractical. There are churches in China with high seating capacity for the sake of providing basic Sunday worship services for the largest number of believers possible; however, they do not have other service facilities that a typical megachurch complex in other countries could provide.

What then would have been the main methods the Chinese church would have employed to achieve such high growth rates? Given that these typical methods are not tenable in China, the Chinese church has had to employ other methods. When I posed this question to them, pastors from ACCs and the TSPM/ CCC almost all answered that they had not done anything specific or intentional other than leaving some gospel tracts at the church reception hall for seekers to read, which led to a high influx of seekers and believers. Some may attribute this to the miraculous work of the Holy Spirit, but if this growth is due to divine intervention, one can hardly harness and transform this into a program that reproduces the effect. In fact, many pastors secretly wished for a slower influx of new believers, as they had been overtaxed to provide even basic faith formation courses prior to baptizing these new believers.

It seems that factors causing such growth may also be sociocultural. If one looks at the entire Chinese religious landscape during the 1980s and 1990s, not only Christianity, but all religions reported significant growth to the extent that the government termed the phenomenon "Religious Fever." During this period, a crisis of confidence prevailed in China over the Chinese Communist Party due to disillusionment from the Cultural Revolution, which was compounded by the Reform and Open policy through which China adopted a dynamic market economy contrary to the very stable planned economy of the past. Chinese citizens lost their trust in ideology as well as faith in the future as the predictable socialist society began to disintegrate. The long-suppressed religions then became publicly offered alternatives for people to lean on when they had to cope with the uncertainty of the days to come. In the mid-1990s, new churches were dedicated at the rate of three per week in Zhejiang Province, which was amazing, especially to Western visitors whose own churches were gradually being closed. But very few Christian visitors from abroad would have noticed the fact that local Buddhist or folk religious temples were also being rebuilt or newly established at about ten times the rate of the church buildings![4]

In reality, the Chinese Christian population grew amid a nationwide religious resurgence. Buddhism grew steadily in the 1980s and 1990s, experiencing rapid expansion as many Chinese media and business celebrities swelled the ranks amid the renascence of Chinese traditional culture. Buddhism also enjoyed state sponsorship, as it had become a cultural image China wanted to project to the world as part of China's Soft Power initiatives.[5] Daoism and traditional folk religion also enjoyed a major comeback after a long period of suppression, especially in rural areas where local deities often became the rallying point of communal identity. Local governments encouraged the reestablishment of local religious icons for sociocultural and tourism reasons. Folk religious practices such as geomancy and fortune telling became popular, especially in business circles. Chinese Muslims also experienced a reaffirmation of their cultural-religious identity as they pushed legal and policy boundaries to ascertain their rights and practices after long periods of denial by the government. As Muslims in China tended to live in clusters, concentrating in specific regions, they had successfully taken administrative control of many autonomous counties, villages/townships, and even prefectures as well as two provincial-level autonomous regions (Ningxia and Xinjiang) through the provisions on policies for national minorities. In these Muslim-concentrated areas, Islamic practices flourished. Orthodoxy and Catholicism also enjoyed encouraging growth rates and drew converts from non-Catholic or non-Orthodox backgrounds. Smaller Christian-related sects such as Jehovah's Witnesses were gaining ground in China. New religions such as Baha'i had been growing popular among intellectuals since the 1980s,[6] and the

4. Professor Chen Cunfu of Zhejiang University did a survey in the late 1990s in Zhejiang Province, but the findings have not been published. Personal communication in Hangzhou, July 1999.

5. Kim-kwong Chan and Alan Hunter, "Soft Power in Chinese Foreign Policy," in *Chinese Foreign Policy*, ed. Emilian Kavalski (Farnham, UK: Ashgate, 2012), 125–34.

6. It started with a few Baha'i expats living in Tianjing, Shanghai, and Beijing, and by 2018 there were estimated about thirty thousand followers all over the country.

Church of Jesus Christ of Latter-day Saints (LDS, the Mormons) had also started in China during the 1980s.[7] Other world religions, such as Judaism and Hinduism, were all making their presence known during this period. Overall, this period was a golden era for all religions in China, since all existing religions had grown, and new religions had gained footholds when all religion had been eradicated just less than a decade ago.

In this socioreligious context, Christianity seemed to have taken advantage of the spiritual vacuum created by the rapid paradigm shift in Chinese society caused by socioeconomic reforms. Protestantism offered healing and a better livelihood to poor peasants when the grassroots medical system collapsed in the 1980s and 1990s. It attracted millions of believers, often the desperate, from rural areas. It gave new hope to the public when the socioeconomic future became uncertain, especially during the economic reforms, when millions of workers were laid off from the state-owned enterprises of the manufacturing sector during the 1990s and early 2000s. Millions of unemployed workers swelled the Protestant ranks, especially in industrial cities, where economic reforms hit the hardest. In the twenty-first century, the church offers high moral values, such as charity, honesty, fidelity, and modesty, as China has entered a period of high economic growth, and many people have been intoxicated by materialism, hedonism, and consumerism. As an alternative to these mindsets, hundreds and thousands of intellectuals, merchants, and professionals have joined the church. Despite this sectorial growth, many churches have reported a slowing down of their growth rates, and some have even declined in number, especially in the rural areas. As the government has deployed significant resources to provide medical, educational, and social welfare systems to the rural populations, especially since the beginning of this century, pews in rural churches have been vacated. When the government devised policies to develop the private sector to absorb the surplus labors from the down-sizing of state-owned enterprises, churches in second-tier indus-

---

7. As of 2018, there are more than ten thousand members in at least ten cities in different regions of China and an officially registered venue in Shanghai. Since 2015, LDS members from mainland China began to serve as missionaries in different part of the world.

trial cities reported they were still stable, but some began to record decline in Sunday attendance. In recent years, the most vibrant churches have been those in major metropolitan areas, which have tapped into the new middle class and professional groups of people who have found Christianity to be an alternative source of moral direction. This dynamic population suggests that the Chinese embraced the Protestant faith mainly for pragmatic reasons, that is, in direct relation with what the faith could offer them in their particular socioeconomic context. There is increasing competition in this religious market as other religions also offer their alternatives.

As the growth of the Chinese Protestant community slowed, church leaders began to reflect on what the church can offer to the Chinese people as their needs for the bare essentials for physical survival have rapidly diminished. As the church faces a new generation of Chinese who are being brought up in a postmodern cultural milieu of ahistoricism, egocentricity, virtual reality, sensuality, distrust of authority, and the search for self-fulfillment and self-actualization as the ultimate goal of life, the pragmatic or ideological fulfillment the Chinese church used to offer becomes inadequate. The church is also at a political disadvantage in an intensely competitive market of religious services when some of the competitors, such as Buddhism, are receiving state sponsorship. All these challenges face the Chinese Protestant community as it attempts not only to retain current believers but also to win new converts into its fold. Perhaps it needs nothing less than divine intervention if the Chinese church wishes to maintain such high growth rates in the future.

THE CHINESE CATHOLICS' IMPACT ON THE UNIVERSAL CHURCH

Catholicism had suffered much persecution by civil authorities in Asia in recent times, such as the banning of Catholic faith in China and Japan during the seventeenth and eighteenth centuries;[8] it did survive, although its numbers dwindled. The expe-

---

8. Shusaku Endo wrote a novel in 1966 on the dilemma that the Japanese Catholics and foreign missionaries faced in the seventeenth century as they were torn between

rience of the Catholic community in China once again demonstrates the resilience of Catholicism even in hostile environments. In 1949 there were three million Catholics, from a total population of about 450 million Chinese, making up 0.67 percent of the population. In 1982, the population was eight hundred million, and the Catholics, after thirty years of harsh suppression and virtual lack of clergy for more than a decade, still numbered around three million, as estimated by the authority, making up 0.38 percent of the population. Since then, this remnant of three million has grown fourfold into about twelve million in a Chinese population of 1.4 billion, making up 0.85 percent of the population, a figure higher than that of 0.67 percent in 1949. The increase of Catholics in China, despite the adverse condition and lack of resources, has even slightly outpaced the population growth. There must be something in Catholicism that attracts the Chinese, even though embracing Catholic faith is a costly sociopolitical liability and what Chinese Catholics receive in return is just the most basic sacramental service, alienated from the Chinese culture. During the same period, the number of Catholics in the West declined, despite the availability of resources on outreach and formation, a positive political environment for religion, and the availability of a wide range of church services to the parishioners. Such a contrast between Catholics in China and Catholics in the West may shed light on the spiritual essence of Catholicism; there is a pearl of great price that the Chinese Catholics are still willing to pay for at great cost (Matt 13:45–46), whereas people in the West no longer treasure such religious merchandise, which may have already gone out of fashion.

In 1949, the Chinese Catholics outnumbered Chinese Protestants three to one, as there were fewer than one million Protestants, a negligible social group that constituted only 0.22 percent of the population. Most of the leaders from both Christian traditions were either expelled or arrested, and both groups were eradicated from the face of Chinese society in the 1970s. In the 1980s, when the Chinese government would allow religion to

loyalty to civil authority and fidelity to the religious authority, which bore different political interests. The movie *Silence* (2016) was based on this novel and has since generated many discussions on this theme.

operate openly, one may have expected that the ratio of these two groups of remnants would be similar to thirty years ago: three to one. However, the government estimated that there were three million Protestants and three million Catholics: a one-to-one ratio. This means that the Protestant population had increased three times in size, whereas the Catholic population remained the same size as thirty years ago, though living under a similar sociopolitical environment as the Protestants. By the end of 2018, the Protestants outnumbered the Catholics at least five to one (the government's low estimate of thirty-eight million and six million, respectively,[9] or my estimate of twelve million Catholics, or 0.85 percent of population, and sixty million Protestants, or 4.3 percent of population), while both groups experienced the same liberal religious policy under the Reform and Open policy. In short, from 1949 until 2018, the Protestants' growth rate, in terms of population ratio, is about fifteen times higher than that of the Catholics in China.

The Chinese government regards both the Chinese Catholics and Chinese Protestants as agents serving foreign interests and exercises strong political control over these two religions. Also, both religions manifest a foreign image, such as Gothic arches, Western music, and foreign feast days, that is alien to traditional folk customs. Both preach a similar religious message of monotheism, Jesus as savior, justice and mercy, the last judgment, and resurrection. With so many similarities between these two groups in the context of Chinese society, yet with such a huge difference in growth, there is certainly room for speculation and exploration as to the reasons behind such a difference. Some may attribute it to the intense in-house fighting between the Catholic underground and the open factions, which took up scarce resources. Others may attribute the high level of laity involvement of the Chinese Protestants in ecclesiastical affairs to be a factor, whereas the Chinese Catholics may have missed the important teaching on the ecclesial role of the laity from the Second Vatican Council, *Lumen gentium*,[10] or the decree *Apostolicam*

9. See "China's Policies and Practices on Protecting Freedom of Religious Belief," State Council Information Office of the People's Republic of China, April 2018, https://tinyurl.com/y96shhpr.

10. Pope Paul VI, *Lumen gentium* (1964), 4.30–38.

actuositatem on the laity.[11] The flexible nature of the nonliturgical and nonclerical Chinese house church movement could also be a factor, or the high involvement of female pastors, the centrality of the Bible in Chinese Protestant spirituality, or the signs and miracles emphasized by rural Protestant populations. All these speculations deserve in-depth analysis beyond the scope of this volume. However, the differing growth experienced by Chinese Catholics and Chinese Protestants in China may shed new light on church growth, evangelization, and ecclesiology in the context of ecumenical dialogues.

One of the most important signs of the normalization of the Chinese Catholic Church was the Sino-Vatican Provisional Agreement signed on September 22, 2018, which paved the way for a new spirit of cooperation between the Vatican and China over the Chinese Catholic community, beginning with episcopal appointment. Prior to this agreement, the most contested issue between the Chinese government and the Vatican was the authority of episcopal appointment: for the Chinese, it is an issue of national sovereignty to not permit any foreign national to appoint Chinese bishops; for the Catholics, it is the Petrine prerogative, not that of any civil authority, to appoint a bishop of the Roman Catholic Church. There has already been a *modus vivendi* in place; most of the openly consecrated bishops in China have received prior approval from both authorities. The signing of this agreement, however, officially confirmed such a practice in a spirit of cooperation. The agreement acts as a face-saving gesture for both parties, as the Chinese authority would submit a candidate for the pope to confirm after investigation. The pope would have the right to reject the candidate should he find sufficient ground to do so, and in such a case, the Chinese would submit another candidate for the pope to decide upon. In this way, both sides can claim that they have authority over episcopal candidates. Furthermore, the Chinese authorities have recognized that the pope is the head of the Chinese Catholic Church, a major concession from China on the issue of sovereignty. With or without such agreement, the reality is that a bishop must receive blessing from both the civil and the ecclesiastical

11. Pope Paul VI, *Apostolicam actuositatem* (1964).

authority in order to function effectively in China. It is hoped that with such an agreement in place, the bishops in China will now be able to operate in a refreshing environment not only to heal the long intraecclesial division and to provide much-needed pastoral care for the faithful but also to search for the authentic expression of the Catholic faith in this ancient land. One may, however, question the loyalty of these coappointed bishops: to Caesar or to God? It is indeed a test of faith to trust those Chinese bishops appointed under this agreement, that is, whether or not one believes that fidelity to the gospel can ultimately triumph over political interest, as witnessed by millions of Chinese Catholics in the past several decades.

This issue of episcopal appointment in China carries far-reaching implications for the Catholic ecclesial structure. Since the Second Vatican Council, the Catholic Church has been catching up with the rapidly changing world, putting an emphasis on adaptation, indigenization, and contextualization. The centrality of the Catholic population has already moved from Europe to the southern hemisphere. However, the authority still strongly resides in the Vatican, with a predominantly Eurocentric personnel and worldview, even though there have been efforts to increase cardinals and senior Vatican officials from non-European backgrounds to reflect the current diverse racial and ethnic composition of the Catholic Church worldwide. The willingness to concede Petrine authority over episcopal appointment in China suggests the desire of Pope Francis, and perhaps some of his predecessors, to reform the Catholic Church beyond the Cold War mentality into the globalized world of the twenty-first century. By dealing with the Chinese authority over the normalization of the Catholic Church in China, the pope dispenses authority from the center to the periphery, trusts prelates of the local church (i.e., the Chinese church), works courageously with even nonreligious civil authorities (the Chinese Communist authorities), and exhibits the humility of believing in the goodness found not only in the Catholic faith but in all humanity, even Chinese atheists. This agreement also implies that the Catholic Church recognizes that the church now lives in a very diverse world that requires adaptation into local contexts in order to make the gospel relevant.

This Sino-Vatican Agreement will serve as a signpost of changes that have taken place within the Vatican vis-à-vis the sociopolitical reality of the world and echoes the *aggiornamento* spirit of the Second Vatican Council.

CHINA: HOME TO THE LARGEST CHRISTIAN POPULATION IN THE WORLD?

Given the growth rate of Christians (all branches of Christian traditions) in China since 1980, a prominent sociologist, Yang Fenggang, has projected that by 2025, China will have as many as 160 million Protestants, and 247 million by 2030, perhaps the largest population of Christians in a single nation in the world,[12] constituting as much as 10 percent of the total world Christian population. As of 2015, there were 2.3 billion Christians out of a total world population of 7.3 billion. Whether Christian population growth can be projected based on past growth rates is a hotly debated issue. However, China would surely not be the same if there were close to three hundred million Christians living in the country, and such a block of believers would certainly affect not only Chinese society but also the global Christian community. Such speculation may be very farfetched, as a myriad of factors will influence the outcome, such as the sociopolitical climate in China, Christian population development in other high-growth areas such as Africa, and global interreligious dynamics.

When one deals with China, one faces big numbers; China has the largest population in the world. Unless one places the numbers in a relevant context, such big numbers may easily project a distorted perception. For example, it is a fact that there are more Catholics in China, as many as twelve million, than Catholics in Ireland, a predominantly Catholic nation with a total population of less than seven million. However, the twelve million Chinese Catholics constitute less than 1 percent of the population, which means that Catholicism wields a low political,

12. Antonia Blumberg, "China on Track to Become World's Largest Christian Country by 2010, Experts Say," *Huffington Post*, April 22, 2014, https://tinyurl.com/y3y62dow.

social, and cultural impact on Chinese society. In contrast, the Irish Catholics, with much lower absolute numbers than their Chinese counterparts, can still shape the whole social, cultural, and political identity of Ireland. Similarly, the 255 million Protestants in the projected Chinese population of perhaps 1.4 billion in 2025 would constitute about 18 percent of the population and would still be a minority social group.[13] Currently, there are perhaps as many as 250 million Chinese, or 20 percent of the Chinese population, observing traditional Chinese religious practices, be that ancestral worship, local deity festivals, or folk Buddhist or Daoist ceremonies. Even such a seemingly high number, constituting 20 percent of the present population, does not seem to have a strong social or ideological impact on Chinese society because the majority of the Chinese population, perhaps 70 percent, is still agnostic, secularist, or atheist. Therefore, even with a high number of Protestants present, the percentage is still very low in comparison to the total Chinese population and may not necessarily cause a significant impact on society.

Presently those who observe traditional Chinese religions, such as Buddhists, Daoists, or adherents of folk religions, have far outnumbered Chinese Christians in China. These groups of followers are not shrinking but growing. They compete with Christians for converts from the same agnostic or secularist pool of the population. They too offer competitive religious services that could dampen the impact of Christianity on Chinese society. Furthermore, the ruling party is an ideological organization that considers itself a quasi religion with its beliefs—dialectical materialism or atheism—positioned as state orthodoxy. Chris-

13. Since 2017, China has lifted the One Child Policy and allows most couples to have two children. This combined with the increasing life expectancy of the Chinese population due to improvement of medical services may result in an increase of the projected population up to as much as 1.6 billion in 2030. However, the current disproportionate gender ratio has led to twenty million marriageable males being without a spouse, likely leading to lower marriage and birth rates in the coming decade. Also, there is a decreasing fertility rate among women due to the increased female presence in professional and senior managerial positions. Many factors may significantly lower the estimated high population projection. Some academics in China suggest the Chinese population will peak at 2025 with just 1.41 billion and will gradually decline; see Fu Jing, "Population Will Peak in 2025," China Daily, October 7, 2015, https://tinyurl.com/y63luol8.

tians have to compete with other traditional religions and their large membership numbers for cultural influence, such as social values, and at the same time compete against the state-supported atheism for influence in the public domain, such as education, media, and social services. In addition, the political elite in China are all Party members who embrace atheism and exclude religious believers from their ranks. With no effective influence in the political system, the Chinese Protestant population—regardless of their numbers—has little leverage to transform the political structure of China other than through radical means such as a revolution. It seems unlikely that Christian values will permeate Chinese society, even with several hundred million believers, due to the simple fact that there are similar or even higher numbers of followers from other religions as well as a predominantly atheistic and agnostic-secularist influence already dominating and controlling the sociopolitical arena.

Currently, there are about nine hundred million Protestants worldwide. If there is no major Protestant surge other than biological growth in parts of the world other than China, the projected 250 million Chinese Protestants in 2025 may constitute about 25 percent of the global Protestant population, estimated at one billion, and may well be the largest national or ethnic block of Protestants in the global Protestant communion. Not only will Chinese delegates be highly visible in international Protestant activities, such as conferences, assemblies, summits, and rallies, but Chinese elements may also shape theological and spiritual orientations. Maybe the Chinese Protestants, through their spiritual journey of suffering, resilience, pragmatism, modesty, and faithfulness, will become a source of inspiration for the increasing number of Christians who are living in hostile areas or under religious discrimination. Additionally, the simple style of ACCs—small, flexible, dispersed in community, closely bonded, nonstructural, and nonsacramental, with an emphasis on word and witness, and a laity-centered mode of ecclesial operation—can offer an ecclesial alternative to the current liturgy-centric, clergy-based Protestant communities commonly found in the West.

THE CHINESE CHURCH AND GLOBAL MISSION: THE LAST BATON OF THE GREAT COMMISSION?

If one looks as the mission history of Korea, its global mission initiative has been based on its growth in economic affairs, especially since the 1980s, as well as the rapid growth of its Christian population since the 1960s. Currently, Korea is the second-largest missionary-sending country in the world with major influence in mission circles. One may wonder if Chinese Protestants will follow in the footsteps of their Korean brethren. China has become increasingly influential in world politics, economics, global affairs, and even in culture as the Chinese language (officially called Putonghua, and commonly known as Mandarin) is becoming more popular, being taught in many high schools in the US, UK, Thailand, New Zealand, and many other countries. China's goods are flooding stores, and the quality is rising. Students from China are flocking to leading universities in the US as well as to educational institutes in most countries of the developed world. Chinese immigrants and merchants are also making their presence felt in virtually every corner of the globe. Given the huge economic success of China and the large pool of Protestants available, China may become the largest missionary-sending country in the world, proclaiming the gospel to all corners of the globe just as her manufactured products currently penetrate the global market. Because this missiological potential of the Chinese Protestants has become one of the most exciting themes among mission circles in recent years, I will discuss this topic in greater detail than other previous themes.

Some Chinese Protestants view China's global mission potential as an opportunity to finish the Great Commission. The "Back to Jerusalem Movement" (BTJ) originated with Chinese Protestants in the mid-1940s to initiate evangelistic campaigns in the northwest of China.[14] Several groups, in the form of Spiritual Bands as mentioned in chapter 3, had the idea of spreading

14. Chinese from the more developed central and coastal areas seldom traveled to the poorer western border areas until the Sino-Japanese War of 1937–1945, when millions of Chinese, especially students, were displaced into the hinterlands. A realization of the underdeveloped nature of these regions may have prompted these young people to organize programs to help develop the "backyard" of the country.

Christian faith from northwestern China (Xinjiang), through central and west Asia, to Jerusalem, thus hastening the return of Jesus to earth under the eschatology of proactive millenarianism. One of these small mission bands was named "Spreading the Gospel All over the Place Band" (*Pinzhuan Fuyin Tuan*), and its name was erroneously, or conveniently, translated by an English missionary, Ms. Helen Bailey in England, as the "Back to Jerusalem Band" in the early 1950s when she prepared prayer letters for this group. This band, numbering in total no more than thirty, had no particular destination in mind at their formation. They moved in a generally westward direction as they "felt the call," without maps, travel plans, money, or information on the region. Despite their geographical and political naivety, more than half of them managed to reach and remain in various parts of Xinjiang, the westernmost province of China. However, none of them had studied the local language (Uyghur), since they had no particular ethnic group targeted in mind.[15] Two members of the band—a couple, Grace Ho (He Enzhen) and Mecca Zhao (Zhao Maijia)—felt the call to travel even farther west. In 1949–1950, they planned to go to Afghanistan because the local people had told them that it was the nation west of China they would have to go through in order to reach Jerusalem. However, the farthest they reached was Kashgar, the last major frontier city in western China and several hundred kilometers from the China-Afghanistan border.[16] By 1950 the Chinese Communist Army had liberated Xinjiang, and all mission activities were banned. Most Chinese missionaries were rounded up and banned from religious activities; many were charged and sentenced, and some died in jail. Grace Ho and Mecca Zhao settled in Kashgar, with no contact with the outside world other than a few other BTJ members within the province. From the 1980s onward, they operated a small ACC at their home and had no idea that the name of their band, mistranslated

---

This idea persists even today in the Chinese government's development effort to help the western part of China catch up with the coastal regions.

15. Personal interviews with Rev. Huang Ziqing, an original member of the BTJ Band, in Xinjiang, August 2002, August 2003, and August 2006, and in Liaoling, April 2004.

16. Personal interview with Grace Ho, in Kashgar, July 2001.

in English thirty years ago, had been known outside of China by others as the Back to Jerusalem Band until I informed them in July 2001.

One of the missionaries from the 1940s mission movement from the central and coastal areas in Xinjiang was Simon Zhao (Zhao Ximen), who had not joined any band but was well known among the missionary circles in Xinjiang. He and his wife were arrested in 1951, and his wife died in prison in 1960; Zhao suffered many years of imprisonment and hardship, and he was finally released in the late 1980s. He wrote many devotional poems and hymns that have been a major source of encouragement and hope to Protestants in Xinjiang.[17] In the early 1990s, he claimed to have received a vision of Chinese missionaries as God's chosen instruments to convert the Muslim world. Later, he settled in Henan and shared this vision with the ACC's leaders. In the mid-1990s, the name "Back to Jerusalem" was seized upon by some leaders in the ACCs in Henan, and they shared this idea with Chinese churches abroad and, later, with Western evangelical mission circles. A significant figure in this movement is Liu Zhenying, also known as Brother Yun or the Heavenly Man, who has managed to unite several large ACC networks and to promote the "Back to Jerusalem" vision. Following his dramatic escape from prison in China and flight to Germany in 1997, he actively promoted this mission idea, which has been well received by mission agencies in Europe and in the US. In addition, the BTJ (or, as some groups later preferred, the BJM—Back to Jerusalem Movement) vision has been disseminated through hymns, books, websites, and enthusiastic discussions at mission conferences. In the process, the original idea of evangelizing the Muslim world in central and west Asia has gradually evolved into a wider vision called the Indigenous Mission Movement (IMM), challenging Chinese Protestants to evangelize the unreached, especially people groups living in the "10/40 Window"[18]—and not only Muslims but also Hindus and Buddhists living between China and Jerusalem. As the Chinese

---

17. See Simon Zhao's poem "The Farewell Blessing," in Kim-kwong Chan and Alan Hunter, *Prayers and Thoughts of Chinese Christians* (London: Mowbray, 1991), 18–19.

18. A concept developed by Luis Bush in 1990 to denote the region between ten

government pushes forward the Belt and Road Initiative—commonly known as the One Belt One Road initiative, a vision of President Xi Jinping to develop the Eurasian continent into a China-led economic zone involving more than sixty countries —which geographically covers most of the population within the 10/40 Window, including the majority of the Muslim population, the Chinese Protestants are furthering their missiological vision by incorporating this China-led geoeconomic project into a platform for Chinese missionaries to gain access to Muslim-dominated areas for the completion of the mission mandate—the mandate given by Jesus to all disciples to evangelize the world—before the end times.

The enthusiasm for the BTJ vision in mission circles seems to be a confluence of the centrality of Israel as a motif of millenarianism and Western fascination with the rise of China and its huge Protestant population growth. In 2007, the BTJ website called for the mobilization of one hundred thousand (revised from the original figure of two hundred thousand) Chinese missionaries to go to the Islamic-dominated regions of central and west Asia, and eventually to spread the gospel to Jerusalem to prepare the world for the second coming of Christ. Thus, the BTJ implicitly regards this movement as the last change of the baton in global missions, with a simplistic interpretation of mission history: the gospel that traveled from the Middle East to Europe, then on to North America and (via Western missionaries) East Asia, will now be returned to its starting point by Chinese missionaries. In so doing, it will complete the mission mandate of preaching the gospel to the whole world. This ethnocentric missionary theme was promoted by some Chinese church leaders in the diaspora as early as the 1970s and now fits well with the new BTJ movement.[19]

The promoters of this movement offer several arguments to justify this mission. First, China has no major political adver-

and forty degrees north of the equator, an area with the highest concentration of non-Christians.

19. This is reflected in the theme song of the CCCOWE (Chinese Coordination Center of World Evangelism). The Great Commission Center also advocates such a theme by portraying the global missions movement as encircling the world, with the last leg being directed by Asians from the Far East (see *Great Commission Bi-Monthly* 48 [February 2004]).

saries and is on good terms with virtually every nation. It can do business both with Cuba and the US, Iraq and Iran, the Palestinian Authority and Israel, North Korea and South Korea. The Chinese can go where Westerners may have difficulty gaining access, especially into Islamic nations, where Western missionaries usually find it hard to enter and even harder to operate. Second, Chinese Protestants (especially those from the unregistered sector) have a wealth of experience in clandestine forms of religious activities, which seem to be appropriate for doing mission in countries generally hostile to Christianity.

Third, the BTJ movement coincides with the Belt and Road Initiative of the Chinese government, which aims to build a circle of Eurasian economic prosperity with China at the center. China has been urging its people to go outward to develop infrastructure and commercial activity, especially in central and western Asia, the very same region that the BTJ would target. Therefore, BTJ missionaries could naturally blend into the increased influx of Chinese into this region.

Fourth, Protestants in China practice a simple form of Christianity devoid of elaborate liturgical, diaconal, and institutional structures. Such an ecclesial form is simple to operate, flexible, and cost effective, especially in an environment hostile to Christianity. The Chinese Protestants have already proven that such an ecclesial form is effective enough in China to achieve a high church-growth rate. Therefore, they are in a good position to duplicate such success in Muslim-dominated regions.

Fifth, even though Protestants are still a small percentage of the Chinese population, their absolute numbers are huge, creating an almost endless supply of potential missionary candidates, whereas fresh missionary recruits are at an all-time low in most churches in the West. Sixth, these Chinese missionaries are used to living frugally, unlike Western missionaries, whose lifestyle is usually on a level with Western expatriates. With the same amount of money, it can be argued that a mission agency can deploy far more Chinese missionaries than their Western counterparts. Therefore, Chinese missionaries can be more cost effective than their Western counterparts in the mission field. Finally, it is not just that Chinese missionaries are cheaper to employ; they also accept suffering as a part of the

Christian reality, and many are ready to be martyred without hesitation. In fact, Brother Yun had even suggested that he had prepared to accept ten thousand Chinese martyrs in the first decade of the BTJ in order to crack open the Muslim world for the gospel.[20] The Adventist belief—an eschatological assumption that Jesus will return once the gospel has been preached around the world—further fuels this disposition for martyrdom.

Reliable sources suggest that there are already several dozen mission-training centers in China, as well as many outside China, and hundreds of candidates are currently in training. At least a thousand Chinese missionaries have already been dispatched in the field, and some vanguard teams are establishing support bases and so-called "caravan stations" along the major hubs on the Belt and Road Initiative's trade routes. BTJ has been getting an increasing amount of international attention and financial support, especially from pro-Israel, Christian Zionist, evangelical, and charismatic mission agencies in the West, and also from Chinese Protestants in the diaspora. Such encouraging news has been highlighted in many mission conferences and rallies to enthusiastic participants, projecting a vision of tens of thousands Chinese missionaries carrying the good news to unreached people and ushering in the eschaton.

The idea of thousands of Chinese missionaries settling in Muslim-dominated areas and evangelizing in secret is attractive to many Western Christians, who are frustrated by the relative fruitlessness of Western missionary endeavors among Muslims. As one veteran missionary in a Middle Eastern country once told me, "We have been so lonely in laboring for many years with little result. We are so frustrated that we are tempted to jump at any idea, however berserk it may seem."[21] The BTJ movement is still in its infancy, and though the current impact in the field is noticeable, the result is yet to be measured. I will take a sober look at the justifications for the participation of Chinese Protestants in global mission endeavors.

Indeed, Chinese churches have a vast supply of potential missionaries. Furthermore, the increasing surplus of Chinese farm

20. Tim Stafford, "Interview with Paul Hattaway: A Captivating Vision," *Christianity Today*, April 1, 2004, https://tinyurl.com/y5e9kw2v.
21. Interviewed in April 2004 (name and place withheld for security reasons).

laborers and semiskilled factory workers, perhaps the largest block of underemployed laborers in the world (numbering more than 150 million), may facilitate the recruitment of missionaries from among the rural Chinese Protestant population. However, church leaders in the Middle East have repeatedly stressed that missionaries to that part of the world should acquire some sort of professional status in the region and have an in-depth understanding of Islamic culture. Few Chinese Protestants could meet those two criteria, especially with regard to quality training in cross-cultural issues with good understanding of Islamic culture.[22] A veteran missionary in the region once communicated to me that he encountered a group of BTJ missionaries from rural China in Iraq when BTJ was still in its early stages. To his surprise, they had no knowledge of Iraq, and certainly none of them could speak Arabic. Furthermore, they were pig farmers, which is not the best profession for gaining acceptance in the Muslim world.[23] Finding it difficult to succeed in their only profession, they subsequently left for another Middle Eastern country. Current BTJ missionaries are better prepared, as an increasing number of professionals from the urban churches are joining the movement.

There are political and commercial repercussions to the BTJ's involvement in the Middle East, highlighted by an incident in which two Chinese BTJ missionaries were kidnapped and later executed by ISIS in Pakistan.[24] They were sent by a Korean mission agency that had recruited, trained, and sent teams of Chinese missionaries to central Asia and the Middle East to evangelize to Muslims. The Koreans provided the funding and training, and the Chinese provide the labor, with a monthly stipend of around USD $300. In 2016, this Korean mission agency sent a team of thirteen Chinese missionaries to Quetta, the capital of Baluchistan, Pakistan, under the guise of Chinese language teachers. In fact, they did door-to-door evangelism with the local people, using the little Pashto and Urdu language

22. "Interview from the Land of the Pharaohs," *Back to Jerusalem Bulletin* 2 (December 2004): 7–8.

23. Personal communication, January 31, 2005 (identity withheld).

24. See "Risky-Road: China's Missionaries Follow Beijing West," BBC, September 4, 2017, https://tinyurl.com/y4qnofkh.

they had recently learned. In June 2017, ISIS kidnapped two of them, Li Xiheng and Meng Lisi. The Chinese government was unprepared for such a crisis, as the Chinese consulate did not know of the existence of these thirteen people, much less about what they were doing. No ransom was demanded, and it was perhaps religiously motivated, as the locals knew about these overt proselytization activities, which were greatly disliked by the local mullahs. The Chinese soon took the remaining eleven members into the safety of the consulate and later sent them back to China. The Pakistani authorities attempted a military operation to rescue the two hostages but failed. Later, ISIS executed these two Chinese missionaries. The Korean boss of this team of Chinese missionaries fled but was caught and expelled by the Pakistani authorities.

The Chinese government was furious; China was investing tens of billions dollars into Pakistan as part of the Belt and Road Initiative to build a strategic China-Pakistan Economic Corridor linking the Gwadar Port at the Gulf of Oman to Kashgar of Xinjiang, China. Quetta is one of the major hubs of this huge infrastructure project with oil pipeline, highway, and railway construction. There were hundreds of Chinese engineers, technicians, and project managers in Quetta. With this incident, many Chinese were deemed not safe, and their construction projects came to a halt, causing billions of dollars of loss and complicating the whole China-Pakistan Economic Corridor Project. The Chinese government swiftly closed down many missionary training centers in China, arrested and expelled some Korean missionaries, and warned Chinese Protestants not to engage in such reckless endeavors that may jeopardize China's long-term political interest in the region. The Chinese Ministry of Foreign Affairs is now drafting a law to deny consulate service to Chinese who go to areas against the warning of the Chinese government. Pakistan has also taken action by arresting the Koreans who operated these teams in Pakistan, and since that incident, it has been much more difficult to grant commercial visas to the Chinese, even for those who are in legitimate business. In summary, these Chinese BTJ missionaries act against the economic and political interests of China. The political fallout is tighter control of missionary training in China, greater difficulty for businesses operated by the Chinese in those regions, and greater limitation of Chinese activities by local authorities in these regions. With the increase of China's investment in regions of the Belt and Road Initiative, the Chinese government will most likely take active measures to discourage groups such as BTJ missionaries, as such mission activity, should it gain momentum, would undermine China's geopolitical plan for the whole region.

Also, the cost-effectiveness arguments of deploying Chinese missionaries in a dangerous mission field seem to be based more on the manufacture-market model for global sourcing of the cheapest manufacture capacity than on the Christian value of equality, where all missionaries despite differing origin and ethnicity should be treated equally. The church has long passed the age of colonialism when whites were superior and were treated better at times in the mission field than locals. Such arguments, although popular and tempting, may change mission into a religious outsourcing service industry to provide proselytization for the lowest bidder that generates the greatest result! Should that be the case, some entrepreneurial Chinese Protestants may subcontract or outsource some mission tasks to newly emerged Christian groups, such as the Vietnamese Christians, who might ask for a lower living allowance than the Chinese do, to further enhance cost effectiveness in downstream outsourcing. It may also transform Chinese foreign mission cooperation to a mercenary missiology, where cheap Chinese missionaries are hired as Gospel suicide commandos to blast through hard-to-access areas for evangelism, even at the cost of martyrdom. Meanwhile, the bosses of those mission agencies, foreigners with their per-life value costs perceived to be higher than those of the Chinese, stay far away in safety, as in the case of Pakistan. Should that be the case, there is little theological difference between the suicide bombers of Islamic extremists and Chinese mission commandos for hire who try to convert their Muslim counterparts!

Furthermore, the severe lack of qualified pastoral workers within China also hinders the recruiting of qualified BTJ candidates. The recruitment of BTJ missionaries to exotic fields may compete with the need for pastoral workers, a situation common to all churches, Chinese or otherwise. Finally, China's increasing commercial presence in Islamic countries, from Afghanistan to Algeria, sometimes involves practices conflicting with Islamic traditions, such as some Chinese restaurants in Kabul selling alcohol and operating brothels. This is already generating fear of Chinese market dominance and of a deterioration of sociore-ligious values. Also, with the increasing influence of Chinese presence in many countries, especially those in the Belt and Road Initiative, more countries such as the Maldives, Sri Lanka, and Malaysia are feeling a greater threat than a benefit from China. There has been a gradual shift from appreciation for the Chinese to fear in many countries, which will work against the Chinese BTJ missionaries, making it harder for them to be wel-comed by the local populations. However, despite all these cau-tions, more Chinese Protestant missionaries are joining global missions, and many more are preparing for such challenges. As to the magnitude, scale, and influence of this new mission con-tingent, only time will tell.

LOOKING AHEAD

Despite its miraculous growth and current strength, there are at least three major challenges ahead for Christianity in China. First, unity has been in short supply among Christians in China. Due to political and canonical differences, Catholicism in China has been split into official and underground factions. Such divi-sions cause tremendous hurt and bitterness between the two camps. Although much hope has been placed on the Sino-Vat-ican Provisional Agreement, memories of past grievances still linger, and animosity between factional leaders may perpetuate. It will take a long time and a tremendous amount of grace for the Catholics in China to heal from this division and to become unified in heart and spirit as an ecclesial entity.

Protestants fare no better than their Catholic counterparts on the issue of unity. Unlike Catholicism, there is no demand for Protestants to be organically joined as one, visible ecclesial entity, and there is ecclesial flexibility to start one's own church should one have some disagreement on doctrines or polity. Such allowances serve as a safety valve; if there is too much tension within a group, instead of fighting each other, one can always protest and form another group in the true spirit of Protestantism. However, as with the original diverse denominational traditions, thanks to the never-ending divisions of the ACCs and internal power factions within the TSPM/CCCs, unity is challenging. The Chinese Protestant community, despite its huge numbers, is divided into endless groups and factions that render it weak, partly due to a lack of consensus and an inability to take collective action. Chinese Muslims, with far fewer numbers than the Protestants, have clearly made more of a sociopolitical impact in China, often successfully challenging the government to address their needs. Protestants in China have yet to unite to champion their common interests. However, as long as Chinese Protestant groups stress the common spiritual needs of their nation above the needs of their own groups, or the situation in the Chinese church in general rather than the achievements of their own particular group, there is still the hope that Chinese Protestants will move in the direction of genuine Christian unity. Should that be the case, this unity will enable Chinese Protestants to impact Chinese society in ways beyond one's imagination.

Second, are we looking at Christianity in China or Chinese Christianity? Christianity has always been regarded by the Chinese as a foreign—or more accurately, a Western—religion, given its historical origin. One of the major challenges facing Chinese Christianity is its need to be accepted as an authentic part of Chinese society, not as an extension of a foreign entity intruding into China. Chinese Christians have paid a high cost trying to gain a foothold in China, and they are now at the highest population percentage since the introduction of Christianity at least 1,400 years ago. However, there is still a long journey ahead for Christianity to be accepted as part of the Chinese social fabric. Church buildings in China today often look Western and incongruous in the surrounding landscape. Worship music in church is often translated Western hymnody, however beautifully written and composed, which is far from the cultural psyche of China. At present, Christianity is still a foreign religion that happens to have been inserted in China, as Chinese Christians in general explicitly choose a Western appearance despite the government call for a Sinicization of all religion in China. Hopefully, a day will come when Chinese Christians are confident enough to incorporate their cultural heritage into their Chinese Christian identity without fearing the betrayal of their Christian faith, which they have kept at great cost.

Globalization and localization of the Chinese Christian community constitute the third major challenge. Globalization seems to speed up the exchange of goods and services, as well as people and ideas, across borders. Thanks to globalization, various ecclesial modes, from the Korean style of prayer and fasting to American charismatic worship, exist in Chinese Christian communities. At the same time, Chinese Christians are also developing their own ecclesial elements unique to their context, such as ACCs, and the spirituality of suffering and resilience that contributes to the richness of the global Christian communion.[25] Will the popular ecclesial trends be the norm of the Chinese Christian community? Or will the Chinese church develop its own ecclesial mode, counterbalancing globalized trends? Should the latter be the case, we will see the emergence of a new form of Christianity that is uniquely Chinese. A veteran Sinologist, the late Father L. Ladany, SJ, once stated a cardinal rule about watching China: "Expect the unexpected."[26] This rule may also best describe Christianity in contemporary China.

25. Daniel H. Bays, *A New History of Christianity in China* (Chichester, UK: Wiley-Blackwell, 2012), 225.

26. In the last issue of *China News Analysis* under his editorship in 1982, he wrote about his thirty years of experience as a China watcher. His last comment was that when one watches China, one must expect the unexpected.